W9-BBM-516

BREAKING WITH BURR

Harman Blennerhassett, 1796.
Courtesy of the Blennerhassett Historical Park Commission.

BREAKING WITH BURR:

HARMAN BLENNERHASSETT'S JOURNAL, 1807

Edited by
Raymond E. Fitch

Ohio University Press
Athens

Printed in the United States of America.

Library of Congress Cataloging-in-Publication Data

Blennerhassett, Harman, 1764–1831.
Breaking with Burr.

1. Burr Conspiracy, 1805–1807—Personal narratives.
2. Burr, Aaron, 1756–1836. 3. Blennerhassett, Harman,
1764–1831—Diaries. I. Fitch, Raymond E., 1930–
II. Title.
E334.B63 1987 973.4'8 86-23814
ISBN 0-8214-0860-7

For my son Matthew

CONTENTS

LIST OF ILLUSTRATIONS

ACKNOWLEDGMENTS

I owe my initial interest in this project to several students in a special Summer Quarter course on the Blennerhassetts I taught in 1979. Charles Sherrill, in particular, wrote a paper from which I learned, among other things, how many changes and omissions there are in the first forty-five pages of W. H. Safford's edition of the journal. That was a beginning. In the intervening years I have benefitted inexpressibly from the generously shared knowledge and consistent enthusiasm of Ray Swick, Historian, of the Blennerhassett Historical Park Commission. Likewise, I am grateful to Dan Fowler, Director of the Commission, and to Professor Philip Sturm of Ohio Valley College for encouragement and practical suggestions; however, these helpful persons are in no way implicated in the shortcomings of my approach to this work.

I also wish to express my gratitude to the Ohio University Research Committee and the Trustees of Ohio University for a Faculty Fellowship leave for the Spring Quarter of 1986 which enabled me to complete this edition. To Patricia Elisar, former Director of The Ohio University Press, and Holly Panich, Associate Editor, I am particularly indebted for their patient and kind attention to the special problems that the publication of Blennerhassett's text presented. Lastly, but by no means least warmly, I wish to thank Helen Gawthrop of the Press for all her generous technical assistance to me in preparation of the texts and illustrations. Beyond all thanks have been the gifts of diligent proofreading and constant encouragement from my wife Guinavere Romine Fitch.

Raymond E. Fitch

INTRODUCTION

"The Fascination of This Serpent"

[*Biographical Foreword*:—Harman Blennerhassett (1764-1831) was the youngest of three brothers in a distinguished family of Irish gentry. He was educated at famed Westminster School in London and studied law at Trinity College, Dublin, from which he graduated with honors and was, at age 25, admitted to the Irish bar. Meanwhile, however, the early deaths of his elder brothers had left him heir to the family estates at Castle Conway. Freed from obligations to a profession, he could indulge his literary interests and travel to the Continent, where he sympathized with the ideals of the French Revolution, read in the *philosophes*, and returned to join the revolutionary movement in his native Eire. In this state of enthusiasm he became enamored of the lovely and clever Margaret Agnew, a daughter of his sister Catherine and thirteen years his junior. Uncle and niece married in defiance of law and decorum. Hostility to their marriage, its illegality, and Harman's political sympathies combined to force them into exile. The family estates were soon sold for some $160,000, and they sailed for New York in 1796.

Perhaps it was their social secret, or the romantic adventurousness behind it, that drove the Blennerhassetts to seek a less restricted life than that afforded by New York and Philadelphia, where they stayed briefly; for they soon went west by way of Pittsburgh, arriving in Marietta, Ohio, in 1797. From there, as if seeking further privacy, they purchased part of an island in the Ohio River, near the site of the present city of Parkersburg, West Virginia. During the next several years they had built there no secluded cottage but a stately mansion for all to see, with well-ordered grounds and "a shrubbery that Shenstone might have envied"—an earthly paradise that symbolized their social ideals and compensated for much they had been forced to abandon. Domestic, cultural, and business pursuits of a great variety engaged their interests; yet it has been suggested that these adventurers were becoming restless in their rustication, that, their wealth eroding, they were ready for some speculative enterprise when Aaron Burr came calling one fine May evening in 1805.

For Harman's account of what followed, the reader should turn to Appendices C and B, then to Appendix A and the main text of his journal of 1807. It will be noted that from time to time in the journal Harman speculates ruefully on those qualities in Burr which enabled him to dupe so many, including the diarist himself. Yet he does not, perhaps cannot, reflect on those tendencies in his own life—the rebellious idealism, the adventurousness—which had ripened him for Burr's plucking. But his journal is not very introspective. Furthermore, it would have been inappropriate for him to remind his beloved wife, to whom the journal is addressed, that the same qualities on which their relationship was founded had also readied him for Burr. Indeed, there had been an earlier fall and exile in his life; and the second, far less fortunate, was prefigured in the first. What makes the Blennerhassetts' story "tragic" is not their loss of paradise but the sense one has of the disregarded inevitability of that loss.]

Harman Blennerhassett began writing the journal reproduced in this book at a quarter past 6:00 P.M. on July 14, 1807, at Lexington, Kentucky on the day he was taken into custody. It had not been a good day for him. Although his first entry is sparing enough (see Appendix A), a letter he wrote to his wife, Margaret, that same evening gives more of the dismaying details of his predicament and his reactions to it. She knew he had been on his way East from Natchez, where she and their two boys had taken refuge after their flight down river from Ohio in December. Harman had been taken there, and soon released, by authorities of the Mississippi Territory, after his chief, Aaron Burr—wanted for treason, yet hoping to avoid falling into the hands of General Wilkinson, who had betrayed him to the President—had abandoned the loyal remnant of his expedition to their fates at Cole's Creek in February and disappeared into the bush. Now, in mid-July, Burr was before a Grand Jury at Richmond, and Blennerhassett was on his way back to see what might be salvaged of his island estate on the Ohio after its ransacking in December by the "Wood County Myrmidons," as he called them, and the following exactions of his creditors. But more pressing demands intervened; it would be another five months before he could turn toward the wreck of his Eden on the Ohio again.

In his enthusiastic commitment to whatever he understood of Burr's plans in the West—at most a "severance of the Union" and the formation of a Western empire centered on Mexico (with Burr its emperor, Blennerhassett in a "diplomatic appointment" of his choice), at least an expedition to settle the Bastrop Grant on the Washita—he had endorsed a number of bills drawn by Burr, amounting to at least $10,000. But "the little Emperor of Cole's Creek," as the diarist would call him, had taken to the wilds of Mississippi without, presumably, means or plans to pay these bills; and although the arch-conspirator had made arrangements with his son-in-law, Joseph Alston, a wealthy South Carolina planter, to settle these claims, some remained unpaid. So it was with a reference to these financial circumstances that Blennerhassett began his letter to his wife from Lexington on the evening of July 14: "On my arrival here to-day I was taken into custody for my endorsement of some of Col: Burr's bills, of which I am now getting clear by an arrangement Mr. [Henry] Clay is drawing up between Mr. Sanders and me, effected by my transferring Col. Alston's obligation, etc."*

---

* For letters to Margaret of July 14 and 18, 1807, quoted on this and the following pages, see William H. Safford, *The Blennerhassett Papers*, 1864 (rptd. New York: Arno Press, 1971), pp. 259-268. For further biographical and background information on Blennerhassett, Burr, and the Burr Conspiracy see below Appendices A, B, C, and the Selected Bibliography. References to Harman's journal in the following pages are identified by date of entry.

But it was beginning to look as though these financial arrangements, even if successfully concluded, might not purchase his release. A messenger had arrived—having made a rapid journey from Richmond in twelve days—with news that both he and Burr had been indicted "for high *treason* and a misdemeanor," that a jury was being assembled from hostile Wood County, and that the trial was scheduled to begin on August 3rd. What to do? Escape might still be possible, he told his wife in the same letter, but he would not consider it. "Burr's situation is thought to be as perilous, as may be my own. If I go on to the Island or Marietta, I must expect to be immediately sent to Richmond. I have no idea of attempting an escape, which I could probably effect by Detroit to Canada. I feel conscious of all want of law or evidence to convict me." And Wilkinson's fall and disgrace would be assured, he thought, whatever might happen to Burr or himself. "I will not fly," he concluded, having the chief danger in mind, "even from Wood County witnesses and juries." This determination not to flee turned out to be ironic, however, because before he could pen his next line to his wife, the possibilities of getting either himself or his letter out had been interdicted. He was, he says, writing the sentence just quoted when he was interrupted by the arrival of David Meade, Deputy U.S. Marshal, "an amiable, kind young man," who placed him under arrest and announced their intended departure for Richmond within a few days.

Blennerhassett's situation, while not physically disagreeable, was becoming more serious and, of course, more significant. He was a prisoner of the state, now, and on the highest charge. A note of deeper gravity seems to enter the letter to his wife that he resumed later in the day. "The same Providence that has ever supported me will let my time and my reflections flow as smoothly here as if I were at liberty. You must serve the same *God*, and by strong and steady endeavors think of this, and the worst that persecutions can inflict upon me, as lightly as I do." The "persecutions" were, for the moment, merely that the government's prisoner was moved to "a new lodging . . . a clean, airy room in the jail," but his was now to be isolated confinement, nonetheless. He was informed by his jailer, Prentiss, that he had "orders to let no one speak to me but in his presence, and to let no letters come to me or go from me."

It was under these new conditions of confinement at Lexington, then, that Blennerhassett began, on the evening of July 14, the first loose pages (printed here as Appendix A) of his journal. "I make memoranda of all these occurences," he told his wife in the same letter, "which I read over to the jailer, and he has engaged to sign." As this last statement implies, we can see from these early pages themselves that they are little more than a bare chronological record of his handling; his letters of the 14th and 18th to his wife provide a more detailed account of his needs, plans and anxieties. On the 18th, for instance, he confided these foreboding remarks about Burr's finances: "I am extremely sorry to find the injury to private individuals of this country in consequence of a *baseless* authority for Burr's financial operations here last autumn, far exceeding my greatest suspicions. If it be shown that he had *not* funds and friends pledged to him to warrant his drafts, his conduct would appear nefarious enough to displace all the friendships he ever formed. These strictures are particularly extracted from me by something I have heard of him relating to myself in a pecuniary sense, which will be examined and come hereafter to your knowledge, if material." He would have many "strictures" on this theme to add in the next five months, and the journal would become his most dependable listener.

Actually the ban on letters was immediately rescinded to the extent that he was permitted to write, to his wife only, the sealed letters in which such statements, with their cathartic value, were possible. But gradually the journal—also written to his wife, but with the significantly enlarged intended audience that might include, he said, "2 or 3 confidential friends"—would supplement the sealed letter as a vehicle of emotional release. As such it had several advantages: the expanded though still confidential audience; the relative security afforded by the little "pocket book" in which he kept his notes; the ritual consistency of daily upkeep, which encouraged also sufficient continuity for the development of themes, characters, even something in the way of a plot; and finally, the diary could be a source for, a record of, and even a kind of dialogue with, the letters. So for these, and perhaps other more practical reasons, the journal would continue—through the journey to Richmond, the period of his confinement and then of his freedom there, his subsequent visits to Washington, Baltimore, and Philadelphia—to end, more strangely than it began, with the bitter knowledge that only its full text can convey to us.

On November 10 Blennerhassett would say of his journal, after four months of keeping it, "I feel I have penned many reflections, and passed many characters with my own, in review, in a light which should be admitted to few eyes, besides those of my wife." Clearly he does not see his diary here as a cold record of objective events; indeed, while his text *is* a valuable document concerning the Burr conspiracy and trials, it is not primarily about those events. The diarist speaks of "reflections" and of "characters," including his own, displayed in a "light" that he thinks of as uniquely personal. What is this "light?" The implication is that it is not primarily a reference to certain facts that are disclosed but an allusion to the developing ironic perspective from which certain actions and persons come to be seen. The "light" issues from the interplay of style and content; it is produced by Blennerhassett's writing, his text, itself. This text will not, for instance, permit the reader to maintain (as William Wirt's famous speech does) an easy polarity between the idea of Blennerhassett as impulsive innocent and Burr as the crafty seducer. In the diffusing light of the diarist's writing we trace an interest in Burr that is governed, from moment to moment, by contempt, rivalry, idolatry, and other factors. The journal is fundamentally a chronicle of his disillusionment with Burr, though Blennerhassett declared (August 29) that this had happened (or had begun to happen) seven months before he began to keep the journal. But the way this perhaps foregone conclusion actually came to happen—the stages by which Blennerhassett released his hopes from the snares of Burr—should be retraced against the background of other events and characters in the journal. Its ultimate interest, perhaps, is in its contrast of two characters who represent contradictions in social ideals of the age, the Romantic rebel, say, against the Romantic outlaw.

In reading the journal "for plot"—as if it were essentially narrative—it will be convenient to divide it into the following "chapters," or phases: (1) from the beginning with the journey to Richmond, through August 23 (p. 52), the night of Col. Duane's infamous visit to Blennerhassett at his quarters in the Richmond Penitentiary; (2) from August 24 to September 7 (p. 81), the date of Blennerhassett's release from "captivity," soon after Burr's acquittal of the treason charge; (3) from September 7 through Burr's misdemeanor trial, September 9 to 15, and the immediately following hearings on charges of treason and misdemeanor in other districts—during all of which proceedings Burr and Blennerhassett are free to socialize in Richmond when their presences are not required at court—to the diarist's dissatisfaction with the end of the "present prosecution" on October 20 and his departure for Washington on October 25 (p. 139); (4) his querulous stay in that city, from October 27 to 30, his bold adventures in Baltimore from November 1 to 4, and the finale in Philadelphia, November 5 through 19.

As we review some of the crucial events of these four phases of the journal our primary concern will be with the vagaries and vacillations which mark what we might call its Burr-plot, the recurrent narrative scheme driven by Blennerhassett's desire to obtain recognition of his "claims" (monetary and emotional) against the arch-conspirator. But we will also notice some others of those "reflections" and "characters" that the diarist valued, as well as a few special features of the text that were suppressed by its previous editor, William H. Safford.

1.

From the opening pages of the first book of the journal we learn that Blennerhassett and his escort, consisting of David Meade and a guard of five made the trek from Lexington to Richmond in sixteen days, covering a distance of 564 miles.

Though there are occasional references to the oppressive heat, the rugged road, the "good house" or "bad house" where they lodged, evidently no incident of the journey was as deserving of record as the humiliating circumstances, for the diarist, of the tired little troop's parade into Richmond. His frank admission that he was "disappointed to see no particular notice taken of the party, except by a little boy, who called out to his comrades 'Oh! See the troop of horse but they have forgot their colours,' " not only shows his eye for the ironic detail but provides a foretaste of the anti-climactic quality of so much that will befall him in the succeeding weeks. Here, at least, with the first entry written in Richmond Penitentiary, the journal becomes a quite different kind of record, more distinctly narrative and subjective, than that promised by the earlier entries, all of which were, perhaps understandably, omitted by the journal's first editor.

As he settles into his "large and convenient" though suffocating rooms, Blennerhassett is greeted by, among other things, the service of a warrant from Chief Justice John Marshall; a supply of tea and cakes sent by Burr's daughter Theodosia, wife of Joseph Alston, the man of means who will figure so largely in the succeeding diary entries; and by a cheerful note from Burr, welcoming him to his "late quarters" in the prison. Though he makes no other remark about it at this point, the phrase "late quarters" presumably alerted Blennerhassett to the fact, had he not known it, that Burr had better quarters, nearer to the center of action, than he would have at the Penitentiary, a mile from town. Burr, of course, had been in Richmond since late March and had even spent a few days in the noisome city locker, but at the start of the Grand Jury hearing in May he had pled weak health and need to be convenient to counsel; consequently, he had been granted specially barred and guarded quarters in a house rented by Luther Martin, his loyal friend and member of his counsel, in a fashionable street near the Capitol. However, between the return of the indictments on June 24 and the start of his trial on August 3, the government, to lessen its expenses, had housed Burr at the Penitentiary in the rooms now occupied by Blennerhassett.

Having been returned to his more costly lodgings for the trial,

Burr was not only physically closer to the theater of interest, he was at the center of the subtle web of his own defense. Therefore, on the second day of his confinement, Blennerhassett is further distanced by another note from Burr advising him of the necessity of, as he puts it, "employing counsel, as the only proper intermedium of our communication." Burr's suggestion is immediately reinforced by a visit from Alston. But this gives the diarist a move to make. He has confidence in his own legal training and skills, and since he has already virtually exhausted the last means of his family's support on Burr's projects, he has resolved not to spend one dollar in his own defense. On Burr's part there is a need to fit Blennerhassett into the overriding project of his, Burr's, defense; for the diarist this is an opportunity to call attention to his financial situation. So in the following entries we have, most significantly, Blennerhassett's account of his declarations to Burr's attorneys, Benjamin Botts, John Wickham, and Edmund Randolph, that he would be glad of but cannot pay for their counsel, though perhaps, he suggests, they may be remunerated by Burr or Alston.

This lesser financial matter leads naturally to negotiation with Alston on the larger question of the endorsed bills; accordingly we learn, on August 5, that he has "enclosed various papers to Mr Alst. showing him how my property has been sacrificed on the Ohio, and praying his aid to recover it for my children by virtue of his respons^{y} for my endorsement of Col: B.'s protested Bills." Visiting the diarist the next day, Alston expresses "concern" for the embarrassments occasioned him by these endorsements, yet he resists Blennerhassett's proposal that the bills be met through the sale of slaves; instead he proposes a plan of deferred payment, "if the creditors will accept one half payable with Interest, next Jany 12 month—the other half—etc. the Jany following—." But this solution is unsatisfactory to the diarist, since his own assets must remain frozen until the agreement is accepted and perhaps until paid; hence his complaint: "my children's property is and will be irrecoverably sacrificed in the mean time."

This demand for indemnification is continuous and crucial in the diary, of course; but it is paralleled by the diarist's less objectified demand for recognition or appreciation, not only for his past services to Burr but for his continued value as a strategist. These latent demands are evident in the rest of Blennerhassett's account of his discussion with Alston on August 6. We learn that another motive for Alston's visit that day is to pose certain questions that Burr wishes to ask. It appears that during Randolph's visit to him, Blennerhassett had remarked that "Burr had sometimes been too cautious; sometimes too little so." Important here is the diarist's insistence that, as example of Burr's lack of caution, there are Burr's disregards of his warnings against commitment to General Wilkinson and Colonel Morgan (both of whom betrayed his confidences), and that he could, furthermore, cite as many examples of over-caution; "God knows, I know 100 both ways." He was about to list some of the hundred examples of over-caution, he tells us, when Alston interrupted him with the remark that "M.rs Blennerhassett had good reason for her opinion of Col: Morgan."

But what Blennerhassett has been trying to show Alston in this instance is that *he*, not his wife, had the qualities of penetration, balance, and restraint that would enable him to weigh and refuse the two extremes of incaution and overcaution. Therefore, if Burr's question implies a word of guidance in the matter of discretion, it is, in the diarist's view, ironically misdirected, since, he notes, "I did not feel that Col: Burr had ever suffered as yet fr. any avoidable indiscretion of mine, 'tho I was likely to do so far more, than I had done already by his Errors." What is still more galling is that the example of caution Alston had "exhibited to the world" was a letter to Charles Pinckney,* containing what Blennerhassett considered a treacherous repudiation of his

* Joseph Alston to Charles Pinckney, Feb. 6, 1807. *The Blennerhassett Papers*, pp. 227–29. For its relation to the famous "cipher letter" supposed at the time to have been written by Burr to James Wilkinson (July 22–29, 1806), see Mary-Jo Kline, with Joanne Wood Ryan et. al., *Political Correspondence and Public Papers of Aaron Burr*, 2 vols. (Princeton: Princeton University Press, 1983), 2:986–90, and below, pp. 224–25.

father-in-law's projects, marking him, of course, as "the most improper organ of . . . Burr's *wishes*."

Finally, on the subject of caution, Blennerhassett is reminded, in this same entry (August 6) of two points that will bring him back to the subject of indemnification, the essential claim he is pressing with Alston. First, he has heard from a third party that Burr has called him a bankrupt, and this thought, in so close an association with the idea of caution, provokes a cathartic outburst of feeling: "Bankrupt! Hah! Who made me so? Oh God of retributive justice!" Second, Burr had also declared to the same person that he did not believe Alston was bound to the diarist by any written document; but here, concluding on the theme of caution, Blennerhassett wants to ask Burr, through Alston, if he recalls "that He himself drafted that very paper, after having censured another which Mr A. had written as insufficient?" And with this the diarist ends the significant account of his second day in prison, having insisted on the validity of both, his losses and his caution.

Two days later, on August 8, in a homely remark that Judge Safford omitted from his edition, the diarist notes that his face continues "very sore with a sort of ring-worm these 10 days." His indignation is also inflamed again, not now by Burr's failure to recognize his qualities or his claims but by another matter that, one might suppose, would occupy him more often than it does: the government's strategies to obtain Burr's conviction. Rumors that have reached him of a "grossly packed" jury and of "the most damning manoeuvers and intrigues" in Wood County, provoke an ironic apostrophe to the President. "Say Thos. Jefferson—thou philanthropic messenger of peace and liberty to this favored country—under thy administr^n are those things unknown to thy tender heart . . . ?" He goes on to predict, with surprising confidence and accuracy for one who is generally seen as a fuzzy-minded idealist, that the Grand Jury will ultimately be found to have misinterpreted Justice Marshall's definition of treasonable acts in his opinion in the recent case of Burr's associates, Bollman and Swartwout. Finally, such reflections as these seem to suggest a deeper reason and larger audience for his writings: while the press will inform his friends of the progress of the trial, only his notes may convey the secret history of its flaws and miscues.

Two days later, August 10, we are reminded of these remarks and of his replies to Burr's questions through Alston, when the diarist treats us to the carefully detailed account of his first visit to the court, and of his encounter there with Burr, the first face-to-face meeting of the two associates since the leader had abandoned his boats at Cole's Creek in February. Burr, wreathed in smiles, as the diarist tells it, expressed pleasure at the meeting; but our narrator adds an ironic qualifier, "observe I had not before heard from him since Thursday." Of course, Burr's counsel do not wish any unplanned intrusion of Blennerhassett's case upon their client's, so they quickly quash the Prosecutor's, George Hay's, sly attempt to proceed with Blennerhassett's arraignment while Burr is preparing his schedule of witnesses. So the diarist, who came to court in a carriage, is sent back to the Penitentiary unarraigned and on foot. There he continues with the writing of his Brief (see Appendix C) which has now reached the 6th folio. The heat, he tells us, has been extraordinarily oppressive, yet there comes a moment of unexpected relief: "tried to get cool by walking and fanning, but was so weak I was obliged to lie down on the floor, where I slept, I know not how long, 'till I was awakened by the name of Mrs Alston, at which I started up, as if electrified and perceived a servant of hers, with a large present of oranges, lemons and limes."

By the 12th there has been a cooling rain, but the prisoner is hot with indignation, first with the word that the government is lax in paying the expenses of defense witnesses, and then with news of the perjured testimonies of Taylor, Albright, and Wallace. But he takes some satisfaction in the idea of faith in "a Guardian *Providence*, that ordains the conviction of perjury to issue in the same breath, fr. the lips of falsehood accusing the Innocent." Furthermore, there are rumors that the prosecution is flagging but that a *nolle prosequi* will go on the record even if Burr is acquitted.

The next day brings a letter from Burr which explains Alston's absence—he is confined to bed—and an important visit from lawyers Wickham and Botts. The essential purpose of their visit appears to be to calm the prisoner somewhat. Though they confirm the disturbing rumor that the government plans to call his wife as a witness against Burr, they opine that the "helpless state of the children would justify her non-compliance." Most importantly, they urge Blennerhassett, whose Brief, we learn, has now reached the 13th folio, not to press for an immediate trial—ostensibly because "party-prejudice" is still too high. Perhaps it is to quiet somewhat the diarist's desire to be involved that Botts promises to advise Burr to have him present in court when witnesses he knows, especially the Hendersons, are called to testify in Burr's trial. We can imagine how aggravating it was to Blennerhassett to hear how "Burr lives in great style and sees much company within his gratings," because he adds, "where it is as difficult to get an audience, as if he really were an Emperor."

Perhaps it is a sense of the disparity between the situation of Burr—now in his natural element as lawyer, politician, intriguer—and his own comparative isolation that causes the diarist, again balancing contrasts, to turn his attention to conditions within his prison itself. Whatever its cause, his critique, on August 14, of the Keeper's scheme to reduce prison costs shows the diarist's practicality and his humanity. Similarly, his capacity for sympathy and his interest in the synthesis of contrasts are shown in the portrait of Vaun, the prison barber, a black man in whom, the "physiognamy of his countenance and the steadiness of his hand, with the keenness of his instrument, admirably correspond with the firmness and sensibility of his heart.—Would to Heaven I could add its purity.—But hideous jealousy entered there, and goaded this wretch to murder and to madness."

The Burr-plot also moves forward slightly in this long entry, for we hear that Burr has replied to the diarist's letter urging that, for reasons he makes clear in his Brief, he be allowed to examine, on Burr's behalf, witnesses he has known in Wood County. Perhaps this proposal may be viewed as another plea for recognition (he too has been trained as a lawyer) or at least for some direct involvement in the lengthening proceedings at the

Capitol. But Burr temporizes on this; and on the diarist's further recommendation that his Brief be reviewed by their counsel, Burr promises, in his note, that one of the lawyers will be sent for the Brief. But, according to the diarist, no one had called for it—nor would anyone. This situation takes Blennerhassett back to the theme that ended the previous entry. Burr is in his element now; he has no time for such details; "the exercise of his *proper* talents now constantly solicited here, in private and public exhibition, whilst they display his powers and address, at the Levé and the Bar—must engross more of his time, than he can spare for the demands of other gratifications." Having sketched Burr's character along these lines, the diarist reveals something of an artistic purpose when he goes on to explain that he will apply the principle of "harmony of contrast" in his effort now to arrive at a "third portrait" of this figure, Burr, now "so differently appearing to my regards at Richmond and on the Mississippi." He has time and reason for such reflection, apparently, since we learn that he has suspended work on the Brief, in expectation of Burr's acquittal.

As the problem of legal exoneration subsides, the issue of reimbursement, like that of recognition, is reemphasized. Alston is able to visit again and, in this same entry, August 14, brings rumors of Burr's probable acquittal on both bills, the treason and the misdemeanor; but at the same time he bears also the ominous suggestion that the Prosecution will probably move, though unsuccessfully, to have the acquitted defendants transferred to other federal districts for trial on the same charges. No mention is made of money at this point, but the subject reappears in the notes for the following day. First, we have the diarist's sardonic metaphor comparing the opening of Burr's treasure chest, in bankruptcy, to the opening of Pandora's; all his treasures, we learn, have flown, except hope (the hope of his suits against the government, after his acquittal), "on which some favoured dependents may yet"—as he himself once did—"mortgage to him, their future services and the property of their children." Money is also the subject, in the same entry, as Robert Nicholas, "a Democrat, furious keen and selfish," appears with one of Burr's protested bills, endorsed by Blennerhassett to Lewis Sanders of Lexington, for which, says the diarist, "I will never give more than my bones," since he is absolutely determined to transfer that obligation to Alston. Indeed, this effort to get Alston to make good on his promise of reimbursement dominates the next several entries.

First we hear, on August 16, that Nicholas has induced Alston to *offer* to make a journey to South Carolina in hope of raising money. But then comes a very dark day for Blennerhassett, "a Black-Monday indeed," August 17, as he has a letter from his closest friend and banker, Joseph Lewis of Philadelphia, who writes "in his *private* capacity" to inform him that the banking-house of which Lewis is the head has been "obliged to dishonour" all the bills the diarist has drawn since the preceding January, in consequence of attachment served on his funds at suit of "the Kentucky insurance co. and Lewis Sanders of Lexington." This means that bills he had drawn at Natchez will rebound and be a source of suffering to his wife. It is perhaps the nadir of Blennerhassett's hope in this period—a moment of personal ruin, embarrassment, and anxiety for his family; consequently, we hear this, among the very few direct outcries of pain and remorse in a journal governed primarily by decorum and restraint: "Oh my Peggy, where will yr sufferings end. We thought we were serving a P***** and have been the dupes of an advocate."

The "P[rince]" in whose prospective Western Empire Blennerhassett thought to have, perhaps, a diplomatic post, is now but a bankrupt lawyer pleading for his life. And for himself, he reflects as he hears Alston's carriage outside, his only hope of alleviating his family's suffering is "to humble pride of integrity before that of wealth—to solicit, read it, my wife and forgive it for the sake of yr children, his charity—for them." This is followed by a long, lamenting sentence, after which he explains that the very syntactic flood is a source of relief. "It is a relief to my heart to fill a whole page with a single sentence. The flood of my sorrows is too copious to suffer the artificial breaks and pauses of critical rules."

But Blennerhassett finds relief also in another literary device that contrasts with free association of ideas: sustained irony. The reader of the journal shares the pleasure Blennerhassett takes in both the enactment and the recounting of the "Agrestis" strategem. On August 17, during a visit from Alston, the diarist happens to praise a pamphlet by "Agrestis,"* the visitor had brought, "being 2 letters on Wilkinson's proceedings at N. Orleans . . . at the same time inquiring, who was the author." Alston permits Blennerhassett to suppose that he is the author, which the diarist thinks impossible: "to suppose Alston the author w^{d} be preposterous. Obscurity may consistently veil the parentage of Hercules; but it w^{d} be ridiculous to suppose him the offspring of a Dwarf." In fact, Blennerhassett attributes the work to his wife, Theodosia, but he sees in Alston's silent claim of authorship a chance to play upon his vanity a tune that might make him more responsive to paying the protested bills, and so releasing his funds in Philadelphia. Consequently, in the next entry, August 18, the reader is treated to the diarist's ironic account of the scene he sets for praising "Agrestis" at Alston's next visit, the devices of his praise, and his assessment of the results. "The organ now wound up, I lost no time to try upon it, the tune my heart first called for. How do you think, my wife, it went? To admiration."

The diarist's spirits are obviously lifted. His writing is as well. He enjoys the trick, the telling, and the sense it gives him of having some power over his life again. He has made some progress toward reimbursement; Alston "was tuned up, to the incredible power of paying the *whole* not indeed to day—but next April 12 month." The diarist, tuned up himself, even mischieviously proposes that his next piece might well be "a judicious combination

---

*In Ralph R. Shaw and Richard H. Shoemaker, *American Bibliography* (New York: The Scarecrow Press, 1961), 7:6, this work is listed under Alston, Joseph, "supposed author," as follows: "A short review of the late proceedings at New Orleans: and some remarks upon the bill, for suspending the privilege of the writ of habeas corpus . . . by Agrestis [pseud.] . . . South Carolina, 1807. 42. p." Reprinted . . . at the office of the Impartial Observer, Richmond, Va., 1807.

of discords to be selected fr. the letter to Pinkney, with some more of the melody of Agrestis."

Blennerhassett has hoisted his spirits by his wit here, and he closes the entry by counting his reasons for feeling better than on the preceding day. But on the following day he is "fretted" again on the recognition theme. Burr continues to ignore his advice to have him present in court during the examination of witnesses he knew. Burr, in the diarist's view, orchestrates all the dances of his counsel; that he—isolated, confined at a distance—would like to be similarly involved might be deduced, not only from his analyses of court strategy, but also from his envious cuts at Burr: "But as a jockey might restore his fame in the course after he had injured it on the tight-rope,—so perhaps, the Little Emperor at Cole's Creek may be forgotten in the Attorney at Richmond."

In reading this journal one is frequently astonished at some new facet of Blennerhassett's interest or competence which, in turn, provides a new glance for his ironic perspective. We have seen Blennerhassett the critic and legal theorist at work. Now, on August 20, we meet the diarist as chemist as he prepares to treat, with "oxygenized muriatic acid gas," the air of his rooms, which is "in no small degree tainted from the effluvia of a certain necessary fixture" at the end of his suite. This activity would appear to have nothing whatever to do with Burr, yet it leads to the diarist's speculation that intense smokers like Burr deaden the "sensibilty of their olafactory nerves." He suspects this, since Burr never complained, during the expedition, "of the bad smell of his boat occasioned by the confinement on board, of a cow, for many weeks." It was because of this same insensitivity, he hints, or a less specialized kind, that "he one night suffered Mrs Alston to sleep in the room at the north end of the passage, opposite to that in which I now am, her room, that night being of course, as it is at present, infected with effluvia from a certain cabinet connected with it.—However she early sought the morning breeze in a *solitary* ramble, on the banks of the river, next day."

Meanwhile, at the Capitol, the government had produced a succession of witnesses to events at Blennerhassett's island estate on the Ohio during December 1806, and especially on the fateful night of December 10, when the expedition's four boats were being loaded and General Edward Tupper of Marietta, according to the government's dubious witnesses, had made an attempt to arrest Blennerhassett, but had been prevented from doing so by "seven or eight muskets pointed at him." This testimony seemed very close to the "overt act" of treason that the government had to prove, but there were problems: it made Blennerhassett, not Burr, the chief malefactor; and, more important, the prosecution could not get General Tupper, who was present, to corroborate this testimony. In fact, his later, sworn deposition would sharply contradict it. Testimony was also heard concerning Blennerhassett's character, opinions, interests, and means, as well as about supplies and preparations for the expedition, and its possible military character. But as this line of testimony began to falter and meander, Burr and his counsel seized upon a decisive opportunity to protest the relevance of such evidence as it was providing.

Chief Justice Marshall agreed to hear objections regarding the admissibility of evidence. Decisively, Burr's chief counsel, John Wickham moved that since the prosecution had not proved an "overt act" of treason had taken place on Blennerhassett's island on the night of December 9, all other evidence concerning what had been said or done elsewhere was collateral and inadmissible. In admitting this motion, which, if it succeeded, would assure Burr's acquittal, the Chief Justice was placing his political life on the line, since the government would claim he suppressed evidence, and cries for his impeachment would be heard. The debate on Wickham's motion, which continued until August 29, has been called the greatest display of forensic fireworks in the history of the American bar, but it figures only indirectly in Harman's journal since he had to make do with visitors' reports of it. However, he does speculate from time to time on whether the Chief Justice's character will be equal to this test of it and on the meaning of Burr's defensive strategy as it might relate to his own case.

Burr is again the subject, now more ominously, toward the end of the entry for August 20, as one of the diarist's visitors questions the position being taken by Burr's counsel, that their client is not responsible for acts of Blennerhassett's, and expresses his fear that the diarist may be sacrificed by "falling a victim between the cunning of Burr, on the one side, and the fury and prejudice of the prosecution on the other." He also hears, on the same day, that Wickham has contended in court that since Burr was not present when the supposedly treasonous "overt acts" took place on Blennerhassett's island on December 9, he cannot—even if such acts are proved—be proceeded against until Blennerhassett, who *was* present, has been convicted. Then the next day (August 21) comes the more troubling revelation that Benjamin Botts, the diarist's respected, and voluntary, counselor is married to the sister of one of the chief witnesses against him, Sandy Henderson of Wood County. "Strange," laments the diarist, "that every embarrassment I labour under, great or small, is derived from the same source."

The embarrassments continue to weigh in. On August 22, C. F. Luckett appears with another of the bills endorsed for Burr—the last of these, the prisoner hopes. That same day he is called to court, but this time, despite his diarrhea, he is forced to walk the mile to and from the Capitol. He is expecting, if not desiring, to be arraigned; but errors he points out in the spelling of his name in the indictment are sufficient ground for a delay, and he is again sent back to the prison unarraigned. So indemnification, court action to clear his name, proper attention from Burr, news of his family—all are deferred or denied; we feel the diarist's frustration. Meanwhile, Burr, he hears, is constantly attended by Alston and Erich Bollman, toward both of whom Blennerhassett feels contempt, mixed with suspicion and jealousy. Burr, he speculates, probably now chooses to overlook his son-in-law's injudicious letter to Pinckney; and he grumbles that Bollman has "probably never heard from *authority*," from Burr, "that I had been offered to choose him or Shaw for my private *Secretary*, when I sh.[d] name a diplomatic appointment for myself."

He has, perhaps, a further reason to feel slighted, yet scornful, when he learns from Alston on the 23rd that Burr, expecting soon to be acquitted and discharged, is planning to form a land company to settle his Washita lands and may be trying to interest Alston and Bollman. Blennerhassett answers Alston's queries about these lands by raising doubts about both the validity of Burr's title and the agricultural value of the lands. He has himself, we learn, refused Burr's offer of 10,000 acres by way of reimbursement for his losses; so he has little doubt "that Burr has been promising to replenish Alston's coffers [,] which he will empty of $50,000 at least, fr. his Eldorado on the Ouashita." The diarist confides that he is by no means surprised that Alston has come to him with such questions: "I well know," he writes, "Burr's address in preventing or evading the simplest questions he does not like to answer." Indeed, he knows these straight answers he has just given may put more distance between himself and Burr, because this "may turn out another instance in addition to many others I have furnished, in which B[urr] may see cause to deprecate my knowledge of him, and curse that candour of integrity that has so often traversed his purposes."

It is in this context of frustrations, anxieties, conflicts, and of increasing alienation from Burr, that Blennerhassett's "integrity"—at least his steadfastness as a "Burrite"—meets a crucial test. In the evening of this same day, August 23, the diarist is surprised by a visit from Col. William Duane, a staunch Democrat and editor of the Philadelphia *Aurora*, an organ of the Jefferson Administration. The sudden appearance of "this Gabriel of the Gov^{t}.," the diarist knows, is for other reasons than the courtesies between Irishmen that they at first exchange. Indeed, Duane, as the diarist tells it, soon gets down to the errand he has been sent on. Protesting his concern for Blennerhassett, he warns that Burr's people are preparing to appease the government by making a scapegoat of him. But if the diarist would confess to "having written certain papers in the hands of the prosecutors" he could count on Duane to intercede for him in Washington, "where nothing he should ask, would be refused him." But the prisoner refuses the offer with the curt statement, he says, that concerning his writings, he "should admit none, 'till fairly proved—wch if any *such* sh^{d} ever appear, I w^{d} justify, if necessary, on the scaffold."

But why, one might ask, does the diarist refuse to save himself now at Burr's expense, especially since he has abundant indications, economic and legal, that Burr would sacrifice him, and he has frankly acknowledged to his wife that they have been "the dupes of an advocate"? Perhaps one practical reason might have been that he could see no better reason to trust Duane than Burr; another reason is clearly that a favorable ruling on Wickham's motion, still being debated, was expected, and Duane's visit was itself further indication of this. More important, however, is the high value that the diarist places on his steadfastness, integrity, and on aristocratic principles that he would compromise by turning to the detested Democrats. Moreover, and this is the unifying force in the journal, he is as yet unready to break with Burr. His relationship to this charming schemer is crucially ambivalent still; his hopes for recognition and reimbursement still work against his common sense. Finally, there is an element of rivalry in his stance toward Burr, and to betray him to the government would be to stoop to his level and thereby lose his valued sense of moral ascendancy over the "little Emperor." It is characteristic of Blennerhassett's idealism that the final value he does see in this adventure is to use it somehow, if he cannot find a "readier means," to "abbreviate the imprisonment of Vaun," the Negro barber.

2.

Only one day, August 24, intervenes between Duane's subversive visit to Blennerhassett at the Penitentiary and Burr's reaction to it. On the 25th the diarist is surprised by an early visit from Alston, whose ostensible purpose is to reassure him that he, Alston, will not be leaving Richmond without having taken action on the disputed bills; he will go because the trial is certain to end that week; because he is bored with the place; and, he tells the diarist, because his "anxiety" to raise money for the debtor's "relief" will hasten his departure. But the diarist remembers a true reason: "He forgot, I suppose, he yesterday told Nicholas, he had just received *letters* that *suddenly* called him home. A propensity to rely more on his witts than his memory is a prominent trait in his character." Possibly it is this awareness of the convenient faultiness of Alston's memory, or perhaps the thought of his own most recent sacrifice in Burr's behalf, that now prompts the diarist to his most definitive statement yet of the extent of his losses: "sales of my effects, wch had been sacrificed, in Wood C^{o} would not be much short of $15,000 which sum w^{d} not replace 2/3 of my Library, my furniture, instruments, House-Linen, etc., etc. with all my farming-stock and implements of husbandry, for all which I had no other hope of indemnity, but what I could derive fr. the honour and resources of Col: Burr and himself."

Although Alston is essentially "*silent*" to this declaration, he understands well enough that the real agenda is the diarist's desire for a reaffirmation of commitment that might somehow balance with his rejection of Duane's offer; consequently, Alston now alludes to Duane's visit by way of a veiled warning to the diarist to be on his guard against "spies." There has even been, Blennerhassett is told, a report "that I now see Burr in a different light, fr. that I first, regarded him." Tempting as it must have been, it would not have been in the diarist's interest to confess *that* much of the truth to Alston; so he responds with an account of his actions with Duane which corresponds with our earlier interpretation of them: "I thought it w^{d} be serviceable to the interest of my pecuniary expectations fr. him, to send him back to Burr, satisfied of my vigilance and perseverance in those duties of honour and good faith, which if they doubted in me, I should never forget, I always owed to myself."

But now, matching move for move, Blennerhassett also seizes the opportunity to turn the screws on Alston, by mentioning a reference he *says* Duane had made—it is not in his notes—to the government's having possession of a letter written by Alston to the diarist. "But what did the rascal, continues he, state to be the purport of the letter? Nothing more, said I, than proving—that you and myself were equally involved in all Col: Burr's projects." The fact that Blennerhassett is here using Duane's visit to press Alston toward a financial settlement is further clarified, a few lines farther on in the same entry (August 25), as the diarist reveals to Alston that when he was in jail in Lexington he was so angered by Alston's failure to answer a letter of his that he declared Alston was as fully involved with Burr's schemes as he, the prisoner, was. Moreover he concludes this section of the entry by telling himself that if the threat that the government has something on him were to keep Alston in town long enough "to carry some of his sincere wishes for my relief into execution—I shall owe Duane more obligations *for* his visit than he is aware of."

But the diarist's satisfaction in the execution of this new device to coerce Alston—obviously a more desperate measure than his "Agrestis" stratagem—is short-lived. It is cancelled in the same entry by his account of receiving "a pettyfogging letter fr. Hen. Clay of Lexington," requesting payment of his fee of $20. This new demand drives the diarist to send another begging letter, which he quotes in the same entry, to Alston; the letter's abjectness seems to draw upon the last of his emotional resources; it certainly marks a crisis point in his journal. "Behold me then; without a dollar" is the theme of a sad passage that concludes his long entry for August 25. The diarist's anguish is evident in the mechanics of his writing—in, for instance, the, for him, uncommon emphases and the totally uncharacteristic upper-casing of "shout": "Be these things only known to thee, my wife, hereafter. But let them SHOUT, and ever be by my first of cares, until I set them right, or perish." (See illustrations on pp. 211–12.)

By evening of the next day, however, he has learned that the "bird" he stalks has not yet flown, and he has regained his composure and with it his wit. "The little animal has clapped its wings in screaming essays toward the Oaks [Alston's plantation in South Carolina] but yet may it remain a little longer on that egg, it has not yet hatched, for the cuckoo that laid it." And, indeed, the following day, August 27, brings a visit from Alston with news of financial settlements on the disputed bills amounting to some $16,000. More surprising, perhaps, is Alston's returning to the diarist of what, he admits, "another man might have kept"—his begging letter, quoted in the entry for the 25th. These actions occasion some grudging words that might be read as respect for Alston's never having questioned his financial obligation to

Blennerhassett in Burr's behalf. Further good news is that the Hendersons, as the diarist hears it, "regret that they are obliged to testify against me." This, he supposes, may have to do with a certain letter written by Sandy to his father "soliciting his consent to his sons' espousing the principles and conduct I confidentially recommended to them, which letter will show what treason I recommended or was engaged in." Still other news that is surely not unpleasant to the diarist's ear is the rumor that Burr, even if soon acquitted, will not soon leave Richmond but must face a host of civil suits. If his new friend George Pollock, a wealthy Philadelphia merchant, "or some other preserving Angel," the diarist crows, "does not shield him from this new Host;—then indeed, will he fall more inglorious than fr. a gibbet."

The total absence of an entry for the following day, August 28, takes us by surprise (the only other such gaps are for October 31 and November 6, while Blennerhassett was en route to Baltimore and Philadelphia); yet the partially blank page, like the occasional blot that appears to be from a drop of perspiration, serves to remind us that our meticulous diarist was not simply a mind weighing the prospects of reimbursement, recognition, or litigation, but a suffering body-self, a prisoner during the dog days of a sweltering summer, when influenza made its rounds, like anecdotes about the Chief Justice. Although Judge Safford saw fit to remove many of the diarist's references to his bodily health, a retranscription of the journal replaces the diarist's thought in a body that is troubled by facial rash, foul air, headache, sleeplessness, and diarrhea. On August 22, for instance, we have a pathetic image of his efforts to get air: "I find it very agreeable this ev^{g} to get upon a chair, by which I am enabled to raise my mouth to the lower tier of openings in the grating of the windows & breathe another air for 1/2 an hour." The next day, the 23rd, we have reference to the diarrhea which had troubled him for several days but is, he writes, now "much abated by the medicine I use." This is followed by a prescription of medication and a regimen. The absence of an entry for the 28th is explained the next day by a detailed description of the remedies the diarist-as-druggist has prescribed to himself. Such details—his medical strategies, like his financial strategies—are an interesting counterweight to the usual view of Blennerhassett as bumbling romantic.

Ironically, it is just at this point, as the diarist's mind is absorbed by very practical problems relating to money and medication, that he is visited by his former business partner at Marietta, Dudley Woodbridge, who gives an account of his testimony concerning Blennerhassett's "talents and studies," and particularly, concerning the value of his island estate on the Ohio. The diarist notes that in this examination it seems to Woodbridge that "the drift of Col: Burr was to show that I c^{d} in no sense be regarded as a military character," and his visitor apologizes for having said Blennerhassett had "more other sense than common sense," explaining that this remark escaped him under the pressure of the examination. The prisoner accepts Woodbridge's apology, but he wonders what motive Burr and his counsel could have "to exhibit me to the Jury as a character less skilled in the ordinary affairs of life than common men." He is particularly unsettled by the news that Burr's current favorite, Bollman, has also been at pains to quiz Woodbridge and has extracted from him "an opinion that I am eccentric."

Blennerhassett is understandably distressed that his character is now being unduly sacrificed to Burr's defense—just as his property was sacrificed in the offense. Surely he has still ringing in his ears Duane's supposed disclosures of an attempt underway to make a scapegoat of him. Of course, it would be to the defense's advantage—and the diarist's own—to show that he was by temperament unmilitary and therefore unlikely to have been levying war on the island in December, and that what may have seemed treasonable in the way of overt acts there, especially on December 9, would have proceeded from Blennerhassett's eccentricity, unworldliness, or impracticality rather than from anything initiated by Burr. The reader of this journal will perhaps decide how much justified irony there is for Blennerhassett in the account of him given to Burr's jury. We do know that the diarist finds all of this "mysterious" and determines to seek opportunities to explore the matter further. There also seems to be irritation in the fact that although the diarist receives by letter that day the very welcome news that he might stand in the entail of an estate in Ireland worth £6000., this same entry (August 29) concludes with his most scathing attack yet on the character and abilities of Burr: "the present trial cannot fail to furnish ample testimony if not to the guilt, at least to the defect of every talent, under the assumption of which, this giddy adventurer has seduced so many followers of riper experience and better judgment than myself. You were right therefore, honest Hay, in observing the other day to Woodge . . . that I must now think Burr had duped me; but you were wrong in supposing I am indebted to you for the discovery. I am possessed of it these 9. months."

But the diarist's consciousness has not by any means been entirely consumed by the maturation of this truth; though this is the journal's controlling theme, it is rich in its digressions. There are, for instance, frequent expressions of affection (generally removed by Safford), for his wife, to whom the journal is addressed, and of anxiety concerning her well-being and that of their boys. There are indications of enjoyment, of delight even, as when (August 30) his friend Mercer, leaves "a present of refreshments, of fruit, good butter; and fine calf's feet jelly on ice, . . . sent me by Mrs Gamble." At this moment also there is much excited speculation regarding the Chief Justice's ruling, expected the following day, on the motion that has been before him since August 20. Will he, the diarist and his friends wonder, "shrink fr. his duty, as an able Judge, or a virtuous Patriot to avert the revenge of an unprincipled Govt or avoid other trials, menaced and preparing for himself, by its wretched partizans"? Has he, as some say, written privately to the *Argus* stating opinions that qualify or contravene those he has delivered from the Bench? The diarist is troubled by such news, yet he is confident that "whatever dust or insects may have sought the Judge's Robes—whilst off his back—none will venture to appear upon the ermine that bedecks his person." At this time also Blennerhassett is "severely affected" with influenza, of which his symptoms are "head-ach, coryza, great defluition fr. the nose, and some fever." It is, he tells his wife, "the 3rd sickness I have had here which has compelled me to resort to medicine." But his indisposition does not prevent him from inscribing into the same entry (August 30) a memorable verbal portrait or "character" of Luther Martin, alone "the whole rear-guard of Burr's Forensic Army," whose prodigious powers of memory and analysis the diarist highlights, along with the contrasting personal characteristics of kindness and coarseness. With this conventional set-piece of literary portraiture he is welcomed into the journal as a recurrent and significant character.

On Monday, August 31, Chief Justice Marshall delivered his opinion on the crucial motion before the court; the reading of it, said to be the longest and perhaps the most important of his recorded opinions, took three hours. To Blennerhassett, over in the Penitentiary, waiting for news, this was "the most oppressive day I have yet endured in this place." He has been kept awake all night, he says, by the "unremitting severity" of his cough. When Mercer arrives with the news that in the Chief Justice's opinion the "overt act of levying war" against the U.S., which must be proved by two witnesses, "was not proved by a single witness," the diarist is "little revived with the news." He has, he writes, "too many other trials to pass." There will be the misdemeanor indictments to be dealt with, and the possibility of being transmitted to another federal district for trial, but foremost among his "trials" will be his effort to recover his property. At least, he notes, the end of his imprisonment will bring a better opportunity to press his claim against Burr: "When *I* shall have access to Burr and Alston it will be my fault if I do not see them when I ought." On September 1 the jury reported its famous verdict that the charge of treason against Burr was "not proved." On the 2nd, his health somewhat improved, the diarist is able to take some pleasure in a visit, still under guard, to the Capitol to hear counsel enter plea for his discharge from the indictment for treason. He delights in the sensation of coolness as they enter the dome, but, more particularly he is gratified as they pass out, by the expression he sees on the face of an enemy, Phelps, "whose visage exhibited so high-coloured a picture of the disap^{t} of his malice that I involuntarily smiled on him." He smiles a bit too, we suppose, when he learns that Burr, expecting his discharge soon, plans to visit him at the prison in a day or two; for now he expects, as he says, to "have the liberty of the town as soon as his Highness."

On September 3, Blennerhassett posts, with evident satisfaction, the news he has heard from his fellow-prisoner, Major Israel Smith, that soon after the Burr expedition's arrival at Natchez the preceding January, Cowles Meade, acting governor of the Mississippi Territory "had seriously taken up an idea of Col: Burr's being then *deranged*, alledging that he could not be mistaken, as he Meade, had very long known him." Nevertheless, the diarist also takes note of the fact that in court the day before Burr had "looked 50 per cent better than I have ever seen him; and displayed a command of tone and firmness of manner he did not appear to me to possess, before the verdict of Tuesday." But there were still delays in carrying out the implications of that verdict. On the 4th the prosecutor, at the President's instigation, made a last-ditch attempt to have the prisoner held for transmittal to another district, where an overt act might be proved; but Chief Justice Marshall ruled against the motion on grounds that the indictment for misdemeanor had to be tried before transmittal could be considered. He accordingly ordered that Burr be discharged from his treason indictment and that the trial for misdemeanor commence immediately.

The following day saw a further delay as the result of a prolonged argument over the amount of Burr's bail. Blennerhassett notes on September 5 that the figure was set at $5000, over the objections of counsel that the Colonel would find bail difficult to obtain because he was still technically in custody "on *civil process*." This is something of a revelation to him. "Strange! I should never before have heard of this arrest on civil process having been made upon him, and still being unremoved." Meanwhile ominous rumors reach his ears about plans to prosecute the accused in Kentucky—"at the moment we are discharged here—provided only, the necessary witnesses can be trained and suborned, and a Gr. Jury packed for the purpose." But there is news also of a more comforting sort; Burr and Botts, looking ahead to the oncoming trial have been examining a witness, A. L. Duncan, who, it is said, can discredit General Wilkinson. "It is pretended," the diarist posts, "D. has proved W. guilty of forgery, in erasing and altering the cipher letter. But I do not place implicit reliance on the full extent of this statement."

Still the "business of bailing" drags on, and this circumstance gives Blennerhassett the occasion to remark, caustically, that Burr's bail, like the security for his own bills, may "undergo some procrastination" in so far as they depend upon Alston, from whom he has heard nothing concerning the arrangements he had promised to make with bill-holders Nicholas and Luckett. But by afternoon of the same day the diarist has to admit he has been mistaken in his "conjectures of the morning, respecting the Hero of these notes." Luckett appears with evidence of Alston's settlements with himself and Nicholas, and he brings news also that Burr has procured securities for his bail and for some $30,000 in civil suits. Indeed, he hears that the former Vice-President "enjoyed a long walk, this ev^{g} with Mrs Alston, in which he exhibited his person thro' the greater part of the town, and will probably honour me with a visit tomorrow."

But while the arch-conspiritor was free to promenade about the town with his bright and beautiful daughter on his arm, his loyal victim and sometime chronicler was still in the Penitentiary and about to enter another moment of crisis. Thus we learn on September 6 that the diarist is undergoing "no small uneasiness" because he fears that Burr's misdemeanor trial could prolong his imprisonment—another loss of his to Burr. So he determines on a strategy of his own: to insist on being brought to court early, before Burr's trial begins, and there to plead in abatement to both his indictments. "My speculation on the success of this manoeuver," he writes, "opens to me, a prospect of no small amusement." The pleasing point of his strategy, he believes, is that the prosecution will be in a dilemma, because to counter his plea with sufficient evidence to justify his continued commitment must force the prosecution to delay Burr's trial, so that Burr "must inevitably, be distanced—unless he can prevent my pleading 'till the present trial is at an End wch I also expect, he will fail in." Soon, however, we learn that the start of Burr's trial has been put off for two days so that Hay can send to Monticello "to learn his master's pleasure" regarding the release of the contents of a letter from Wilkinson. Blennerhassett's mock-heroic allegorical account of the way in which the contents of this letter were leaked in the meantime is a witty diversion in his notes of September 6. We are therefore taken by surprise when he announces on the 7th: "This day at 11 o'clock A.M. ended my captivity which has lasted 53 days." Hay has simply agreed then and there to Botts' request to have the diarist's treason bill discharged. He must be detained for the misdemeanor, but bail is allowed, and Blennerhassett readily accepts Dudley Woodbridge's offer to be his security for the $5000. So now the diarist, as Burr, is free to seek society in Richmond, provided he presents himself in court on September 9th.

3.

The third of the major episodes into which the journal can be divided includes the entries from September 7 to October 25; it includes Blennerhassett's comments on the progress of the misdemeanor trial and the transmittal hearing, as well as scenes, characters, and reflections drawn from his involvements with the social life of Richmond. These materials are too detailed and diffuse to be fully discussed here; however, it will be possible to call attention to certain highlights, especially those which clarify the diarist's relationship to Burr.

One such highlight is Blennerhassett's account of a meeting with Burr on September 9, the day of the opening of Burr's misdemeanor trial. This is his second call on Burr, we note, since the diarist's release on the 7th. Burr is living in the former residence of Alston, who has gone off, we learn, "in the way he has so long threatened, i.e. without taking leave." The visit with Burr is under some constraints, evidently, because the diarist catches a glimpse of another visitor, "this old sly-boots," General Dayton, "sequestered in another room," though Burr does not offer an introduction. The conversation, we are told, "turned altogether on the subject of my involvement in pecuniary claims upon him." Blennerhassett explains his losses and his expectation of indemnity "distinctly and with firmness." And he declares that he holds Alston "answerable" for his notes and the interest in them, unless Burr were to settle these claims himself. All is very clear and direct, it seems; and Burr, perhaps mindful of the third presence, is equally so. He will "adjust all such demands whenever he can be freed from the present prosecutions." To Blennerhassett this must then have seemed a not very distant prospect, since earlier in the same entry he remarks that the defense would be adopting the same strategy they had used in the treason trial, moving to arrest all evidence that was not specific to the charge, i.e., that Burr's expedition had been military in character and had been intended against Mexico, a possession of Spain, with which nation the United States was then at peace.

Burr's acquittal of the misdemeanor charge is even more distinctly in prospect by the time the diarist next visits him, on September 13, in company with Major Israel Smith, another loyal associate who had been the diarist's neighbor at the Penitentiary. It is Burr's response to the expectation of the end of his prosecution that makes this meeting, or the diarist's record of it, particularly fascinating, though no reference is made at this time to financial settlements. We learn that Burr is "gay as usual, and as busy in speculations on reorganizing his projects for action, as if he had never suffered the least interruption." Their former leader urges that "our schemes" could all be set in motion again within 6 months, and with better chance of success, since they would now have "a clearer view of the ground, and a more perfect knowledge of our men." The diarist pauses here to note that this remark Major Smith and he "did not fail, I believe, duly to apply both to him and to ourselves." Then he delivers an appraisal of Burr that is among the most significant in the journal for the insight it gives into the hidden Blennerhassett, particularly into the sense of rivalry the inner man felt toward Burr: "if Burr possessed the sensibilites of the right sort, with 100th part of the energies for which, with many, he has obtained such ill-grounded credit,—his first & last determination with the morning and the night should be the destruction of those enemies who have so long and so cruelly reaked their malicious vengeance upon him. But time will prove him, as incapable in all his future efforts as he has been in the past."

On September 14 the Chief Justice ruled in favor of the motion of the defense, doing so in what the diarist calls "as able, full, and luminous an opinion, as ever did honour to a Judge, which has put an end to the present prosecution." As he had done with the treason indictment, Hay attempted to forestall a verdict of acquittal with a plea of *nolle prosequi*, but the jury was ordered out, and within half an hour had found Burr not guilty of high misdemeanor. Hay then agreed to the pleas of *nolle prosequi* to the indictments of Blennerhassett and Smith, and thus, for the diarist as for Burr, the second act of the Richmond trials came to an end on September 16. But a third and most convoluted act began immediately, as Hay, playing the last of his trumps, moved that the alleged conspirators be committed to the Federal Court in Chillicothe, Ohio, on charges of having committed treason and/or misdemeanor in that district. What followed was a hearing, with the Chief Justice now sitting, without Jury, in the role of examining magistrate, hearing all testimony, in order, as the diarist puts it, "to separate, and apply to each [case] such evidence of overt acts as the testimony might disclose." The court was now thrown open, in effect, and the stage set for the government to produce as many of its 140 witnesses as it wished. It would take five weeks to hear them out, during which time the defendants enjoyed the freedom of society.

On the 16th we have the diarist's succinct summary of Botts' "perspicuous" four-point opening argument against transmittal, an argument, we learn, "which Burr very neatly summed up and condensed before Court adjourned about half past 3." In the evening he again has Burr under observation, now at a dinner party at Burr's house, for he "had at *last* tho't of asking us to dine with him." In his account of this dinner ("neat and followed by 3 or 4 sorts of wine—Splendid poverty!") we are treated, through the diarist's eyes, to Burr's anecdote of the perfumed letter. In the story, Burr tells of a trick played on him by one woman to detect, through his reaction, the recent presence of another with him. But the reader's real interest may be in the question of why the diarist recounts this story of the betrayer betrayed with such particularity—for his wife. (That he does so tells us, as so much does, about *her* interests as his intended reader.) The moral that Blennerhassett gives to his own account amounts to a two-pronged attack on Burr's way with women in relation to the American way of love. "I have given it place here," he writes, "only to convey an idea of that temperament and address which enables this character on certain occasions, like the snake, to cast his slough, and thro' age and debauchery, seems to uphold his ascendancy over the sex in a country where sensuality is love, and sentiment but a name." It seems evident from the phrase "like the snake, to cast his slough" that Blennerhassett is setting forth Burr as the Satanic betrayer—here of women—much as William Wirt, in a famous speech that the diarist will copy into his notes, had imaged Burr as the Satanic serpent in the Blennerhassetts' Eden on the Ohio. But here perhaps there is also a trace of envy in the diarist's account, like the woman's in Burr's story—of the great deceiver's compelling vivacity; for the diarist, as he will tell us in connection with an anecdote of his own, was by no means inattentive to "the sex."

While the diarist, during this period, enjoyed occasional evenings dining or merely conversing in elegant company, or in playing an instrument at the Harmonic Society, his days were mostly spent as a passive auditor of the courtroom drone. But on September 18 his attention is awakened to indignation as he posts his response to the Judge's ruling on Botts' motion of the 16th. He is furious at the idea that, having failed to prove treason against the defendant in a district of its choice, the government may now, it appears, prosecute the same offense from district to district till it finds a conviction. The absurdity of this, in the diarist's view, is that, in his and Burr's cases, the government would return to scenes (Kentucky and Mississippi Territory) of its earlier abortive efforts to prosecute the defendants. Since these are the maneuvers of a vindictive administration, he suggests, they must be judged in the light history, not of law, which government may coerce. Hence he hopes his comments may "serve to furnish some ingredients in the History of the pres.^{t} administration." In the next day's entry (September 19) we learn that Burr has likewise been disturbed by the Judge's apparent inconsistency with his own earlier decisions, so much so "that he would not trust himself to rise to sum up and condense the forces displayed by his counsel into compact columns . . . as is generally his practice." However, despite the check his defense has received, Burr "has no fear of the final result."

In this confidence of his eventual release, Burr has been making new plans that arouse the curious speculations of his former associates. On the 20th of September the diarist posts the news that he has heard from De Pestre, and later, Smith, that Burr "sets off immediately for England, after his liberation fr. the present motion before the C.^{t} to collect money for reorganizing his projects." Though Blennerhassett doubts that Burr would return to these projects, or even return at all, if he could get to England, he can readily imagine how Burr would entice creditors here with the idea of his having liberal sources there, then deceive sources there with empty promises of projects here, etc. Still, he is most troubled by the thought that Burr "should never have dropped even a hint to me of his projected trip to England. I have had more of his confidence than either Smith or de Pestre." This hint of a still further betrayal leads Blennerhassett to what may be the sharpest condemnation of Burr he has yet uttered: "whatever feeling this man possesses, is confined within the sensuality of his temperament, if indeed his conduct . . . does not warrant suspicion of Cowles Meade, and fully prove . . . . that there is at best a method in his madness."

There is more of Burr in the next day's (September 21) account of the diarist's conversation with Col. De Pestre, who has told him how the arch-conspirator met his match in trying to dupe the Spanish minister Yrujo, who "pierced the cobweb tissues of Burr's intrigues with him at a single glance" and "laughed at the awkwardness with which Burr endeavoured to mask his designs on Mexico." The diarist takes evident satisfaction in this example of Burr's apparent incompetence in foreign intrigues, shown in this instance as well as in his failure to make use, during the past winter, of the small arms, supposedly placed at his disposal, from two French warships. "If he had not talents or spirit to use them," the diarist concludes grandly, "he is where he sh^{d} be."

A similar dismissal takes place in the next incident that must be spoken of. This occurrence, however, is only very obliquely related to either the diarist's accounts of Burr's schemes, or to the procession of government witnesses in the transmittal hearing. Perhaps this is why Judge Safford omits entirely from his edition Blennerhassett's astonishing account of his Circe episode, in the entry for September 24. The segment is a kind of prose-poem—perhaps the most striking stylistic display in the journal—complete with mock heroic classical embellishment, entrancement, epiphany, and disillusionment. Blennerhassett, performing that evening with the Harmonic Society, becomes briefly captivated by a "very handsome woman," whom he apparently first notices in the audience, has entwining glances with, then fancies their co-participation in the erotic spirit of a glee which is being sung. But when he is introduced to her after the performance, the soul-mate illusion is dispelled for him, by her conversation, and she is dismissed as a mundane, unsophisticated person, whose conversation, lacking wit and culture, had little of the charm of her figure. The diarist—writing all this to his "first *beloved*"—was, by his superior sensibility, "released thus fr. the captivity in wch this Circe bound me for a moment, I hope not thereby degraded from the favour of a more amiable Penelope than ever really furnished a model to Homer." With this graceful compliment the diarist is fully in control, but we notice that this story illustrates the romantic sensibility that enabled him—the "devoted victim"—to be also entranced by Burr, whose conversation was all that the widow's was not. His wit, we know, would never have missed the invited play on "horns" that ends their conversation.

The diarist's romantic sensibility is manifested also by an interest in visions of quite another sort. Four days later, in the entry for September 28, he notes that he has had a long letter from his wife; in it he learns that she has been troubled by a "complaint in her chest" and that the two boys have both had fevers, but Harman has suffered most. The diarist is convinced that a dream he had, while in the Penitentiary, of Harman's death from a dog's bite must have announced this disease to him, since it came at the moment that must have marked the climax of the fever spoken of in Margaret's letter. But now he must wonder if the more recent "second dream" he has had may announce a relapse that has happened since the letter. This thought leads to the general reflection that while "reason," as he writes, "shall continue my only guide to faith, I will yet wonder in mysterious awe of—such dreams as these, which my understanding cannot scan whilst they appal my heart."

Back in the courtroom, meanwhile, the climax of the transmittal hearing has been reached two days earlier, on September 26, with the long-foreshadowed appearance on the stand of General Wilkinson, Burr's one-time friend and his betrayer, whose word was more instrumental than any other in disposing Jefferson to proclaim Burr a traitor. His confession at this point that he had altered a duplicate of the famous cipher letter in such a way as to remove a phrase in it that would reveal he had been in previous communication with Burr, showed ultimately that he had betrayed both his friend and the President. Blennerhassett recounts this, we note, after a particularly sardonic impression of the General as being typical of American military leadership. We now have it as it was before Judge Safford removed the offensive reflection on the army. "The General W^{n} exhibited the manner of a sergeant under a C^{t} Martial rather than the demeanor of an accusing Officer confronted with his culprit. His perplexity and derangement, even upon his direct examination, was no unfaithful picture of the talents and resources under which the American army is marshaled and his cross-examination has placed beyond all doubt 'his honour as a soldier and his fidelity as a citizen.' "

It was to have been expected that this appearance of Wilkinson in the witness box, the climax of the hearing, would have been the occasion for a dramatic confrontation of Wilkinson and

Burr. The fact, however, as the diarist tells us on the 26th, is that "Burr who was very unwell with a Diarrhea, preserved a composure inspired by W.[s] self-condemnation and supported by his indisposition." The next morning, Burr, with surprising confidence in his loyalty, summons Blennerhassett to his bedside, asking him to prescribe something for the complaint. Although the diarist, in his capacity as chemist, obligingly has some pills made up immediately, when he calls again that evening he finds that Burr hasn't taken the medicine but a dose of laudanum instead. The consequence is, perhaps to the diarist's satisfaction, that Burr's diarrhea is "much worse" the next day and the court cannot sit, owing to his absence, so Wilkinson's examination is delayed. These circumstances coerce Burr into taking Blennerhassett's medicine—perhaps as much of the desired recognition as the diarist ever gets from him—with the result that the defendant rests well and is much better on the 29th, though the diarist learns he "has prudently declined attending Court: tho' he is evidently mortified he is not able to witness the progress of his recrimination of Wilkinson, conducted by his counsel, in which he is so desirous to take a part." But Blennerhassett is present, his pen dipped in acid, with neo-classical color. "Then came on the Little Upstart Brigadier—whose demeanor to day, was no doubt as opposite to that bloated arrogance in which he strutted at Orleans during the reign of his brief authority, as was the carriage of Dionysus at Corinth compared with his royal port before at Syracuse." Wickham's conduct of the examination, in Bott's absence, is "masterly and ingenious," casting both the prosecutor and his eminent witness into "confusion." The diarist is aware that the government's case is eroding and Wilkinson's testimony has done little to shore it up.

Later that day Blennerhassett is with Burr again; although Bollman and Major Smith are the only other persons present, Burr offers no introduction to Bollman. The diarist is incensed at this exclusion, and his remark on it shows the urge to rivalry that is a feature of his relationship with Burr. "Both no doubt have discovered long since, I am not of a temper to further their intrigues. But they are short-sighted in not perceiving how effectively I can and will assuredly frustrate them." The same element of antagonism develops later in the same entry (August 29) as the diarist refuses his "services as a runner to beg for him" when Burr suggests a canvas for funds to restart the *Impartial Observer*. He is pleased with his resistance to Burr in this but aware that the great schemer may have had a hidden purpose in this request. "Was it to remind me to smother any rising thoughts within me, to renew my hints to him of other calls for money?"

Burr is again the subject of the diarist's contemptuous analysis on September 30, when, in the presence of Robinson and Smith again, Burr argues that Cowles Meade had violated his agreements made with the leader "last February or January in what was called the *armistice*, at Natchez." Blennerhassett is appalled that Burr would claim Meade had broken any agreement to let the expedition members keep their arms, "when we all knew the solicitude with which he afterwards had them all *hid* and sunk in the river." This line leads the diarist to what he now sees as his duty: it is that young men, particularly Robinson and Swartwout, "whom I can redeem fr. future connections with every incapacity but the talents for intrigue must not be entangled in those snares so imprudently or so rashly laid for their credulity." He again calls to his aid (for the third time in the journal) Cowles Meade's "impression last winter that Burr was at *times* deranged as the only means of accounting for his occasional rashness of his assertions." (On October 7, referring to Burr's apparently contradictory attitude toward Col. John McKee, he will allude once again to Meade's impression, but with a crucial change of tense: "Can he find no better friends? or is he really deranged?")

It is at this moment—perhaps thinking of the implications of such words of his as "redeem" and "snares," and seeing Burr as the great antagonist—that the diarist mentions William Wirt's famous speech of August 25, which he has first seen in print and quotes at length in his entry for October 3. In his speech, Wirt, making a distinction between principle and accessory in treason, launches into a long allegorical portrayal of Blennerhassett as the contented Adam into whose island paradise on the Ohio, stole the serpent, Burr, bringing temptation, fall, and exile to the innocent Adam and his Eve. The symbolism is as attractive to the diarist as it was rhetorically useful to the lawyer. But Blennerhassett, as we have seen, appears to have been ambitious, worldly, sophisticated—even exiled—before Burr appeared; and Eden was not so much his estate as what it replaced. Moreover, the journal constantly shows that the diarist has a litigious and scheming mind of his own, but he is clearly less secretive and self-interested than Burr and is guided by ideals that are more clearly public, religious, and aristocratic. It is from this standpoint that he sees himself as the serpent's antagonist rather than victim (more nearly St. George than Adam) whose task is to "frustrate" Burr's new schemes and "redeem" the younger associates from his influence.

We notice this pattern again in the entry for October 4. As Wilkinson is discomfited and the hearing draws toward a close, Blennerhassett hears personally from Burr of his rumored trip to London, and listens to his request for letters of introduction to the diarist's aristocratic connections. Harman, as we have mentioned, sees Burr's duplicity in this, noting that "he has no serious purpose of reviving any of his speculations in America" but is motivated more by "anxiety to elude his creditors," including the diarist. So he begins to form a counter-scheme of his own. Meanwhile, in the same entry, he embraces the task of saving young Robinson, the only child of a wealthy father. "To save him," he writes, "my breast heaved with indignation against his tempter, whilst my heart laboured for the danger of my young friend." But his intervention, "had seasonably prepared this y^{g} man, who will tomorrow, make his escape to Pittsburgh, fr. the fascination of this serpent." St. George has done his work.

On October 10, with the "motley proceedings" at the Capitol nearing their end, the diarist outlines his ultimate stratagem for forcing Burr to meet his claims. "My plan," he writes, "is to hint to him—my ability to introduce him into the first circles in England, by introductory letters, at the same time showing him my expectations of becoming soon possessed of a large fortune, in Europe: fr. which, I doubt not I shall be enabled to engage his most warm interest. This plan I shall put in execution tomorrow, of which I will note the effect upon him." The irony with which, in the next entry, he depicts the effect of this bait on Burr is quite delicious. "Hey-day! Behold the wretched and beggared Blennerhassett about to rise out of the misery in which I have plunged him and his unhappy family, into wealth and consequence! Heir too, of a nobleman! . . . all this, and probably much more to the same purpose, entered and pervaded the mind of this arch-financier, with the velocity of light in an instant. Be it so. Let him outwit himself." The hook, of course, is that Burr must first exonerate the diarist from the demands of Miller, the last of the bill-holders. "Otherwise we break upon a *writt* and for everything else, I fear not his address in future." But, we wonder, does the hook have a barb? Will he really withhold the promised letters until Miller is paid, or will the diarist, in his desire for recognition, reverse the stratagem upon himself, giving everything away to get the attention he really wants from Burr?

This latter possibility is suggested, oddly enough, by the anecdote which closes the entry. As he is departing from his visit, he notices a "French heroic poem" that Burr has been reading; as he looks on into it he sees it is no decorous neoclassical epic, but a "repast of blasphemy and obscenity, better suited to his [Burr's] vitiated palate." They are, indeed, quite unlike those pious and sentimental verses, composed in memory of Miss Gray by his friend Banks, lines that he would deem worthy of "preservation" and so copy the whole poem (perhaps as an outlet for self-pity) into his entry two days later on October 13. But with the French poem, the diarist, though he condemns the subject as appropriate to Burr's morals, is himself hooked by the wit of the piece, retells most of it in his own notes, and ends by wishing he had a copy. We can anticipate that his stratagem with the letters abroad is likely to collapse just as this critique of Burr's reading does, because he cannot keep his distance from the exotic charm of Burr's world. When on September 24, in setting down the Circe episode, he speaks of "that accursed sensibility to which I am a devoted victim," or, speaking of fortune, on October 18, he says "I am already her puppet," he refers to the pattern of desire that will make his final break with Burr difficult.

For the moment, however, his attention is drawn to a new crisis that makes his design against Burr a secondary concern. On October 20, the Chief Justice delivered his opinion in the hearing. It is to the effect that none of the defendants can be transmitted for treason; however, Blennerhassett is ordered to appear in Chillicothe, Ohio, on the 4th of January to answer charges of misdemeanor. Burr, too, is "ordered on this new dance." Stunned by the idea of extended prosecution, diarist is immediately determined to "leave the little Emperor to exhibit it alone." The thought of escaping to Florida occurs to him; then comes the idea that Col. Duane might be induced to shift things for him. It is with these two large plans uppermost in mind—to use Duane for leverage with the Administration and to "close my pecuniary affairs with Burr there," that he sets out for Philadelphia, by way of Washington and Baltimore, on October 24.

4.

Blennerhassett's last few days in Richmond appear to have been troubled, though one can sense something like enjoyment in such moments of the journal as his lampoon of the overfigurative language of Wirt's last speech (October 17) or his account (October 18) of meeting Mrs. David Randolph, the "near relation of the President" who "uttered more treason than *my wife* ever dreamed of." The 20th brings word of a "new calamity," his wife's recent fever, which leaves him in a state of "lethargic absence," from which, he says, he wakes in wonder to find life still going on. "Oh! Melancholy," he complains, "how long wilt thou brood upon me." In this mood and on the same day he learns of his commitment to Ohio for the misdemeanor trial. It is perhaps quite natural that he should think (October 22) of escaping with his family to Florida, "rather than play a part in a second farce." This intention is reinforced the following day when he learns Wickham's opinion that if the government wishes his conviction at Chillicothe, Woodbridge's evidence would be enough to secure it. "Another call to Florida," he notes. And with all, there is still the humiliating suspension of his credit at the counting house of his friend Joe Lewis in Philadelphia. So it is with much pending that he sets out for Philadelphia; with his projects for dealing with Duane and Burr in mind, he anticipates also the solace of his friend, Lewis. "His counsel will soon direct my distracted cares to peace."

But distraction in another mode comes sooner. As they are "jolting and jarring" in the coach over the roads toward the Federal City, Luther Martin's unchecked loquacity, his phenomenal memory, his gifts for anecdote and satire often embellishing his alcoholic monologue, hold the diarist's interest all the way. And once they are settled in their hotel, Martin's boozy gregariousness and brilliant discourse, which he carries freely "into the enemies' country, I mean to the public room," is a source of continuing excitement and engagement with others. Yet Blennerhassett's thoughts are soon returned to the rankling issue of his continued prosecution. A paragraph in the President's Message to Congress raises the possibility of impeachment proceedings against the Chief Justice "by signifying a doubt—whether we have not still the use of our necks, thro' misconduct of the Judge." For Blennerhassett, incensed over the committal decision, the Judge's impeachment would merely be "penance" for that "timidity of conduct," which, while it restrained him from hanging them, nonetheless induced him to continue the prosecution as a sop thrown to "pacify the clamorous yells of the Cerberus of Democracy," but moistened with the tears of his family. As a sop he is still in danger.

Burr, meanwhile, has remained in Richmond to arrange securities in the civil suits pending there against him and amounting, the diarist says, to some $36,000. What particularly annoys Blennerhassett concerning this is the news that Burr has used the information concerning his expectations "of succeeding to a large fortune in Europe"—communicated as part of the diarist's own strategy to get money from Burr—as a device to persuade his securities in Richmond by indicating that he will control

Blennerhassett's new funds. "Such is his honor," the diarist laments, "such his unerring purpose to take every chance of converting even the hopes of his acquaintances, to his own interest." But he allows that he can accept "this last liberty he has taken with me," if it can further his own demands against Burr.

He has, however, a more immediate project, which is to discover the government's intentions as to his further prosecution in Ohio. On October 28 he begins this with a letter to Caesar Rodney, the Attorney General, by way of Martin, requesting to be informed officially if the government will require his appearance at Chillicothe. It is while waiting for Rodney's answer that he pens the interesting but unrelievedly contemptuous description of the "misled city" on the Potomac that dominates the entry for this date. He finds the major structures of the city as ill-proportioned and incoherent as the authority they are meant to symbolize. "After all," he concludes, "every foreigner after his arrival here will inquire for 50 years to come, as is now very common, 'where is the city of Washington?' "

His mood is not much improved the following day, October 29, by a visit to the Attorney General, whom he finds "a trifling negative character," and a "sniveller," who "shall not have even a nitch amongst the worthies of the present admin." His impression of Rodney, as of the city, may have been partly conditioned by the shadow of continued prosecution, projected in part by the perfunctory and non-committal note he has had from the Attorney General, stating that he could only observe "at present" that Blennerhassett would be bound to appear at Chillicothe. Despite the forceful tributes in these entries to the loyalty and benevolence of his companion, Luther Martin, he cannot but admit that "this place has been extremely tiresome to me." Burr, he notes, is somewhere in the city, but his appearance can no more be depended on "than on that of a new comet." So it is with relief to the diarist that he and Martin, "wedged in amongst 10 other passengers in the coach," set out for Baltimore on October 31.

It might be argued that, just as Blennerhassett met with frustration and ennui at Washington, so he met with their opposites—gratification, of a sort, and excitement—in Baltimore. The four Baltimore entries (November 1–4) are crowded with arresting comments and details, sometimes unelaborated. For instance, we learn without other comment that Dr. Cummins, who has traveled with them from Richmond, "has bro't on a fever by his debaucheries." Burr, of whom we are told "no 2 persons of his acquaintance will ever understand him alike," has also appeared in town, but has "sneaked into obscure quarters," namely, "the French hotel in Gay-street." But the main event of the diarist's Baltimore stop, his encounter with a Democratic mob, is given rather full dramatic development in his account, with something like foreshadowing, diversion, rising action, climax, falling action, and resolution.

The incident is foreshadowed on November 2 when the party of "Burrites" is serenaded with the "Rogue's March" by a company of the city regiment drawn up under the window of the dining room—the salute is "a manifestation of the public regards" for the alleged traitors, and a kind of warning. On the 3rd the diarist treats his reader to a most interesting diversion as he is taken by his friend "Hayden the Dentist" to observe the operation of a powerful new electrostatic generator which "charged a Battery about 15 feet of coated glas in ten turns which killed a duck." On his return to Martin's house, one of the lawyer's students informs the diarist that a mob is expected to attack the house that evening and do some kind of violence to Burr, Martin and himself. Indeed, the handbills that have been circulating, of which the diarist offers a full copy of one in the same entry, promise no less than "execution" of all the accused malefactors. Alarmed by what appears to be brewing, the diarist seeks out Burr "at his shabby quarters in *Gay Street*" because, curiously, "his vigilance I had before proved, tho' lively at all times, was most sharp on the approach of danger." But whatever support he may have expected from Burr at this point Blennerhassett is disappointed of. After being kept waiting in an outer room for fifteen minutes, he is admitted to Burr, only to find that the vigilant one has been "packing up his things to escape in the Mail, which was to leave in 10 minutes."

From this point in the narrative on, one senses that Blennerhassett becomes not only the hero of his own account but of his own desire; to act decorously, calmly, and, to an extent, bravely at this crisis, gives him the nearest thing to gratification that his romantic temperament receives in the period of the journal. From reports he has heard he concludes that there is some danger of receiving at least "a suit of tar and feathers" in the promised demonstration. But he reflects on "how naturally Burr might expect to receive unwelcome obloquy for his flight," and at once determines to stand his ground. Here, indeed, could be a chance to upstage Burr for once. Thus at dinner, as the time set out for the "*spectacle*" approaches, he is a study in composure, conversing cheerfully with, and ordering drinks for, the guard of city police sent to protect them. As the mob approaches noisily, Blennerhassett ascends to the garret of the house, from which he climbs through one of two trap doors to the roof, intending to take his station there, though the street cannot be seen clearly. As he is about to shut the second door, cutting off his return to the garret, he hears the "uproar" of the mob's passing outside, drops back into the garret, and from one of its windows sees the procession pass below, "to the amount of about 1500 as well as I c^{d} estimate, in full huzza, with fife and drum—playing the rogue's march." Later on, after the mob has dispersed, he can comment that "an American mob is as tame as it is unweildy or immaleable." But the situation from which he views the people as they pass seems symbolic of his life, suggestive of the very altitude of his political ideals that led to his becoming one of their villains. Yet there is, for him, a kind of gratification, a consummation (the journal's high point, perhaps evident in the care taken in the telling) in this his own (by comparison with Burr's flight) relatively close and steadfast encounter with his dreaded enemy—the "Mob-ility."

Arriving in Philadelphia two days later, on November 5, he goes, it appears, first to Burr and then to his "worthy friends" the Lewises. Burr, he notes, "pretended" he would have stayed on in Baltimore had he not believed the demonstration would have ended with the handbills—thus we have the narrative's resolution. But there is also a curious concession on Burr's part as he offers the diarist a long-withheld introduction to Bollman, then his closest associate; however, Blennerhassett appears somewhat suspicious of the motive here, since Bollman appears not to wish his acquaintance, never having called on him at Richmond—a circumstance "B. tried to excuse but failed." When the two associates (rivals, perhaps, for Burr's attention now) meet properly on November 7, the talk gravitates toward Bollman's proposition that another investor or two join with him in purchasing a plantation near New Orleans. The reader wonders, of course, if Burr is using Bollman here to verify Blennerhassett's financial prospects—the possible inheritance, or any expectations he may have by way of the Lewises—or to improve them.

On November 10, the diarist pays another visit to Burr, who has "again opened an audience chamber, which is much occupied." There he meets George Pollock, a reputedly wealthy man whose "education" Burr has lately been seeing to. Blennerhassett likes Pollock, but he notes that, "with respect to Burr, whatever may have been the ground of his present intimacy with Mr P. I can venture to affirm, it has already been abused, on the part of the former, altho' the latter as yet, is evidently unaware of it." The diarist takes this occasion to condemn, in his notes, Burr's abuse of another loyal friend, Martin, "for he fled fr. Balt^{o} with^{t} waiting even to thank his friend for the long and various services he rendered him." This behavior Blennerhassett finds singularly contemptible, since Martin, in his benevolence, has resolved to appear for them both at Chillicothe in January. The diarist goes so far as to raise this matter with Burr directly, and we learn, after Burr's protestations, that he means to write to Martin (Indeed, years later he cared for the senile Martin in his home until his former counsel's death in 1822), but his immediate concern, as the diarist puts it, is that "Martin's too great zeal and indiscretion" would be a liability to them in the Ohio trial.

We recall from Blennerhassett's remarks on October 20 that he would have two purposes in Philadelphia, apart from visiting the Lewises: first, to obtain, if he could, Duane's assistance in extricating himself from further prosecution, and second, to settle his claims against Burr. In his discussion with Burr on November 10 he now moves from the problem of Martin to his plan to appeal to Duane. Burr must approve of this, which he does, if it is not to seem to be a betrayal; furthermore, it may bring some slight pressure to bear on the second project, to which he now turns—the financial claims. In this complex conversation Burr offers nothing at the moment despite the diarist's allusion to his "splendid hope in Europe" and his "means of advancing him," Burr, there. Against this the master strategist offers two inducements: first, that two persons who may help are now out of town but should be heard from in two or three days; second, that Blennerhassett has his (and Mrs. Alston's) permission to take any steps he can to recover from Alston. There are references to Burr's continued annoyance with Alston for his disparagements of Burr in his letter to Pinckney, which letter, the diarist sneers, even imputed "to Burr a design to deprive his infant grandson of his patrimony." We note, incidentally, that this "irredeemable passage" in Alston's letter Blennerhassett appears to regard as containing, nonetheless, a fact about Burr, and one that is largely his own find, since it has been overlooked by "many persons of penetration and intelligence who have indulged an eager interest in investigating every thing during the last year relating to Burr." However, the diarist seems to take no warning from his own detections, and he leaves the interview convinced that he still has some leverage with Burr—that, as he says, "the baits I have thrown out to him, do not yet glitter in vain." On the 12th, Thursday, we learn that Burr is out of town on an excursion up the Delaware; but on Saturday, the diarist determines, he will make his "last demand upon him so long projected" for security against his claims, amounting to "about $9000." Meanwhile, there is Duane to be dealt with.

This "long-projected interview" with this "high priest of Jacobinism" which the philosophical diarist now conceives of as a remedy for his toothache, the greater pain displacing the lesser, seems almost a moment of comic relief from the intensifying pathos of the Burr-plot. We enjoy the fully realized detail and sustained irony with which Blennerhassett can recount a scene which must have had intense practical interest for him. Ultimately, of course, the diarist must refer to the offers Duane had made to him at Richmond. We note with interest that the basis of his appeal is that he no longer feels obliged "to undergo endless persecutions" in order to "vindicate whatever concern" he had in "Col: B's speculations, especially, as he probably, will never renew them." We marvel, of course, that the diarist should have imagined that this position would give him any real leverage with Duane, since he really has nothing much to exchange, even less than the "baits" he has offered Burr. Consequently, the reader is not surprised that Duane offers nothing, nothing, that is, but the startling opinion that "the chief of the nation is still very much afraid of Burr." Finally, it is little wonder to us, knowing the diarist as we now do, that the Colonel "twirled in his seat" when Blennerhassett allows that during the "late rising in Baltimore," on the day his "effigy was executed," he was little alarmed to dine in public, since he is "always provided with a brace of pistols."

There are, of course, many passages in the journal which, like this last, illuminate Blennerhassett's character—and, by reflection, that of his primary intended reader, his wife. As we read along from entry to entry we seem to take up residence in a consciousness that is the crossways of surprisingly diversified interests, many of them quite unrelated to the policies and trials of Burr. Counterpointing the continuous concerns of father, husband, and anguished provider he also shares, from time to time, the interests of the philosopher, pharmacist, musician, planter, and critic of the arts. So in the entry for November 19 it is no surprise to meet the diarist as art critic, accompanying his friend Lewis on a visit to the nascent Academy of the Arts. Yet the details of his observations, the specificity of his brief critiques—"a want of embonpoint below the navel, which is rendered more objective where it stands," etc.—is still surprising when we reconsider how preoccupied his mind must have been with his intentions for the following day.

By now, with winter coming on, rapidly closing the season for descending the Ohio, Blennerhassett has determined upon the final confrontation with Burr over the matter of his claims. He has set the next day, November 20, as that on which to "burst the cob-web of duplicity of all his evasions with me upon money matters." He appeals to his reader, who must have seen "everywhere in these notes, how long and insidiously he has trifled with my claims upon him." All his strategy for trading influence or later prospects in Europe for ready money here are forgotten; this is to be a direct assault. The nuances by which the force of this appeal is slyly deflected and trivialized are fully and ironically recounted. Burr at first delays him while he continues "trifling" with his previous visitor, a shop-boy, about some articles of dress. He then digresses to other claims upon him; makes the diarist recount his claim, already presented in Richmond; he then utters a "sneer at the amount," calling it "*pretty small*," and finally, claims he has yet to examine the account. In these actions the diarist sees as if by the sudden flight of luster from the master-schemer's eye, a Burr whose subtle chains upon his hopes he can now finally break; he sees "a little man indeed," and later explains that this exhibition of "a heartless swindler in the last swoon of his disorder . . . determined me to hasten my departure fr. this disgusting spectacle of a quibbling pettifogger who will never have a friend but amongst idiots swindlers or bankrupts."

He has been treated, he sums up, in this last interview with Burr, "not as a former associate ruined by my past connection with him, but rather as an importunate creditor invading his leisure or his purse with a questionable account." The final indignity to the diarist—and to us an adequate symbol of the kind of recognition he had failed to obtain from Burr—is the notice he takes, on the journal's last page, of the agitated Burr's mispronunciation of his name. So the journal breaks off, not in mid-sentence yet in mid-page. There are many unfilled pages in the new notebook, the third Blennerhassett had begun, but *this* story, the great misadventure of his life, was at an end.

[*Biographical Afterword*:—Although this was Blennerhassett's last meeting with Burr, his claim continued; and through this his journal came to assume a position in his life that was more significant yet, in a way, degraded. The day after their conclusive interview the diarist wrote Burr a caustic letter, referring to the evident contradiction between Burr's remark the previous day about not having examined the diarist's claim and his statement earlier at Richmond that he was satisfied Blennerhassett's claim was correct and wished to see no vouchers in support of it. He demands that Burr reply immediately, "in the course of this evening," stating any objections to his "charges." Furthermore, he continues, in consideration of "the close of the late interesting intercourse that has long subsisted between us," he must withdraw the offer he had made to write letters introducing Burr to influential acquaintances of his in England; this is because, as he puts it "I could not solicit their attentions to you as my friend; and I should wish to decline doing so on any other grounds."

He received no satisfactory reply, if we judge from the letter he wrote to his wife on November 30. Here he explains that he has just dispatched certain items to her aboard the brig *Mary*; among these was a trunk, in the bottom of which she would find "two small volumes" of his notes, "intended for no eye at Natchez but [Lyman] Harding's and your own." He gives very strict instructions concerning these volumes: "You will, therefore, when not in *your* hands, always keep them under *lock and key.*" From these notes, he explains she would see that "I have broken with Aaron Burr upon a writ," his ultimate effort to recover "a demand upon him of $8000., as you shall better understand hereafter."

In February, 1808, he rejoined his family at Natchez, having passed through Ohio and witnessed the desolation of his former Eden. Soon they purchased "La Cache" a 1000-acre cotton plantation near Port Gibson; there, after two years of anxious separation, the Blennerhassetts' found, for a time, a home again. But mounting debts, falling cotton prices, and the dailiness of dirt farming were hardly conducive to forgetting his claim against Burr. From "La Cache" in 1811 he addressed to Joseph Alston, then governor of South Carolina, a strangely magniloquent yet bitter letter. In it he speaks of a long "suspension" of their correspondence and of having "long since despaired of all indemnity from Mr. Burr," so much so that he would "never more consider a reference to his honor, good faith, or resources in any other light then as a scandal to any man offering it who is not already sunk as low as himself." However, he reminds Alston of his promise and duty to make good the writer's losses by "our expedition." Accordingly he estimates his total damages at $50,000, subtracts $12,500 Alston has already paid, leaving a balance of $37,500, "of which sum," he affirms, "I now demand $15,000. payable at New Orleans or Philadelphia, in August next."

Of course, Blennerhassett was not assuming that Alston would be overcome by a new sense of duty toward his father-in-law's old confederate; indeed, he would now propose "other motives of action besides those already offered." Now his journal, so carefully locked away, could be brought into play, along with other papers, in a last effort to squeeze a payment out of the presumably prosperous Governor. He regrets, he continues, that it has fallen to his lot to disclose to the public, especially "the honest Democratic electors of South Carolina," every aspect of Alston's connection with "our confederacy," including his pledge to make good their losses, but especially his betrayal of his father-in-law, and would-be emperor, "the *shabby treason* of deserting from your parent by affinity, and your *sovereign* in *expectancy*; and then, finally, in your letters to your Governor, to vilify your father-in-law, and perpetrate an open perjury by publicly denying all privity or connection with his views or projects." His book containing all these notes, sketches, and damning documents, Blennerhassett declares, is entirely ready for publication, but would be withheld if Alston complied with his demand, "by forwarding a credit of $15,000, payable as before mentioned, and accompanied with your obligation, or some other equivalent proposal, for adjusting the balance."

Alston evidently did not comply. It has been suggested that falling cotton prices after the embargo imposed by Jefferson in the War of 1812 had shrunken his means, just as they would doom Blennerhassett's own plantation. Much of this is implied by a still more desperate but grandiose final letter Blennerhassett wrote to Burr from "La Cache" in April, 1813. In it he cites the same balance due him, threatens publication of the same compendious "book," which has been "hitherto postponed only by sickness." At this point, however, he would be willing "to accept from any other source $15,000, in lieu of the balance I claim of $37,500." As an added inducement he cites the threatened book's over-killing title: "A Review of the Projects and Intrigues of Aaron Burr, during the years 1805-6-7, including therein, as parties or privies, Thos. Jefferson, Albert Gallatin, Dr. Eustis, Gov. Alston, Dan. Clark, Generals Wilkinson, Dearborn, Harrison, Jackson, and Smith and the late Spanish Ambassador . . . . exhibiting original documents and correspondence hitherto unpublished, compiled from the notes and private journal kept during the above period; by H. Blennerhassett, L.L.B." So he had come to the ultimate and despairing purpose to which the journal he had written to his wife might be put, in a ponderous blackmail. He did, at least, add a motto to his book, which, he wrote, would find "applicability in every page"; it is one he might have taken less unconsciously to himself: "It is only the Philosopher who knows how to mark the boundary between celebrity and greatness." (For letters quoted see W. H. Safford, *The Blennerhassett Papers*, pp. 516-18, 533-38, and 550-52.)]

HARMAN BLENNERHASSETT'S JOURNAL, 1807

[*From last page, verso, of book three.*]

Journal of
Harman Blennerhassett Esq.
Whilst in the Jail at the
City of Richmond Va.
awaiting his trial for
Treason & Misdemeanor

Saint Louis Dec. 25th

[*Followed by partly legible, undeciphered inscription, as shown on page 210.*]

[*Centered, top of endpaper, book three.*]

JOURNAL
commencing
July 20, 1807——

Lexington K^y July 20. 1807—[*]
Monday.

At 11 o'clock a.m. I was conducted by the Jailor, fr. prison to Wilson's Inn, where I was rec^d by Mr Dav. Meade, the Dep. marshal with a Guard of five persons. I at once mounted a horse—prepared for me, and proceeded, under their escort, on a Journey to Richd Virg^a We stopped to dine etc. at Col. Meade's—for 1½ hour; and then proceeded on to Delhams at the Kentucky river where we supped and spent the night.—

---

20 miles fr. Lexington.—

Tuesday

Continued our journey and reached Tate's, on what is called The Crab-orchard Road.—where Mr Meade informed me, he did not mean to keep any night-watch over me, as had been done at Dulham's, where I was called upon at bed time to retire with, the Guard, owing he said to the presence of much company at the house.—Dist fr. Lexington 62^m

Wednesday

We proceeded, and reached Johnson's, about 9 o'clock p.m. without any remarkable occurrence—Distance from Lexington.—100 miles

Thursday.—

Proceeded and reached Wilden's Dist fr. Lexington—136 miles

[* *Superscript numbers in brackets refer to textual notes; annotations, keyed to page and line, are not indicated in the text.*]

Friday

We only got to Bean's Station, owing to very hilly roads and bad weather. dist. fr. L.^{n} 164 miles.

Saturday.

We reached Rogersville about two o'clock p.m. and continued—there the rest of the day to rest on account of the extreme heat of the weather, during which, I got an opp.^{y} of sending a few words by post, to my wife to be forwarded by Major Boyd of Lexington distant 187. miles.———

Sunday

We arrived at the Widow Noley's dist. fr. Lexington 220 Miles [*Small blots in lower rt. corner.*]

Abingdon Virg.^{a} July 27. 07—
Monday

Reached this place a good house within a mile of Craig's dist fr. Lex.^{n} 257. miles—

Tuesday.

Continued the journey as far as Atkins'. dist. fr. Le. 296 miles.—

Wednesday.

Reached Ellis's in pleas.^{t} weather. Dist. fr. Lex.^{n} 334 miles. —N.B. Two last houses bad & dirty. [*Page torn along rt. edge.*]

Thursday.—

Travelled to the Whits House ill—dist. fr. Lex.^{n}——372 miles.

Friday.

Reached Sherman's good house. dist. fr. Lex^{n} 411 miles.

Saturday. Augt 1.—

Arrived at du Priests good house—dist. fr. Lex^{n}——448 miles.

Sunday

Reached Francisco's bad house. Dist. fr. Lexingt^{n} 486 miles.

Monday.—

Arrived at Scottsville distant fr. Lexington.—531 miles.

Richmond Virginia Augt 4.07.
Tuesday—

We set out as usual fr. Scottsville before day, rode 12 miles to breakfast; then proceeded to Triberos 8 miles on our way where we rested ½ hour in excessive heat; afterwards, proceed^{d} to Richmond where we arrived at 45 minutes past 2 p.m. Dist. fr. Lexing^{n} 564 miles—From Triberos Mr Meade sent a note to Major Scott The Fed. Marshal for the District of Virg^{a} to inform him of our approach. We travelled this last stage as usual, 'till we got within 3/4 of a mile of Manchester where Mr Meade left us at a turnpike gate and rode off at a quick pace. Now Capt. Sattawhite took the command of the party, and observed to me, that it w^{d} be proper to observe some order, to which I answered I had no objection. He then ordered Mr Morton the High Sheriff of Kentucky and Mr Willis Morgan to form a file in front; M^{r} McCally & Mr David Todd to form another in the rear, directing me to ride single, between the files,—whilst he took his station in front, of the whole. In this order he led the escort, with the prisoner in an easy walk, under a broiling sun, over a road, in which I was almost suffocated by the dust, owing to a long drought with which the country seemed to have been affected and a smart breeze in our rear. During this embarrassment, I called to the gent^{n} in front of me to observe; "that I supposed it was not necessary those in the rear should ride so close to me." They did so probably fr. the Captain's having used the words "close order," in forming the procession. Those in front however that is Mr Morton or Mr Morgan answered me in the negative; upon which, the rear file fell back a few paces. We continued still in the same order, in wch I endeavored to keep my station—as was assigned me, as nearly as possible, 'till we drew near to Mayo's bridge, over James River—when the Capt. left his station, in the front, and rode back to the rear, I suppose to order them to ride closer up; for they immediately afterwards, did so.—We now reached the bridge, on which the Capt. shook hands with Col. Mayo, en passant—and telling him one of the Gent^{n} in the rear w^{d} pay the toll, which Mr Todd did very expeditiously, without much deviation fr. his station. We proceeded at the same gait, 'till we entered the main-street commonly called the Brick-row where I was disappointed to see no particular notice taken of the party, except by a little boy, who called out to some of his comrades, "Oh see the troop of horse but they have forgot their colours."—The walking gait was still preserved 'till we got in sight of the Washington Tavern,—when the Captn was pleased to trot up to the house, in which pace we followed him as closely as possible.—On alighting fr. my horse I was welcomed by Mr Meade in the presence of many gentlemen standing in the portico. He then asked me to go up stairs, ordered dinner, etc. after which he delivered me into the custody of the Deputy Marshal of the Virg^{a} District, by wh^{m} I was conducted in a carriage to the Penitentiary, Mr Meade and the Capt. accompanying me.—In the evening, I was visited by Mr Alston, Mr Mercer and Mr Randolph, the latter having obligingly tendered me his services and advice as a Lawyer.—Here, my apartments are large and convenient, but very warm fr. the height of the windows' preventing a free admission of air.—The Dep. Marshal on taking charge of me, read a warrant by Judge Marshall, but refused to leave it or a copy with me.

I had a friendly lively note fr. Col: Burr this evg to welcome me to his late quarters in this prison. Wrote a close page or two to my wife,—partook of some good tea and cakes sent me by Mrs Alston, with Mr Mercer, who kindly gave me 2 hours of his interesting company—and after getting a bed and a few other necessaries fr. the tavern I went to sleep much fatigued after midnight——

Richmd Penitentiary Virginia
Wedny Aug. 5. 1807.—

Slept 'till 7 o'clock this morning—had a light breakfast fr. the tavern; hired a servant @ $13 a month, by the week, he finding himself—was visited by Mr Julian Dandridge with whom I used to assist here 7 years ago at the Harmonic Society; by Prichard the Bookseller whose hospitality I remember to have then recd and who tendered me his best services reminding me of some pecuniary accomn I had conferred upon him, which I had forgotten. Visited again by Mr Alston who brought me a letter fr. Col: Burr; also by Dudy Woodbridge Junr, Edmd Dana with letters fr. Miller and Col. Cushing: [*blot*] by Mr Jno. Banks, who reminded me of my gold chronometer in his possn; by Mr Craighton, who conferred great civilities on me 7 yrs ago at Fredericksburg, and now warmly tendered me his best services. Mr Alst. repeated orally to me, the necessity Col: Burr observed in his letter for my employing Counsel, as the only proper intermedium of our communication. I assured him I was very desirous of such aid, but was determined not to strengthen my defence, however disastrous the issue of it might prove, by drawing fr. the exigencies and sympathies of my family a single dollar to defray its charges. He still urged me to write a few lines to Mr Botts which I did, stating that I was solicitous of the aid of Mr B's talents on terms I wished to propose to him in person.—On Mr B's appearance soon after in my room, I stated to him that Col: Burr and Mr Alston had expressed a desire

(Richm^{d} Penitentiary Virginia
Wedn^{y} Aug. 5.—1807.—)

that I w^{d} employ him, tho' they were apprized of my determination not to spend a dollar in my defence—being a resolution the exigencies of my family imposed upon me. But Mr Alston having assured me Col: Burr w^{d} arrange the matter with Mr Botts, I wished Mr B. to believe I sh^{d} regard the aid of his talents on my trial as most beneficial to my interests and flattering to my wishes. Mr B. handsomely replied to me by assuring me that he would think it dishounorable to withhold his professional aid fr. my inability to make him a pecuniary compensation. I returned that fr. the state of my affairs, that inability w^{d} probably be permanent, and again referred him to the contingency of Col: Burr's, or Mr Alston's remunerating him on my acc^{t} as well as on Col: Burr's, as it was in this view and at their special insistance, I had given him the trouble of calling upon me, tho' I could sincerely assure him, that were I in circumstances to remunerate him in a degree proportional to the sense I entertained of his talents etc. he would be one of the first Counsel I sh^{d} employ.—Mr B. seemed perfectly satisfied, and was pleased to say he w^{d} with my leave bring Mr Wickham to see me, who, he was sure w^{d} be happy to assist me in the same way with himself. I thanked this generous and enlightened stranger with all that awkward embarrassment which the impetuosity of gratitude suffused upon my countenance making every pore of my face, an outlet to the flow of my heart, which found too narrow an issue at my mouth. It will soon appear how necessary it was to explain the occasion and manner of my interview with Mr B. I took this opp^{y} to observe to

(Richm.^{d} Penitentiary Virginia
Wednesday Aug. 5 . 1807—)

Mr Botts that Mr Edm^{d} Randolph, had last ev^{g}, called upon me and obligingly tendered his *advice* by wch I said, I could not presume to suppose Mr. R. meant I should consider him as my Counsel, gratuitiously engaged to defend me on my trial. Mr. B. was in the act of taking leave when I made this remark to him, which prevented my distinctly understanding his reply.—I was visited this evg. by my Lexington Escort en masse, who took *that oppy.* to inspect this building and the armoury—took their grog and then took leave. Morton, who arrested me so rudely, whilst engaged in conversation with Mrs. Jourdan and & Miss Van-Pool at Lexington, endeavoured by the most assiduous attention on the road, to repair that outrage—and now I thought, exhibited in his countenance every concern for my situation. The foregoing innuendo, therefore, wd. avoid him.—I find I have every liberty allowed me, but those of passing fr. under the *roof* of this building by day, or out of *my room*, at night: the door being locked upon me at 8 o'clock, and opened at sunrise. I have got a supply of groceries & liquors; my dinner is furnishd. by the tavern and I have every prospect of living well!—This evg. I have enclosed various papers to Mr. Alst. showing him how my property has been sacrificed on the Ohio, and praying his aid to recover it for my children by virtue of his responsy. for my endorsement of Col: B.'s protested Bills.—Continued my labours to comfort my poor wife by another page of a close written letter and went to bed at midnight.——

Richmd. Penitentiary Virga.
Thursday Aug 6. 1807—

Woke this morning with severe headach and genl. lassitude, took a little breakfast with no appetite. At 10 a.m. took small dose of Ipecach, repeated at noon. Still indisposed with much sickness at stomach—had a long conversation with Alston, in which he expressed gt. concern for the embarrassments occasioned me by endorsemts. of the bills,—declaring, that for my *sake* he would do any thg. in his power; observing, however that it was impracticable to raise money in Carolina by sale or mortgage of lands; that thro' his anxiety to have all the protested bills *taken* up, he now had a friend employed in this town endeavouring to raise as much money as would cover all the demands; that I should learn the result today or tomorrow —which if successful would remove all difficulties.—I proposed to him an alienation to me or some of the holders of the bills, of some negroes to be sold at Natchez, where I suggested he might avail himself of the advance they w.d fetch upon their value in Carolina; and by that means he w.d probably sink half the demand upon him. But after some *consideration* he stated the value of Slaves in Carolina full as high as it is at *Natchez* —and at last observed that his *estates* needed *more slaves* for their cultivation th.n he owned.—He offered however to assume all the demands upon me, if the creditors will accept one half payable with Interest,

(Richm.d Penitentiary Virg.a
Thursday Aug.t 6. 1807)

next Jan.y 12 month—the other half—etc. the Jan.y following—But my children's property is and will be irrecoverably sacrificed in the mean time. Quiquid delirant Reges plectuntur Achivi.—M.r A. next referred to some memoranda he had in his pocket of some inquiries to be made of me on the part of Col: Burr—of which two are remarkable—1st. Had I written or w.d I write to Emmet to come to the trial? 2d. In what Instance did I intend, when I observed to M.r Edm. Randolph that Col: Burr had sometimes been too cautious; sometimes too little so? To the first I answered that I had no doubt Emmet's friendship for me w.d bring him hither to assist in my defence, if he thought I stood in need of him. But as I was, on the one hand, determined to expend no money in my own defence, I was on the other equally averse to bringing my friend a journey fr. his large family and withdrawing his industry fr. that harvest on which alone that family depended for their support where they were settled. But could I engage M.r Em. a suitable compensation I w^{d} write to him forthwith—Mr A. said his *expences* sh^{d} be paid. I replied I couldn't say what Mr E. might understand by the term expences, but sure I was he w^{d} never hand in an acc^{t} of his tavern bills or travelling charges.——I must therefore, at present, decline to disturb him. Mr A. was now led by some association of ideas to remark that Mess^{s} Randolph and Botts

(Richm^{d} Penitentiary Virg^{a}
Thursday Augt 6. 1807—)

had signified to Col: Burr or himself that when they offered their professional services to me, I seemed rather to desire to decline them or consider them as intrusive.—Read my notes of yesterday on this subject my adored wife, and pitying friends —Learn further that this ev^{g} Mr Botts brought Mr Wickham to my room.—When I asked Mr Botts if he understood me in the sense Mr^{r} Alst. said he did? On the contrary, he Mr B. declared he did not, nor did he think Mr Randolph did. Mr W. added a few words in compliment of my candour and, said all three considered themselves voluntarily engaged with^{t} any expectation of pecuniary compensation *from me.*—In answer to the 2^{d} Inquiry I informed Mr A. that in making use of the expressions reported to Col: B. by Mr Randolph, I alluded to no particular instances; but could readily cite some. I then instanced the confidence reposed by Mr Burr in Gen: Wilkinson, on wch Col: Burr had known my opin^{n} long since;—and the commitment of himself to Col: Morgan & Sons both as examples of defect of caution on his part; and was proceeding with equal ease to call up errors of an opposite nature (God knows, I know 100 both ways) when I was stopped by M. A's shaking his head expressing his assent to my remarks on Wilkinson and interrupting me by saying Mrs Blennerhassett had good reason for her opinion of Col: Morgan. I was the less scrupulous to enter explicitly upon these explanations for the satisfaction of Col: B. and Mr A. because

(Richm^{d} Penitentiary, Virg^{a}
Thursday Aug. 6. 07—)

I did not feel that Col: Burr had ever suffered as yet fr. any avoidable indiscretion of mine, 'tho I was likely to do so far more, than I had done already by his Errors. I suspected he had sent M^{r} Ed. Randolph to deliver me a lecture on *Caution* and above all, I should least of all examples I could imagine—wish to emulate that caution Mr A. has exhibited to the world. Him theref. I regarded as the most improper organ of C. Burr's *wishes*. Nor was I yet without another motive. I had occasion to inform Mr A. when on the subject of the protested bills—that Mr Barton who had had an interview here, with Col: Burr on that business informed me at Lexington that Col: Burr told him, I was a Bankrupt not worth a Dollar, words or others fully of the same import, which Mr Barton protested he would at any time or place, repeat and support.—Bankrupt Hah! Who made me so? Oh God of retributive justice! That Col: Burr also declared to him that he did not believe Mr Alston had executed any writing by which He A. could be bound to me. What! did his memory, perhaps the most energetic of all his talents, here lose its polish by the abrasion of his own calamities? Did he forget that He himself drafted that very paper, after having censured another which Mr A. had written, as insufficient? But Mr Barton has shown him a copy of the original, and he has probably recognized his own composition.—

At 4 o'clock p.m. took some suip., rec^{d} some visits this ev^{g}

(Richm^{d} Penitentiary Virg^{a})
Augt 6. 1807.)

Could get no tea, because Mr Douglas the Keeper, and Harwood one of his assistants, were not in the building.—and another Turnkey, with whom I had not yet got acquainted would lock me up at night-fall. Head-ach still continuing, I went to bed about 10 p.m. being unable to write this night.

Friday Augt 7. 07.—

Was visited by Mr Mercer who staid nearly 1 hour with me, begged, on the part of a lady unknown to me, who did not wish to have her name mentioned—I would accept of soups and jellies fr. her if they were desired by my appetite or state of health. I told Mr M. my gratitude impelled me to take a liberty wth the lady which I hoped her goodness wd pardon. It was to engrave her name on the tablet of my heart and enable my family to consecrate it in their regards. He then mentioned Mrs Carrington. I prayed him to offer thro' his own manner, a more just return of my sentiments than I cd express.—Soon after this Mr Ormsby of Louisville Kenty called upon me to show me a letter signed H.L. directed to him by Genl Henry Lee stating that he understood H.B. meaning myself was friendless in this place, and tendering any service wth warmth, I might stand in need of:—This offer I declined, charging Mr O. with a suitable *verbal* answer of grateful acknowledgements to the General of whom Mr O. cautioned me to beware in case of any dealing with him, at the same time acquainting me that the character of the Genl was, as I had long before

(Richmd Penitentiary Virga
Friday Augt 7. 1807—)

been apprized, that of a man equally violent in his friendships and his enmities—Fr. the numerous Instances of a violation of private confidence and public faith that have of late disgraced the Govt and the country by liberties that have been taken or permitted at the post offices—I procured, thro the friendship of Mr Mercer the means of sending my letters and during my stay here, receiving those fr. my wife thro' Rob. Taylor Esq., Atty at Law, Alexandria. Closed a long letter to my wife begun as long ago as tuesday evg on my first arrival in this prison. Began to brief my case for my Counsel of which I finished the first folio. Had a return of health and appetite, and dined heartily. Have not seen or heard from Mr Alston or Col: Burr today—read the papers, and continued this Journal till past m.night.

Saturday Augt 8. 07.—

3 o'clock p.m., overslept this morning. Spent more time th^{n} I could spare well in getting combed and shaved, my face continuing very sore with a sort of ring-worm these 10 days.—Read the papers. The Fed. one stating that they learn my arrival here: that I speak confidently of my Innocence and desire a speedy Investigation. Those on the other side dropping the Mister mention my name in conformity to the style of the Pres^{t} and his Wood C^{o} Myrmidons, insinuate that I was caught as it were fortunately in Kentucky, fr. wh^{ch} I was brought hither under guard meaning no doubt, like a felon or a murderer convict——

(Richm^{d} Penitentiary, Virg^{a}
Saturday Augt 8. 07.—)

as I should be. For to day, my only visitor Mr Hendren, a Lawyer, who resides in Charles-City County, and has generously offered to come to town and subsist himself at his own expence, whenever I will permit him to serve me. Oh God! Dost Thou so guide the Hearts of Strangers thy Servants, to comfort that piety, that thro' affliction, will dwell on Thee as The Forest thro' the Storm, on the mountain top!—This Mr Hendren repeated assurances I had before made to me by Mr Jno. Banks and Mr Ormsby—that the Jury, not only so far as that part of the panel that was returned fr. Wood C^{y}, but all the rest that completed it fr. the body of the State, was grossly packed, with the exception of not more than 2 or 3 of the Jurors: that Col: Burr and myself could not be too much on our guard; for he was persuaded, that every Democrat to a man, now in this town, was thirsting for our blood; and Jno. Jourdan, who has returned here today fr. Wood Co^{y}, has told me this evening, he has brought with him ample evidence of the most damning manoeuvers and intrigues that have been practiced in that quarter. Say Thos. Jefferson—thou philanthropic messenger of Peace [*blot*] and liberty to this favored country—under thy administr.^{n} are those things unknown to thy tender heart; or are they the unhallowed doings of thy worthy industrious pastizans, to overcharge or adorn the canvas already burthened with the splendor of thy renoun?—The papers will inform my friends of the progress and conduct of the

(Richm.^{d} Penitentiary, Virg.^{a}
Saturday Augt 8. 07.)

trial of A. Burr. But they may learn only perhaps fr. these notes, that the issue of it, whether it prove serious or comical, will be the product of Error in the Gr. Jury that found the Treason-Bills. For 2 of the most respectable and influential of that Body, since it has been discharged, have declared, they mistook the meaning of Ch. Justice Marshall's opinion as to what sort of acts amounted to Treason, in this country, in the case of Swartwout and Ogden; that it was under the influence of this mistake, they concurred in finding such a bill ag.^{t} A. Burr, which otherwise w.^{d} probably have been ignored. I am well today, and had a keen appetite at dinner, soon after wch Jourdan stepped in, with no particular news regarding my affairs on The Ohio. Saw Robinson and Mr Simpson summoned with him on the part of Col: Burr. Wrote directions for Mr J. Banks to inform him how M.^{rs} B should prepare and make use of a vapour-bath to remove her rheumatism and went to bed at eleven o'clock p.m.—

Sunday Augt 9. 07.—

Visited by Prichard at 9 o'clock a.m. He stayed full 2 hours, during which he confirmed many former accounts given me of the meanness and cowardice of Jefferson's Attorney Gen. Geo. Hay, whose insolence to poor Prichard, some years ago, occasioned P. to throw a plate at his head, which terminated the affair, and kept Mr Att.^{y} ever after, within the bounds of civility.

P. informs me Negroes now sell in this place at the same prices they could be bought

(Richm^{d} Penitentiary, Virg^{a}
Sunday, Augt 9. 07)

---

at, when I was here before 7 yrs. ago. He has offered to get me a woman aged about 30 yrs with two sons 12 and 8 yrs. old belonging to his Sister in law—for $500. Eh! Mr Alston, are Negroes so much lower here than in S. Carolina?—He has also promised to get me Molly's 3 children, 2 girls and a boy, if the owners will part wth them, upon like reasonable terms, as he thinks they will.—After P. left me, continued the briefing of my case for counsel, and completed the 3^{d} folio.—If the prosecutors attempt again tomorrow to put off the Trial to a 4th adjournment—I shall not think it unwarrantable to begin to suspect they fear to advance upon the ground they've taken lest the mines of Mexico or of Tartarus be sprung upon them. This suspicion seems to be somewhat countenanced by the circumstance of their being correctly informed of the places-where Genl Dayton has been for several days, and will continue, near this town, without the Marshal, who is certainly a vicious partizan, having yet made any attempt to disturb him:—whilst the Dernean and once redoubted Eaton has dwindled down in the eyes of this sarcastic town, into a ridiculous mountebank, strutting about the streets—under a tremendous hat, and girt with a Turkish Sash, over coloured clothes, when he isn't tippling in the taverns, where he offers up with his libations, the bitter effusions of his sorrows, in audibly bewailing to the sympathies of the bystanders, "that he is *despised* by the Federalists,

(Richm^{d} Penitentiary, Virg^{a}
Sunday Augt 9. 07.)

---

mistrusted by the Democrats, & *here,*—too long for his fame, too long for his purse." Quis talia fando temperet a lachrymis?—

Genl Dayton however, I hear will offer himself up, tomorrow or the next day, and will therefore live, rent-free like myself for some time. But how far reasons of *State* may prevent my partaking of his society here, I cannot yet tell. It is so close and warm in this room as generally I find it 'till after midnight, that I am obliged to get rid of all covering but my shirt. It is now 11 o'clock. p.m. I will walk about for some time, with a fan, and then endeavor to sleep, to preserve my strength and appetite which still continue good.—

Richmd Penitentiary Virga
Monday Augt 10. 07.—

Rose at 6 a.m. dressed and walked till 8. Had a call from Col: Quanir a violent Democrat who calls every one Tory, that is not of his own Party, and talks a great deal of nonsense about ruining England in the expected war with the United States. D. Woodbridge stept in, whilst I was at breakfast and returned me in frames, the two drawings presented me by Miss Vanpool at Chaumire Col: Meade's place near Lexington, the day I left that town under guard, for this city. After Quanir took leave D.Wge informed me, he was told sometime since by Col. Morgan, a subpoena had actually been dispatched, a fortnight past to Natchez for my wife—And he heard somebody say last evg

(Richmd Penitentiary, Virga
Monday Augt 10. 07—)

General Wilkinson had asserted the same thing. I immediately addressed a letter to Messrs Randolph, Wickham, and Botts, stating this intelligence and appealing to their feelings to vindicate fr. this outrage of party the Rights of a wife, the fundamental principles of Law and Justice.—Mr Mercer called in, as I was folding up the letter, and kindly took upon him the charge of delivering it for me, as well as of inquiring at the post office for any letters, he could bring me from thence—I had but half finished the last sentence but one, when I heard the voices of strangers coming up stairs, and Mr Douglas entered my room with the Dep. Marshals to invite me to take an airing—that is to attend the Court—I was ready in 3 minutes, and on reaching the outside gate, perceived a Carriage and 2 Horse-guards in waiting. I stepped in—found the air and exercise very agreeable;—was told, by the way I should have the trouble to pass thro' a large crowd, to which I answered I was indifferent,—and soon arrived at the Capitol, where, without doors, I did not perceive near as many people as I expected. Within, The Court is held in the Hall of The Assembly, which is spacious and handsome, and was pretty full at my Entrance. I was first led by the Dep^{y} Marshal below the *Bar*. Soon after, somebody else invited me to walk within it pointing to a bench; and again I was directed to walk to the opposite side, directly in front of the Ch. Justice's Seat—where I sat down

(Richm^{d} Penitentiary, Virg^{a}
Monday, Augt 10. 07—)

---

near a table, at which Col: Burr's counsel sit. The Court was not yet opened—. I was soon accosted successively by Mess^{s} Randolph, Wickham, and Botts; who all inquired what had occasioned my appearance in Court;—I said I was ignorant, but supposed, for arraignment. The Counsel did not know I had been furnished 3 days ago, with a copy of the Indictment. But I told them I had not yet rec^{d} a list of the witnesses that might be called to testify ag^{t} me, wch I submitted to them whether I was entitled to before arraignment. I then entered into a conversation upon a hint fr. him, in French, wth Mr Wickham—who upon a first address to a stranger, possesses a talent of infusing into his manner, an air of ease and friendly interest that is truly adapted, at once to engage the hearts of his acquaintance. Some considerable time after the Court opened, it was engaged in a desultory way, with applications fr. Jurors to be excused from serving on the Trial of A. B. on various grounds and excuses. During such occupation, Col: Burr entered—came over to that side where I was, shook me by the hand, and was smilingly pleased to say "he was extremely glad to see me indeed." Observe I had not before heard fr. him, since Thursday—The prosecuting Counsel seemed occupied with those of the Def^{t} A.B. in completing those lists of witnesses with the places of their abode, and agreeing upon some form of an acknowledgement to be made by A.B. that he

(Richm^{d} Penitentiary, Virg^{a}
Monday Augt 10. 07)

---

had been duly served with—the same—for which the Court was patiently waiting—when Mr Hay observed upon his seat coolly, that it might in the mean time be as well to arraign Mr Blennerhassett. To which Mr Botts objected for want of preparation by me and my Counsel—Mr H. replied, that if it was not done to day, a great deal of time would be lost. Mr B. said he could not help it: it would be improper—on which Mr Hay returned, that I might then be remanded—which I soon after solicited fr. the warmth of the place, and a wish to get back to my writing.—I therefore left the Court, having bowed to the Bench, under charge of another Dep. Marshal and another gentleman, with whom I returned hither on foot,—much heated by the walk, about 15^{m} past 2. Saw and saluted many faces on leaving Court, amongst them Wm Love, who appeared glad to see me and inquired particularly for my family, also Dav. Wallace, arriv^{d} yesterday. Dined with less [*blot*] appetite than I had yesterday. Oppressed in the ev^{g} by the heat of the weather; tried to get cool by walking and fanning, but was so weak I was obliged to lie down on the floor, where I slept, I know not how long, 'till I was awakened by the name of Mrs Alston, at which I started up, as if electrified and perceiv'd a servant of hers, with a large present of oranges, lemons and limes. Wrote her in form of a card 3 lines of devotion and gratitude,

(Richm^d Penitentiary Virg^a
Monday Augt 10. 07.—)

---

seizing, the opprt^y of inquiring after Alst. who is confined to the house & to pray her to let me hear again fr. her tomorrow.—Drank tea as usual at night-fall, and was soon after locked up. Thro' excessive heat, have written the 6th folio of my brief, and will now take a drink and try to sleep, it being 2. o'clock the 11th—

Tuesd^y Aug. 11. 07

Rose late.—Saw Jourdan whilst at Breakfast. He staid all day to copy my [*blot*] Brief. Visited in the evening by Dav. & Robert Wallace, with Perley Howe. Had a friendly sympathizing letter to day fr. Mr Wm Thompson a lawyer of handsome talents, tho' a violent Democrat, the Bro^r of the author of the Letters of Curtius. I got acquainted with him at Abington on the road hither.—I do not hear any more of Mrs Alston's intention to attend the trial of her father. I hope neither will add this, to the many indiscretions already committed by him.—Jupiter might invisibly elude the guards of Danae. But the Bonne amie of Col: does not I suppose, occasionally pass his keepers with the same address. Proh pudor! Worked today chiefly on my brief of which I have to night ½ past 12 entered on the 11th folio.—

Richm^d Penitentiary, Virg^a
Wedn^y Augt 12. 07.

Rose at 7 a.m.—was visited by Dav. Meade who tells me, himself and the guard that escorted me hither fr. Kentucky, will be allowed only one half of what they expected viz. instead of 10 only 5 cents per mile for coming and returning. And he expects his bill ag^t the Un. States will not be paid under 2 years after his having advanced his money for them: also, he understands the Marshal Major Scot will not pay Burr's witnesses, whilst he answers all the calls of those on the part of the prosecution. Does a culprit then with an empty purse, look in vain to the provisions of the constitution which declare, that the accused shall have compulsory process to enable him to enforce the attendance of his witnesses.—and may he be hanged, peradventure, for want of money as well as of Innocence? I fear the murmurs of agents and returning officers will be so widely diffused that no one will undertake to serve subpoenas for me, on witnesses however material to my defence, whilst I will not lay out a dollar for promoting its success.—A considerable fall of rain, last night and this morning, has very agreeably lowered the temperature of the air, the high degree of which has for a week past been so very oppressive—I have had by Mr Meade another advance fr. female humanity. Mrs Chevalié, wife of the French-Consul, has solicited by him, my acceptance of any refreshments or delicacies she could send me.——

(Richm^{d} Penitentiary, Virg^{a}
Wedn^{y} Augt 12. 07.)

Read the 3 papers published here of which the Inquirer incorrectly and rather impertinently notices the occasion of my Counsel's declining to permit me to be arraigned last monday.—Was interrupted by idle visitors desirous of gratifying their curiosity to survey my countenance and my Quarters. One of them a rejected Juryman fr. Wood C^{y} of the name of Morrison with whom I am not acquainted—the others, strangers to me, and come, like many others before them—without recommendation, to solicit employment of serving subpoenas on witnesses.—Had a friendly visit, in the evening, fr. Mr Fowler in company with Jourdan; and procured, thro' a friend, copies of the depositions, before the Gr. Jury, of Peter Taylor, Jacob Albright and David Wallace. The first having sworn that I told him we would Stab all those that went with us to get land and would not go on our expedition; the second, that General Tupper arrested me on the Island the night I left it, fr. which I effected my escape by my friends directly presenting 6 guns at the General; and the 3rd, that I offered him the post of Surgeon Gen[l] if he would embark in the expedition. "O. God of truth and justice," avenge such murderous villainies, in mercy. And then, my beloved wife, behold and adore a Guardian *Providence*, that ordains the conviction of perjury to issue in the same breath, fr. the lips of falsehood accusing the Innocent.—M[r] Fowler assures me, M[r] Hay begins to feel sick of the business, and doubts not a nolle prosequi will be entered on the records on Burr's acquittal of the Treason.—11 o'clock p.m.

Richm[d] Penitentiary, Virg[a]
Thurs[y] Aug[t] 13. 07—

Rose at ½ past 6. read 20 pages of Tully de Officiis. walked dressed and breakfasted. Had a friendly letter fr. Prichard, requesting me to command his heart and hand. Also a long letter sent by Phelps, but last by Col: Burr, fr. Tom Neale, confessing at last, that 'twas He bought Ransom, whom he will return to my wife or to myself at the same price he gave for him. Heard by letter from Col: Burr, in answer to one I wrote him, covering another for him to forward, if he wished it, to M[r] Hendren, requesting him to come to town to assist Burr with his knowledge of the Jurymen,—that Alston is to day, confined to his bed. Visited by Dav. Meade with two gentlemen of his acquaintance, summoned as tales-men, or on another venire, pro defectes juratorum, on the last. To one of these, finding he was acquainted with Will. Thomson, see my notes of 11th. Inst., I was fortunate in procuring an opportunity connected with the subject of conversation, to show M[r] T's handsome letter to me.—As this party were taking leave, Mess[rs] Wickham & Botts appeared at the door. They seemed pleased to find the ennui of my confinement was relieved by Company, sat half an hour, and conversed on my case, during w[ch] they told me they understood, the Hendersons would swear much against me; but seemed to think, wth me, their story could bear but little on either count of the indictm[t] They concurred in opinion that I should not hurry my trial but, sh[d] rather wait till party-prejudice was

(Richm[d] Penitentiary, Virg[a]
Thurs[y] Aug[t] 13. 07.)

---

more allayed, and the great crowd of witnesses now in town somewhat dispersed. They confirmed to me the fact of a subpoena having been actually issued for my wife, her name being one, on the list of witnesses furnished to A. Burr.—My complaints on this head, they seemed to regret, as irremediable, because A. Burr is not her husband. In how many instances is the letter of the Law at war with common-sense and its own principles! Are not all accomplices principals in treason; are not Burr and myself charged, by exactly similar indict[ts] with the same overt acts; at the same place,—and consequently, can the same Jury, if I should chuse it or any other in my case, shut their eyes to testimony, upon which Burr may be, by possibility, convicted?—I hinted these ideas to these generous and accomplished advocates, their silence seemed only to reply; sed ita lex scripta est. They however were of opinion that, the helpless state of the children would justify her non-compliance with the summons. The moment they left me, therefore, I dispatched a few lines to her to that effect, which I hope were time enough at the office to go by this even[g]'s mail.—

The slow, march of the trial I am told, has put Wilkinson out of all patience. He has been heard to swear in his wrath, that if Burr is not hanged, he cares not how soon himself were stretched on the same Gallows. M[r] Botts said he saw the Querist at Old Henderson's, and will advise my presence in Court, when the sons are produced to give their testimony—.

(Richm[d] Penitentiary, Virg[a]
Thurs[y] Aug[t] 13. 07—)

Progressed with my brief of which I entered on the 13th folio, bringing the narrative of the case, so far as I hope I can prove it, down to the period of my first interview wth Graham on Burr's affairs at Marietta, in last Novem^{r}—I hear or conclude by letters I have received, Old Richd Neale and James Wilson must be in town. I have as yet, seen neither.—Jourdan tells me Burr lives in great style & sees much company within his gratings, where it is as difficult to get an audience, as if he were really an Emperor. If these things be so well founded as is the hint in last tuesday's notes, I fear Wm Thompson is sketching his portraits of the characters connected with the trial, too far West, not to lose some lines of certain features that w^{d} not escape his pencil if he were *here*.

Friday Aug. 14th 07.—

Went down to the Kitchen, after Breakfast, in this wing of the Building, my servant having gone to town, to beg of one of the cooks there to request a keeper to bring the Barber to shave me. Cooks were preparing the Dinner for the Convicts, now confined here, to the number of about 130. This meal I learned, generally consists of 3/4 lb of meat, 1½ pint of soup and 1 lb. of corn meal-dow, which suffers, by baking, a diminution of ¼ of the weight. The Breakfast, the only other meal allowed in the 24 hours, consists of the like quantity of the same sort of bread and half a gill of molassis diluted with a pint of water. Not having, before spoken of the police of this establishment, I will now mention what has fallen under my own observation regarding it.

(Richm^{d} Penitentiary, Virg^{a}
Frid. Augt 14. 07—)

The convicts are confined for various terms of years according to their several offences for which the heaviest sentence is I believe, for the space of 18 years. They are kept to labour in the respective trades or occupations they had been bred to, with no allowance of rest on any day, but sunday, except during meals, being set to work at daylight, and leaving off at S.

set.—The present keeper is a smart intelligent man, who tells me, before he came here, the value of the annual labour of the prisoners, did not exceed $5000, the expenses being nearly as at present, $11,500. But he speaks confidently of raising the former, in his first year, to $14,500. I believe great diligence will be necessary in him to effect it. The men have not now, as under his predecessor, the benefit of any work they might try to do over and above the limits of their task. Mr Douglas assigns 2 curious reasons for discontinuing that little indulgence to these wretches. 1st. that it was found to occasion expense to the state by encouraging some folks to commit and *confess* small offences, in order to get boarded here *gratis* for 6 or 12 months, when they would be turned out with a sum of money in their pockets, for their extra labour, during their confinement, which they would soon *renew* in the same way. 2dly that those confined for a long term of years, w^{d} probably soon debilitate them selves thro' this stimulus to an increase of industry; by which their maintenance would become a dead charge

(Richm^{d} Penitentiary Virg^{a}
Friday Augt 14. 07)

---

without any return to the State. The Stimuli of Mr D. therefore or his superiors thro' him—are dark confinement in the cells—and the cow-skin, with short allowance of bread and water, which is not very well calculated to prevent the last evil (the debility) now sought to be avoided. My unfortunate Barber I hope fell upon a lucky day for *his* punishment, well or ill deserved, for I was soon told in the Kitchen, that he was in the cells. But expressing my concern for the poor fellow's misfortune, one of the cooks stept out, I suppose, to signify to the proper authority, the maturity of my beard, no doubt, rather than the expression of my sorrow—and in 10 minutes, Vaun was in my room wth his whole apparatus. This Vaun, my friends, is only here for 18 years, merely for cutting his wife's throat, with precisely the same sort of instrument with which he operates most delicately on mine, every other day.—Nor do the largest cities I have ever lived in, boast an artist in his line, that sh^{d} supplant him in my favour. The physiognomy of his countenance and the steadiness of his hand, with the keenness of his instrument, admirably correspond with the firmness and sensibility of his heart.—Would to Heaven I could add its purity.—But hideous jealousy entered there, and goaded this wretch to murder and to madness.—A Gentleman of Petersburg, who called in last ev^{g} with Dav. Meade assured me, that Vaun, on the day he killed his wife, sat

(Richm^{d} Penitentiary Virg^{a}
Frid. Augt 14. 07)

---

at his door for an hour or 2.—showing the bloody razor to the passengers in the street, and telling them how he had used it.—The Gent^{n} declared, had he been of the Jury, he sh^{d} not have concurred in the conviction.—This convict is black; was born free, lived in good circumstances, has been to Europe, and always supported an excellent character. Poor Vaun! the gloom of thy soul is now as dark as thy countenance: but yet may one ray of Divine mercy enlighten it! Thou shalt still shave me.

Col: Burr wrote me today that he was so surrounded by company he could not make up his mind upon a communication I made him by letter, of which he said, he perceived all the importance and advantage. I wrote to him to summon Henderson the father for reasons that will appear by my Brief; urged the advantage that w^{d} result fr. my cross-examining all the witnesses that I knew, particularly the Hendersons, which may be produced against him, if in my present character, I could be allowed to act, during his trial, as an agent or advocate for him; or if that sh^{d} not be permitted, that I sh^{d} at least be in Court, when such witnesses appear.—I also submitted to him the expediency of one of our counsel's seeing my Brief so far as I had written it.—He added in his letter that one of them sh^{d} call upon me for that purpose and to confer on other matters this evening.—

(Richm^{d} Penit^{y} Virg^{a}
Friday Augt 14. 07.—)

But I have rec^{d} no such visit, and must confess, I am rather led to ascribe my disappointment less to the negligence of the advocate than to that of the client—The vivacity of his witt, and the exercise of his *proper* talents now constantly solicited here, in private and public exhibition, whilst they display his powers and address, at the Levé and the Bar—must engross more of his time, than he can spare for the demands of other gratifications,—whilst they display him to the eager eyes of the multitude, like a favourite Gladiator, measuring over the arena of his fame—with firm steps and manly grace the pledges of easy victory. Man is prone to what St. Pierre aptly names the harmony of contrast, in which the mind & the eye are as much delighted in physics and in ethics as the ear is in music. My reflections will perhaps borrow from this principle, hereafter, in attempting to do more justice, in expression of character, to a third portrait of an Original—so differently appearing to my regards at Richmond and on the Mississippi.—Was visited this morning by Bellknap—and Pool; the latter, one of the most active in seizing the boats and provisions at Marietta, last december; also by D. Woodbridge, who read my brief, but to whom, as well as to every one else that calls upon me, I never speak on the subject of evidence yet or hereafter to be given by them in these trials. Had a very friendly letter fr. Col. Cushing,

(Richm^{d} Penit^{y} Virg^{a}
Frid. Augt 14. 07.)

---

lamenting my situation, and assuring me of every exertion of his friendship to serve me.—another fr. Thos. Neale exactly to the same effect as his last.—also a very friendly one fr. Mr Jno. Banks, thanking me on the part of Mrs B. for my prescription, and accompanying a present fr. her of 2. bottles of cordials, and a large cake, sent me by her. Visited by Alston, this being the first day he could venture out in a carriage. He says appearances every day strengthen the expectation of Burr's acquittal on both bills—Hay, having been heard to say, out of *Court* he does not think he will be able to substantiate the charges. It is believed however, a motion will be made to the Court, on the acquittals, but he rejected, to transmit us to other districts for trial according as evidence may appear or be procured as may be contended to implicate our conduct as treasonable elsewhere out of this District. Douglas has also heard Duane confess, that he too, is fearful Burr must be acquitted. Had this evening an obliging visit and 1. hour's interesting french conversation with Col: de Pestre; who informed me his brother-in Law, a promising y^{g} man of various merit, has been turned out of his place as Clerk in the War-Office, because he could not accuse the Col: of Burrism. And afterwards some honourable friends of the Govt. had the delicacy to insinuate how handsomely the Col: might be provided for in the Army,

(Richm^{d} Penit^{y} Virg^{a}
Frid^{y} Augt 14. 07.)

---

if his principles or engagements, were not adverse to the admin^{n}. The Col: replied that he understood the hint; but it neither suited his honour or character to serve in such employment.—Wrote to Colonel Cushing requesting him to forward to me an Inventory of all my effects that have been sold under attachments, and all my Negroes, to my wife or Col. Scott or Mr Harding at Natchez for her.—Have not worked to day, on my brief. Fr. prospect held out by many of my discharge on Burr's acquittal. Chatted as usual, in the morning with Douglas, and having left a letter I began to Miller for tomorrow, continued this diary till midnight.——

Richm^{d} Penit^{y} Virg^{a}
Sat^{y} Augt 15. 07.

Half past 8 p.m. Have not today, seen a face but that of my servant, Billy, who by the comfort I derive fr. his remarkable neatness and assiduity, my wife will not think undeserving of mention in this diary, which I have only resolved to keep for her gratification. Every one is probably at Court, where, this is a day of some interest, as the Jury will probably be empanelled. Have done nothing but walk and read the papers, my face continuing very sore with a disagreeable eruption. Will now finish my letter, begun yesterday, to Miller, and conclude the notes of to day after tea, by which time I may possibly collect something worthy of notice fr. Jourdan whom I hourly expect.—

(Richm.[d] Penit.[y] Virg.[a]
Sat.[y] Aug.[t] 15. 07.)

Whilst at dinner, M.[r] Ellis called in to know, if I c.[d] yet inform him when I might want him to serve subpoenas for me. Otherwise he sh.[d] soon leave town; seeing no prospects of getting any money fr. Col. Burr, against whom he has a demand of about $1100 for a boat and cargo sold him, in 10.[r] last, on the Ohio. B. it seems, has disposed of all such claims by a declaration, it is said, he made in Court, before my arrival, of his being a Bankrupt. But in emptying his strong-box, which seems to have lost all its treasures as quickly as those that took wing from Pandora's, he has I am told, like that Goddess, closed the lid—time enough to prevent the escape of that Hope, on which some favoured dependents may yet mortgage to him, their future services and the property of their children. It would even baffle the acuteness and exhaust the deliberation of our worthy Harding, to estimate the amount of this treasure, or conceive the structure of the debenture by which it is secured. I must, therefore, explain both. Know then, that it has been whispered to me, with the important gravity so confidential a communication required, that the sum is $50,000—the security—a claim upon Gov.[t] for the damages sustained by the Culprit, now trying for his life, but who will probably obtain his acquittal of the Treason ch, with more ease than he can procure one on another charge recorded against him in Kentucky of having robbed the W.[n] Country of $100,000; to say nothing of the absurdity

(Richm.[d] Penit.[y] Virg.[a]
Sat.[y] Aug.[t] 15. 07.-)

---

of sueing the Un. States—in the face of a positive Statute—As I was closing my letter to Miller, Jourdan stepped in, with Robert Nicholas a Democrat, furious keen and selfish, in chase of Alston, to secure and hasten the pay.[t] of Bills protested and endorsed by me to Sanders, to amt. with charges, etc. of $10,000., for which I will never give more than my bones; and the holder believing me determined, now depends on Alston's responsibility to me w.[ch] I have transferred to him. Tomorrow I shall be visited by M.[r] Edm. Randolph on the part of Sanders, and on my own business. I anticipate the conference with much interest. Jourdan is quite desolate and dispirited by the treat.[t] of B. of which he will give me particulars to-morrow; midnight.—

Richm.[d] Penit.[y] Virg.[a]
Sund. Aug.[t] 16. 07.

Rose late this morning very ill—but satisfied I was affected by no influence of confinement or the place; a severe headach, under which I've all day laboured, proceeding only fr. a derangem.[t] of the functions of the stomach, to which I am frequently subject. Whilst at breakfast, I was visited by M.[r] Poitiau, a merchant of consideration here, who had not before called upon me, for which he apologized, and in whom I admired here, in the spring of 1800 the most amiable manners, with a fine musical taste and handsome execution on the violin; he and myself, during my stay, being the principal performers in the Harmonic Society.—My worthy friend Prichard led the way, as much heated by the warmth of his friendship, as of his 2 miles' walk—bringing also, wth him, Wood, the late Editor of the

(Richm^{d} Penit^{y} Virg^{a}
Sund. Augt 16. 07.)

Atlantic-World a paper which is now extinct, and may be truly said to have been the last faint effort, save these trials, of expiring Burrism, under the relentless fury of Democracy. Wood is a singular looking-man, with a countenance expressive of gr^{t} oddity if not of genius.—of few words, with embarrassed [*blot above*] delivery, but said to be skilled in mathematics. His appearance altogether inspired some interest to know him better, and he will, by my desire, enable me to improve our acquaintance—I was agreeably occupied with this party, 'till Genl Tupper appeared. The news of his arrival in town, brought me yesterday ev^{g} by Jourdan, must have caused some little mental uneasiness last night and this morning, of which I was unable to render an account to myself.—This intelligence could not reach my ears, without arriving, in the same instant, at my heart, where it was at once amalgamated with all my hopes and anxiety for my family. With what rapidity did I calculate over and over, and conclude that I must hear fr. Natchez by the Genl I had written to my wife fr. the Chickesaw-Nation, whilst in my journey; I knew not how many dates before the date by the postmark, of that only letter fr. my Peggy of 23^{d} June, which was brought to me, in Lexington Jail, the first night of my confine^{t} there,—to direct to me at Marietta, under cover, to the Genl I hardly permit myself to conclude an interchange of salutations with him, when I eagerly-inquire for a letter.—He has none, and he left home, as late as the 5th Inst.—But a few more mails fr. Lexington and Marietta, without the blessing of a letter fr. you, my beloved, and I shall endeavour to prepare myself for more awful trials

(Richm^{d} Penit^{y} Virg^{a}
Sund. Augt 16. 07.—)

---

than the death warrant of a wicked or a jealous Gov^{t}.—Genl T's. conversation, which lasted about 1 hour with me was very interesting, both to my curiosity regarding the intelligence I would derive from him on my own account, and my admiration of that honourable independence he will yet make the Gov^{t} feel more of on his part than they wish or desire from the experience they have already had of his temper. It seems, much of the artifice of intrigue on the part of the Gov^{t} or their Runners has been put in requisition to endeavour to mould the Gen^{ls} disposition in the temper of the present prosecutions: He has next encountered attempts upon his honour indirectly, to induce him in some degree, to countenance the testimonies of Taylor and Albright, to the facts of his having arrested me, with my rescue and escape fr. him mentioned 12th Inst.: outrages upon his character and feelings, which he has repelled with that disgust and contempt suggested by his honour, but not without, thereby incurring what 'till then, the conservators of Jeffersonian fame never thought of—insinuations of his concern, and threats to involve him in the pains and penalties of the conspiracy.—Either before or after this analysis of the stuff which w^{d} not take the dye proposed;—it was politely signified to the Gov^{t} that altho' he had been recognized as a witness on the part of the Un^{d} States, the prosecutors, in kind consideration

(Richm^{d} Penit^{y} Virg^{a}
Sund. Augt 16. 1807—)

---

of the inconvenience another journey might put him to—w^{d} dispense with his further attendance. He said, however, he would return, were he obliged to travel on his hands and knees.—He also tells me—Doctor Wallace is alarmed at my presence here to confront him, when he shall dare to offer such testimony again as he has ventured before the Gr. Jury; and is terrified, for he is no Doctor, at the thought of being examined publicly by those who are of that profession, to prove he is not one.—See my notes of the 12th Inst. and it will appear how properly I wanted to fill the place of Surgeon-General in the *expedition* with such a Doctor—But G^{l} Tupper says he knows a person to whom Wallace said I was *jesting* with him when I spoke of his going with me as Surgeon-Genl.—I have not been gratified by the visit I expected, to day, with so much interest, fr. Mr Randolph: But have had a long one fr. Alston, which was taken up chiefly with the subject of an arrangement of the demands of Sanders and Miller: The agency of Nicholas has been so far effective as to induce Alston to offer to take a journey forthwith to S. Carolina to try to raise the money, leaving Mrs A. here till his return. He cannot offer hopes of success of this attempt; and no final adjustment, I believe, will be effected but by the opinion and advice of *Mr Randolph.* Mr Craighton call'd this even^{g} after a severe walk of 3 miles staid 2. hours; my headach continuing till 9 o'clock.——midnight———

Richm^{d} Penit^{y} Virg^{a}
Mond. Augt 17. 07.—

This is a Black-monday indeed wth me, whether the cloudiness of my mind or of the sky makes it appear such. Tho' I feel well to day, and took breakfast with some appetite, during which Col. de Pestre entered, and kept up an interesting conversation with me till noon, which, from the complete coincidence of our opinion on certain characters—and the reflections arising fr. the notes we had to compare on our *past* interest and connection with them, could not much tend to fortify me for encountering the new mortifications occasioned me by a letter I have just received fr. my estimable friend, Jos. S. Lewis, in his *private* capacity, informing me that the House of w^{ch} *he* is the head, had in consequence of attachments, served on my funds, my last pecuniary resource of my poor family, in their hands,—been obliged to dishonour all the bills I had drawn, that were presented for acceptance, since 20th of last january, the day such attachments were served at suit of the Kentucky insurance Co. and Lewis Sanders of Lexington. What discredit and embarrassment, the return of Bills I have drawn at Natchez, to am^{t} of 7. or \$800. will occasion my afflicted wife, I fear to estimate. Every day's trial seems to inflict a new wound upon my heart, if some part of it has not yet bled for my wife and children.—My *own* sufferings have long since destroyed the tone and established the apathy of every nerve that vibrated to the first impulses of the perfidy and injustice, that by their continued action, since the beginning of last 10.^{r} to the present hour;—

(Richm.^{d} Penit.^{y} Virg.^{a}
Mond. Augt 17. 07.—)

---

have relieved my mind fr. all care for the duration or issue of my confinement.—I have just dispatched a letter to Alston requesting to see him—and another to Prichard, desiring him to retain, or if disposed of, to try to take up a small bill I drew on Phila.^{da} a few days since for $100. Joe. Lewis tells me, *He* will honour Harding's Bills, drawn on *himself* for $500 in consideration of my wife's situation. Oh my Peggy, where will y.^{r} sufferings end. We thought, we were serving a P.····· and have been the dupes of an advocate. de P. has justly taken up the ideas suggested in my notes of last friday.—This generous *Foreigner* has narrowed his means of maintaining a large family besides some orphans, to the am.^{t} of $5000. for which he has not been thanked.—I hear Alston's carriage, must now close; for what purpose, but to hear a repetition of the same professions already made me of concern, to which is added, however an offer to go to Carolina in 2 or 3 days, to try to raise *some* money, the success of which however, I must understand is very problematical. What could I reply to the professions of one of the richest men in the Union—offering to assume these demands; ready to sell or mortgage, but yet unable to get the money I never used a cent of, and for which the cries of rapacious creditors rend the walls of my prison. Ah! that would be indifferent to me, did I not fear they are loud enough to reach & swell that heart that will echo them back to mine. For what purpose cou^{d} I desire to see him again on this business, but to make the last sacrifice I had to offer, alas! I once thought it impossible, I blush to name it,

(Richm^{d} Penit^{y} Virg^{a}
Mond. Augt 17. 07.)

---

to humble the pride of integrity before that of wealth,—to solicit, read it, my wife and forgive it for the sake of y^{r} children, his charity—for them.—I have thus sought relief thro' the storm, by every effort of skill or diligence I c^{d} make, 'till wearied and exhausted I have sat down, in the humility of my heart, to drift perhaps to that shore, where the mercy of heaven will recompense me in the participation of the rewards prepared for the fortitude and virtues of a wife I have been so long blest with. It is a relief to my heart to fill a whole page with a single sentence. The flood of my sorrows is too copious to suffer the artificial breaks and pauses of critical rules. My Peggy will feel this, if no one else can.—I wrote a very long letter to Joe. Lewis, which I immediately began when Alston left me, to acquaint him, that bills with my endorsements, on account of which one of the attachments had been served on his house as my garnishees had long since been paid by Alston's agent, Mr Sam: Allen of Phila^{da} that I had, in addition to the arrangem^{t} I made, with Sanders at Lexington K^{y} a prospect of making further arrangements here, thro' Alston wth Robt Nicholas the agent and Mr Edm. Randolph the Lawyer of Mr Sanders, by which I sh^{d}, I expected, in a few days to have the attachm^{t} at suit of Sanders taken off, and in the mean time 'till I could see Mr Randolph, which I could not do to day before the mail closed, I hoped Mr L. would believe his house w^{d} not be proceeded against, as my garnishees—and that whatever obstruction to their currency the little resources I yet possessed thro' his house in Phila^{da} were incumbered with, would be removed. I have to night also written to

(Richm^{d} Penit^{y} Virg^{a}
Mond. Augt 17. 07)

Mr Randolph to request him to call upon me tomorrow, before Court opens.—Speaking to day, whilst Alston was here before Col. McKee, of what was doing in Court, wither I wrote to Alston to come to me—A. said they left Hay stating the case, on the part of the prosecu^{n}, damned the speech and declared he would whip a son of his, were he only 12 yrs. old, that could not make a better. This led me to praise a pamphlet entitled Agrestis which Alston yesterday brought me, being 2 letters on Wilkinson's proceedings at N. Orleans, which for its arrangem^{t} and strength as well as for some imagery of the language I observed, w^{d} not be unworthy of a Curran; at the same time inquiring, who was the author. A. said that *was* not known. I then repeated the question to Col. M. who said, "it was a friend of ours" at least Mr A. was suspected. I mention this trifling occurrence for the sake of observing, that Alston was now silent, thereby appropriating to himself the merit of the book, which his wife I have no doubt, might produce; for by the title-page of the 2^{d} edition—as printed here—it appears, the former or the first edition was published in S. Carolina; or else it has proceeded fr. some other genius of much mind and erudition. But to suppose Alston the author w^{d} be preposterous. Obscurity may consistently veil the parentage of Hercules; but it w^{d} be ridiculous to suppose him the offspring of a Dwarf.—Take this trait and test it by the fact.—There is a provincial phrase or two in the pamphlet which I will keep, that proves it first saw the light at N. Orleans.—Sleep you sweetly my boys? and peace be with the heart of yr. excellent mother. I will go to bed and wake to bless you. My watch is down, no wonder. The centries cry all's well. God grant it.——

Richm^{d} Penit^{y} Virg^{a}
Tues. Augt 18. 07.

It may easily be conceived how difficult it must be for one in the state of mind in which I last night, closed my notes of the heavy hours of yesterday—to fall into that oblivious repose, thro' sleep,—which easily ensues upon the cessation of ordinary labour of body or mind, and enables us, by recreation, to perform the task of misfortune alloted for the morrow.—Accordingly, I did not find my bed, what it always proves to the peasant or the mariner,—the grave of care. The tumult of my mind had so inflamed my body, that irritation on the surface could not be allayed whilst trouble revelled within.—I was restless—for I was sick at heart and slept not soundly, till towards morning.—Yet I rose betimes, and had an early visit, as I expected, from M[r] Randolph, who called upon me in pursuance of my request to him by letter last night.—I stated to him my embarrassment, by M[r] Sanders attaching the only remaining funds I had that were tangible—and insufficient for the support of my family, observing, that if M[r] S. did not withdraw the attachment, which I hoped M[r] R. w[d] forthwith as S.'s lawyer persuade his Agent, M[r] Nicholas to do, I sh[d] consider my arrangement at Lexington, with M[r] S. to secure and settle his demand, thro' M[r] Alston, as abrogated.—This seem[d] to engage his reflections. But I was sorry soon to find he had the indelicacy, not only to inquire what was the am[t] of my funds in the hands of Mess[s] Jos. S. Lewis & C[o]—, but even to tell me, that if a sum of $1,000 or even $500 could be got immediately for Nicholas and Sanders, who, he knew

(Richm[d] Penit[y] Virg[a]
Tuesd. Aug[t] 18. 07.)

---

wanted money—such an expedient, he rather believed, would tend to give effect to *some* arrangement into w[ch] M[r] Alston might be induced to enter: adding, as he was taking leave, that, I knew how much a little ready cash helped these sort of things forward.—I had before observed to M[r] R. that he must know now, fr. the nature of my financial embarrassments, detailed to him in these transactions—how little I could presume upon counsel, I could not renumerate. Before he left me, he s[d] Burr has an excellent Jury in the whole, with the exception of

Parker, alone, who, he acknowledged, is a worthy, honourable man, but a violent Jeffersonian partizan. I expressed my surprise at B's accepting him, after he had avowed in Court, as strong prejudices as some who had been rejected. This indiscretion on B's part, he censured. He then told me, Hay was very weak yesterday, in stating the case; and he had no doubt of an acquittal; but to save time and labour, he very much wished the Ch. Justice shd concur in opinion with the Counsel on the defence, who yesterday contended in a lengthy argt with their opponents, that no evidence of intentions shd be gone into till overt acts had been first proven. How the Court have decided I shall know in the morning.

I now soon dispatched a note to Alston; and fortunately continued reading Agrestis, till I heard his carriage-wheels, which seemed to rattle in my ears "read on," till after he had entered the room. i.e. a thought struck me, that possibly, he might have had something to do in the composition, and I might do more with him, thro' his vanity of author-ship, than I had yet been able to effect thro' any other channel— "Admirable," cried I, before I answered his salute. He smiled, what, said

(Richmd Penity Virga
Tues. Augt 18. 07.)

---

he, "Agrestis, are you pleased with that little thing? Well, I did not care to notice it yesterday, but I will now tell you in confidence, 'twas I, wrote it."—I then pointed out to him, an image or two, particularly one in the 1st. letter, of Justice surrounded by the Laws, in the sanctuary of her temple, poising in their presence, the balance with her *own* hand—which, I said, wd be a fine subject for the relief, alto relievo—whilst the stations of her executive officers, assigned them without the sanctuary, might beautifully form the intagio, or background of a good piece of sculpture; adding with a frown, but such opportunities are lost or thrown away in this wooden country. Here I threw down the book—which he as readily took up, to descant on other merits it possessed, or point out errors of the press.—all of which engaged my most profound attention, but are not essentially necessary to be crammed into these notes.—The organ now wound up, I lost no time to try upon it, the tune my heart first called for. How do you think, my wife, it went? To admiration. The instrument was so much now improved, the piece so often tried upon it before, was now, not only performed in half the time, it used to be, but was worth double the money it would fetch yesterday. In plain English—instead of paying one half the money, next January 12 month-and the other half the January following according to his utmost powers, 'till this morning—to day, he was tuned up, to the incredible power of paying the *whole* not indeed to day—but next April 12 month. Who knows yet, but a judicious combination of discords to be selected fr. the letter to Pinkney, with some more of the melody of Agrestis, might produce a harmony, which if it cannot move

(Richm.^{d} Penit.^{y} Virg.^{a}
Tuesd. Augt 18. 07.—)

---

the *Oaks*, may still solicit the responsive *cadence* of the Dollars?—He left me with animated assurances of seeing Nicholas to day—and myself again, upon the business—not however with.^{t} some pretty simpers about Mr Randolph's hint of the $500—which, he regarded as soliciting a douceur, for Nicholas. But even that, he hinted in the suavity of his self-complacency w.^{d} not be impossible, when I assured him it should go in part of the demand.—I have had two or three reasons to day, of lightening my heart of the load that oppressed it yesterday. After Mr Randolph left me, I walked about, invoking the saving providence of Heaven over my wife and children, and wept. 2.dly, better prospects opened to me, fr. my interview with Alston and 3.dly the sincere pleasure I felt in writing to another Eugenius; as dear to me as the first was to Yorick—to communicate to Harding, a transcript of my melancholy notes of yesterday, and a short letter of today, to enable him to observe the better, under which part of the tottering fabric of my affairs, he may set the firm prop of his care and fr.[d]ship for my family, a service in which I feel he will not dally. The regards of my wife may one day, give him a perusal of these notes, as a supplement to his comments on Agrestis, which I have also sent him. I feel no tedium loci, and have no want, but that of letters fr. the best of wives and mothers.

Cock crow announces the morn. Grant oh God! it bring health to my family.—

Richm.[d] Penit.[y] Virg.[a]
Wedn. Aug.[t] 19. 07.

Saw Dud. Woodbridge before breakfast, who told me Eaton, Truxton, Taylor and Albright were yesterday examined on the trial. This intelligence has fretted me, because I find, Burr disregards the caution I gave him, to have me present during the exam.[n] of the witnesses I knew, as they sh.[d] be produced against him. I have heard, He alters the notes of his Counsel, increased yesterday, by the addition of M.[r] Lee, and for the most part, marks out the course they pursue in his defence. I hope his negligence of the suggestions I have made to him, will not furnish more cause of repentance than he is already burdened with. Hay having again called for my arraignment, and M.[r] Botts having I am told, said he would try to be ready by saturday I being now occupied in preparing a Brief for my Counsel—I must again revert to my labours on that work, which I shall resume this ev.[g]—The Ch. Justice has, I think properly, allowed the prosecutors to follow their own course in adducing their evidence, provided, they offer none of any other Treason than what is laid in the Indict.[t] It will appear fr. a correct report of the trial, how far Hay contends that the doctrine of constructive treason is Law, in this country: how candid he is, and what a virulent disposition M.[c]Rae manifests to insinuate bias in the Court toward the accused.—M.[r] Jno. Banks brought me, this morning a paper, containing Bollman's long letter to Duane, respecting B's communications to the

Prest which if not quite a justification of the writer, settles however, forever, the honour and good faith of Jefferson—I have not seen Alston according to my expectation and his promise. The general interest and curiosity engaged at the Capitol must suspend all other concerns. This evening, Gen. Tupper tells me that Hay boasts of having a number of witnesses to establish the credit of Albright! Eternal justice then support my innocence of the facts he has ventured to swear against me, 'till I shall appear before thy tribunal, where the vicious shall only testify to their own crimes. G. Tupper has also a suspicion that Meigs may venture to injure his credit as a witness. But the slightest attempt of that sort shall exhibit Meigs branded in the next papers, as a liar and a coward.—Eaton's manner and delivery in giving his evidence is highly extolled in the 2. Democratic papers the Argus and Inquirer, but I am better informd he strutted more in buskin, than usual, on that occasion—and the effect was as diverting to the whole Court, as it probably, was beneficial to the defence.—Still, Douglas, who is pretty regular in his evening visits to me or to my grog and Segars—tells me, Burr is cheerful as ever, tho' he cannot feel insensible to the advantage the prosecutors have taken in framing the indictt in a manner to correspond, in its form wth the *substance* of the opinion given by Ch. Just. Marshall in the cases of Bollman and Swartwout, and the industry they practice to train and back their witnesses to support it. But as a jockey might restore his fame in the course after he had injured it on the tight-rope,—so perhaps, the Little Emperor at Cole's Creek may be forgotten in the Attorney at Richmond.—I have been weak all day, and again put off briefing 'till tomorrow. 11 o'clock p.m.—

Richmd Penity Virga
Thurs. Augt 20. 07.—

I had Mr Douglas called to me, to request him to treat me to a walk in the yard this morning, before breakfast. My visitors in the course of the day, generally complaining of the closeness of my apartment, and some telling me, they chuse to reside in certain quarters of the town for the sake of high elevation and more air; others that they prefer country quarters, near town, for similar reasons,—and wishing me soon to partake of like [*blot*] advantages:—my walk, for half an hour in the yard this morning, being the 2^{d} time I have been from under the roof of this building, save the day I was taken to Court, 10th Inst. was not unaccountably agreeable, notwithstanding its narrow limits both of time and space and the high walls and buildings, in defiance of all which my lungs seemed to me to quaff their aerial draughts wth a spring and vigour I have seldom felt before. This sensation in the yard, reminded me how justly Darwin reckons, the desire of fresh-air amongst our natural appetites. But the patience and good health with which I not only bear more constantly a lesser share of vital-air, but also an atmosphere in no small degree tainted from the effluvia of a certain necessary fixture at the opposite end of my suite of rooms, recalls more frequently to my reflections, the bounty of providence, in affording me a proof experimentally of a more general maxim, viz l'homme s' habitue à tout. I have however procured materials fr. the Druggist, for making some oxygenized muriatic acid gas, with wch I will perhaps, tomorrow, destroy the noisome miasmata that infest the air of these rooms. Do intense smokers hurt the sensibility of their olafactory nerves? I suspect it. For Col: Burr never complained in the Mississippi, of the bad smell of his boat, occasioned by the confinement on board, of a cow, for many weeks. But what is yet more strange, during his late sojournment in these rooms, he one night suffered Mrs Alston to sleep in the room at the north end of the passage, opposite to that in which I now am, her room, that night, being of course, as it is at present, infected with effluvia fr. a certain cabinet connected with it.—However she early sought the morning breeze in a *solitary* ramble, on the banks of the river, next day; for her husband *left* her the night before, at 10 o'clock.—Continued my labours on my brief of which I completed the 17th folio, by dinner-time, when, who will believe it? I was visited in the most friendly manner,[1] [by David Wallace] [....] by too much folly to mean seriously to commit the crime of a 2^{d} perjury to swear away my life. It is impossible David Wallace could ever *mean* to practice so black a villainy. But it is equally inconceivable how he will profit by the hints he has had fr. Genl Tupper, or, if called upon again, which he seems to dread, how he will travel out of his deposition before the Gr. Jury. I rec^{d} him with the courtesy of a *prisoner now* in his own quarters. He sat a little, and brooked it.—then took leave, confused. I was not afterwards left 15 minutes alone, before every muscle of my face had relapsed fr. the rigour in which Wallace had bound them, to wanton in the liveliest welcome of—little Gates—who hurried to take my hand wth an ardour and frankness, that testified the sincere interest he felt in seeing me well—He had been in town since Sunday; but his duty of attending to the chance of his being called, as a witness in C^{t} and the irresistible interest excit^{d} there since his arrival, prevented his calling on me sooner. He stayed better than l. hour; during wch his conversation was full of interest and entertainment, fr. certain communications he made me of men and things, of which I shall make use in my brief—as well as fr. 2 or 3 anecdotes and stories he told me of some military characters and their achievements—at Marietta on the night the boats were seized there—of all which he acquitted himself with great humour and spirit. I shall expect the fulfilment of his promise to visit me often, with as much interest as I felt this evening.—Visited by a sensible genteel man, with a hard Dutch name I forget, having lost his ticket. He reminded me of having seen me 7 yrs ago in this town, and invited me to his house, when I recover my liberty.—My last visitor was Stokely, who declared, had he been in Wood Co. at the time of the troubles, by which my family and property so much suffered; he w^{d} have exerted whatever influence he had, to prevent them. He said he was very sorry to observe the counsel, on both sides agreeing in one thing at least, that is to keep me, so constantly as they do, in the front of the fight. He c^{d} not understand the policy of A. Burr's Counsel contending that their Client is not *answerable* for any acts of mine; and affected to lament deeply his fears, that in addition to all I had already suffered, I should end at last—by falling a victim between the cunning of Burr, on the one side, and the fury and prejudice of the prosecution on the other; I thanked him; and said I had thoughts of summoning him as a witness for certain purposes, that might be connected with my defence, hoping if I should do so he would excuse the trouble of the journey, to which he assented.—with expressing great desire to see me again settled in the White-House, on the Island. But how much sooner should I suspect treachery in this man 12 months past, than in others who have since, been seeking my ruin. Old Neal will not come to see me, partly, fr. scruples as to the obligations of Duty, being summoned on part of prosecution, and the aversion he would feel to see me in this place.—Hay I hear, having yesterday, stated, he would rest the evidence as to the overt acts—Wickham has today, spoken very ably for 4 hours, chiefly to contend that the acts not having been *proved* no evidence sh^{d} be offered of the intentions,—or that if the acts have been proved, Burr, as an accessory at a distance fr. the scene of action, can not be proceeded against, 'till I as a principal, shall be convicted.—If I have been correctly informed, the ground has been judiciously taken, and will no doubt be ably maintained by Mr W. and the Host that will follow him.—I can not expect at such a [*blot*] crisis, Alston will give a thought to anything out of Court.—I should have added, when speaking of Stokely that I learned fr. him, James Wilson has lost his wife, and left Wood C^{o} for another residence.—How has he left my business? and what has he done with the valuable papers I entrusted to his charge? My children——Will y^{r} unhappy father yet have days and health, sufficient to gather together, the little fragments of your property, so widely scattered over the face of the earth! If he but live, to finish that task—he will then be ready to take the last journey for his wages.—My wife will seek, if I can't, the obligations of D. Woodbridge Senr and others fr. Wilson—before she spares a sigh to time.—

Richm^{d} Penit^{y} Virg^{a}
Frid. Augt 21. 07.—

D. Wood^{ge} called and sat with me this morning longer than he has done altogether since I have been here. He has got over the care of his exam^{n} which worried him yesterday in Court nearly 2 hours and was I understand rather a disservice to the interests of the pros^{n} than otherwise. No witnesses are yet discharged, and all are as uncertain how long they will yet be detained, as ever, unless there be grounds for an opinion Mr Botts has given to Duane—that the trial will be over by wedn. or thurs. next. Mr B. must think, Hay, who I hear has demanded time to examine the authorities cited on the other side in support of Wickham's motion—will not succeed in opposing it. It appears my name is as often made use of in Court, during my absence—as it will again on my own trial, when some curious contrarities of facts and testimonies may come out if I ever shall be tried.—D.W. fr. looking over that part of my Brief, narrating the conduct of the Hendersons, in betraying my confidence to Graham etc. was led to acquaint me with a fact, I was not a little mortified to learn; viz. that Botts is married to the sister of Mrs Sandy Henderson. Must I then, withhold to defend my self against the most serious witnesses against me because my generous benefactor and enlightened patron, engaged to protect my life and character, against the—deadly assaults of his own relatives with no other recompense than the pride of interposing the barrier of his talents between a distressed family and its menaced ruin:——must, be averse to listen to a stat^{t} he w^{d} still less chuse to advocate ag^{t} his connexions. Had I been apprised of this difficulty in my first interview with Mr B. I know not how he could have relieved me fr. it. I must see him on the subject, before I send him a Brief. Strange, that every embarrassment I labour under, great or small, is derived fr. the same source. Dudley tells me, my Peggy's favorite horse Robin was stolen, with other things, by l. Welch, who has not been, since heard of; that Jones the honest, returned him the $40.; that Mun the zealous, kept the other \$20.—"Falsehood! thy name is, man"—not Woman.—Willey visited me to day, and was truly glad to see me again. I made him give me a detail of his adventures fr. leaving the boats. He had traveled in his story, as far as Fort. St. Stephens, on the Tombigbee River, where, he was arested—after having lost 1 of his horses, and lived with the Mulatto-boy, Harry, for 6 days on damaged Corn. Having missed his way, he had not seen Col: Burr fr. the time he left Judge Bruin's 'till he found him at Washington-City; midnight—

Richm^{d} Penit^{y} Virg^{a}
Sat^{y} Augt 22. 07.

Whilst at Breakfast, Little Luckett step^{d} in.—He produced to me, I hope, the last bill with my endorsement drawn by Burr. I had no note or recollection of it. It was drawn on the same baseless authority with all the rest, for \$2,500 and had, of course, suffered a like fate. Yet Luckett had not attempted any proceedings ag^{t} me; tho' he showed me an acc^{t} stating a balance against Burr of upwards of \$8000. by which and losses he has sustained, he says, he has been quite ruined. He intreated my best interest with Alston, and never expects any thing fr. me. I hope soon to be able to state the details of a final arrang^{t} with Burr and Alston to extricate me fr. all these embarrassments. Having learned fr. Luckett, I was to be taken to court today at noon, to be arraigned, I was in the act of dressing, when two Deputy-Marshals called upon me, half an hour earlier than was necessary, excusing themselves by saying, my watch was so much too slow tho' it was exactly with the town clock. The distance fr. hence to the Capitol being nearly a mile, and as I am affected since yesterday morning with a diarrhea, for which I am taking medicine, I had sent my servant to town to procure me a horse. But as he had not yet returned I asked these Gent^{n} if they had brought a carriage, as had been done the last day I was taken to court, telling them my reasons for not wishing to walk. They answered, the Law did not make any provision and the walk would serve me.—So I soon attended them, tho' not in the style that was provided the 10th Inst. My two attendants in fact to day, were unarmed both going and returning. I had time enough before Court was opened, to prepare for my Counsel, a list of 39 witnesses, I should have time allowed me to get here, before I c^{d} be ready to go to trial. Of these, I informed Mr Botts, 12 I deemed material, to disprove all evidence that did or might yet attempt to prove my having committed any overt act, the rest to prove I had in nothing, manifested a traitorous design; and of this number I wanted subpoenas, duces tecum, for 5 or 6 to procure the production of various documents that might be necessary to my defence. My other witnesses are summoned on either side, in the present trial; so that the original list I took with me to Court today, contains no less than 55. I next suggested to Mr B. my discovery of a misnomer in the Indict^{t} where, in my Christian name an e. is used, instead of an a; and in the surname an a. is used instead of an e. Mr B. informed me, that objections for these variances w^{d} procure an arrest of judgment but w^{d} only be sufficient to support a plea in abatement.—He then stated to the Court, after I had stood up to learn the Indictment, which the Clerk read against me—the discovery of a misnomer, which had been just suggested to him, without any desire on my part to take advantage of it; but as my other counsel were absent he wished to confer with them on this defect; and as several of a long list of witnesses I had furnished him, lived as distant fr. hence as the Natchez, it seemed best to postpone my arraignment 'till the opinion of the Court should be known on the several points, made on the part of A. Burr which w^{d} equally affect my case & his—when if necessary, I sh^{d} be prepared to state at what time I c^{d} expect the forth-coming of my witnesses—so that I might be arraigned by wednesday. To this Hay agreed—the court, which sat to day, only on my account, was adjourned, and I returned to this prison, as I left it—that is unarraigned.—I hear Bollman is wth Burr constantly, and no doubt, busy.—If it does not appear that

Burr can boast, as Chas Fox did—amicitiae sempiternae—yet may he say—inimicitiae placabilis. Alston's purse and Bollman's talents for intrigue, are recommendations; or anodynes to a mind, that finds no difficulty in obliterating the impressions of sensations heretofore received fr. either, by the letter to Pinkney, which is before the public, or the process-verbal of the interview with Jefferson whch is not yet given to the world in detail.—Enough has already appeared in these notes, to warrant my suspicions as to Alston, and in addition to the hint given to day and 19th Inst. of my opinion on Bollman's manoeuvre with Jefferson, I am the more confirmed in a disposition to mistrust both the motive and the matter of the interview, as well as his letter to Duane, because he has not, as yet had the curiosity to see me. Neither a community of interest or suffering has affected him. He has had no other motive probably to suggest to him a wish for my acquaintance, for he has probably never heard fr. *authority* that I had been offered to chuse him or Shaw for my private *Secretary*, when I shd name a diplomatic appointment for myself—This would have been an useless and dangerous humiliation of Mr B's pride, which, no doubt, his master has long since found more accommodating to his views than mine. My Visitors, this evening were Genl Tupper, D. Woodge, Belknap, Wood and Doctor Bennet.—the last, who has been brought here, to support R. Taylor's evidence of my having written to him a treasonable letter, by Taylor, is friendly, and can swear that I wrote nothing to him of a traitorous nature, tho T. told him the letter was of that sort, when he gave it to him. The Doctor says he supposed I wanted the arms, I wrote to him to endeavor to borrow for me, 10 or 20 guns, to defend my family and property agt illegal outrage, he knew I apprehended at that time, fr. the Wood Co Volunteers—in the same sense—in which in my Brief, I have stated this part of my Case to Counsel. Genl Tupper read over a most humorous Lampoon on most of the military characters engaged in the Heroic feats of arms, they performed on the night of the 10th 10r last at Marietta.—of which I hope I shall obtain a copy, to relieve the ennui of these notes. I find it very agreeable this evg to get upon a chair, by which I am enabled to raise my mouth to the lower tier of openings in the grating of the windows & breathe another air for ½ an hour. m'night.

Richmd Penity Virga
Sund. Augt 23. 07.

My Diarrhea still continues, tho' it is much abated by the medicine and treatment I use, which as they—may be serviceable in my family in similar affections of the Bowels, I will here set down. Med..l. pill, going to bed, containing l. gr. opium l. gr. calomel, [*blot*] and 3 grs. ipecach: the Regimen is, abstinence fr. spiritous liquors and indigestible food—particularly unchewed, salt and high seasoned victuals,—with a small increase of clothing, in a degree that will not feel unpleasant, to help and *keep up* the action of the ipecach by *the skin.* If Alston could not make the same excuse for not calling on me yesterday, he might have offered some days back. Still less could he do so today, when, I suspect, he has been sent to me. Luckett, this morning, told me it was Col: Burr's wish, that I should write to Alston to do the best he could for him, about the dishonoured bill L. holds with my endorsement. Suspecting the correctness of this statet I replied, that Col: B. was a ready-pen-man, and in the habit of *writing* to me on matters of business: that L. therefore, must endeavour to get him to specify under his hand, how it was necessary Mr A. shd learn his wishes fr. me—whilst they saw each-other every hour. My *own* wishes for the relief of L. I had no objection to signify to Mr A. in my own way——L. posted off and has procured by his importunities, not a letter from Burr, who never puts pen to paper, but under the influence of necessity—tho' he is perhaps, the most constant writer in Amera—but a visit fr. Alston. When he came in I inquired, what were Col: Burr's expectations of the fate of the motions now before the Court? He said, they, or some of them, would prevail, and the Trial would be over by wednesday or thursday; that he and Mrs A. would very soon leave town; and that Col: Burr, on his discharge, wd immediately occupy himself with the business of forming a Land company, and settling the Ouashita Lands. Perceiving he had an interest in thus abruptly informing me of this project, I encouraged him to——dwell upon it, when I found, that tho' he had been conversing with Burr on the subject, he wished *me* to inform him whether B. had ever *seen* the lands? I told him I was not certain, but believed not, adding that Tyler and Smith who once had been very intent on settling there, had long ago abandoned the scheme, believing fr. information they had procured and c.[d] rely upon, Lynch's title was bad—and they were accordingly busily preparing to settle in the Tuckapaw Country, very distant fr. the Ouashita, where the Lands were condemn'd by very good Judges I named to him, who had visited them. A. seemed surprised at this intelligence, and said, the commissioners had confirmed Lynch's title. I told him—I doubted that: but said it was immaterial, as Lynch had long ago been a Bankrupt; so I had not much thought of accepting or purchasing 10,000 acres of those lands, which Col: Burr had offered me. I should not be surprised to learn very soon, that Burr has been promising to replenish Alston's coffers which he will empty of $50,000 at least, fr. his Eldorado on the Ouashita. I well know B's address in preventing or evading the simplest questions, he does not like to answer. I have seen A. often yield to it, and wonder not that he should seek fr. me, that information of which he found B. so tenacious. This then, may turn out another instance in addition to many others I have furnished, in which B may see cause to deprecate my knowledge of him, and curse that candour of integrity that has so often traversed his purposes. Bollman's cautious skill perhaps, will never betray him into similar *indiscretions*. But Major Smith, will be here tomorrow and then bursts the bubble. After I had next, given A. some account by his desire, of the country about the Natchez, in which I also took liberty to correct many errors in C. Burr's view of that subject—I contrived to let him broach the business he came on. He asked me, if I had seen Nicholas to day; I said, no, but Luckett had been here with another of my endorsements, and an account he showed me, with a balance struck ag[t] Col: Burr of something better than $8000. Thus said I, almost every week, I discover some new demand upon me on account of this business, and I have now ascertained, that besides other losses, my name has made me responsible for $21,000. By God says he, it will cost me at least $50,000. I mentioned the bill and balance together, to try if he w[d] offer any objection to responsibilities I had entered into, exceeding the amount of his guarantee to me. But finding he did not, I then told him the am[t] of the bill was only $2500; with the account between Col: B. and Luckett I had no concern, and recommended the latter to such present relief as he could afford him.—He seemed pleased, said Nicholas w[d] probably accept his terms, should remove the incumbrances on my property in Phila[da] etc. invited me to Carolina, and promised soon to see me again.—Then returning to the subject of the trial, he told me a piece of news which well deserves a place here, as so much secret history, characteristic of the feelings and energies of the Ch. Justice. It seems, after the Judge had determined to give the prosecutors time fr. friday till monday, to prepare to answer the arguments of the opposite counsel on 4 points, any one of which being supported by the Court, the trial ends,—a friend of Gen[l] Marshall asked him, if in suspending a criminal prosecution, by granting this indulgence, he had not made a rule that had no precedent. To this, he answered—He knew it, but if he sh[d] decide *against* the prosecutors, on any of these points, he would be reproached with not being *disposed* to give them—an opportunity to answer them. And that he will probably not overrule them all is more probable, fr. an expression of his, whilst playing at chess, with Wickham, since the latter made the points. "Don't you think," said he, "You will be able to *stale mate these fellows*, and relieve us fr. being kept here, 3 weeks more?" See last thursday's notes.—In the ev[g] Gates called, and soon left me to give way to Wickham and Botts as they entered. This visit proceeded fr. a wish I yesterday expressed in Court to M[r] B. to see him in the course of this day, my object being to state to him candidly the objections I had lately discovered to his appearing as advocate for me, in my defence, which might expose the breach of confidence and honour I complained of, on the part of his connections. But as he brought Mr. Wm. with him, and it seemed their joint opinion, that the decision on the points now before the Court, would probably this week, put an end to Burr's trial, and occasion the relinquisht. of mine;—or that if that did not happen, they had determined upon a plea in abatement, for a misnomer, to the indictt. in my case, which they thought must prevail; and then the prosecutors would probably despair of success in getting another Gr. Jury, to find another Bill against me: or if they should make such an experiment—I should most probably, in the mean time, be admitted to bail.—Fr. this view of their opinions, I said I hoped, it wd. not be necessary to trouble them, with my Brief; and I could not venture the appeal to Mr. Botts feelings, which I proposed to make in this interview. My accomplished friends now terminated their visit, with their accustomed kindness; and left me in a sublime reverie on their virtues and talents, which was soon broken in upon, by the appearance of Mr. Douglas with a Stranger, I should rather have said, by two apparitions. For it was now near night-fall and Douglas no sooner appeared than he turned on his heel, saying, "Colonel Duane, Sir," and ran down the stairs. The surprize of this interruption, the stranger, whom I had never before seen, did not suffer to endure long enough to allow me to invoke the angels and ministers of grace for my protection. I was already within the grasp of this Gabriel of the Govt.—He seized my hand, and bad me dismiss my surprize however natural it might be, on his appearance before me. I handed him a chair, and said I had lived long enough in this country to be surprized at nothing it could produce or exhibit; but yet, desired to learn, fr. what cause I had the fav. of this visit. Having heard Mr. Douglas observe, said he, that you wd. be pleased to see me—Sir, Mr. D. has made a mistake; he must have meant somebody else. No matter continued he, having known and seen yr. present situation, I could not, as a man and an Irishman (here he digressed to show, how he both was and was not an Irishman) I wd. not leave this town, without warning you of the sacrifice now preparing to appease the Gov.t by yr. *friends*, of which you are destined to be the victim. You can not desire any other key to my meaning, than the course the defence has this week, taken.—But if you think the Gov.t will not cease to pursue that justice they possess the *means* of insuring, & suspect as you ought, the designs of *those* you have too long, thought yr. friends it might yet appear, no better on my part, than a nominal service, to give you these cautions. I have therefore sought you, not to tender you words but deeds. The only return, on your part will be, that care of yourself, which will find a shield in my honour, (here he very awkwardly struck his breast, and grinned a ghastly smile) and that confidence I can *command* in the Gov.t whose good faith is not misplaced in the zeal I have testified to serve it.—To this harangue, delivered somewhat less perhaps, with the action and manner of Satan, personating Duane, than that of a felon, he added violent protestations of his wishes to serve me saying that for that purpose he would put off his journey back to Phila.da which otherwise was irrevocably fixed for wednesday, and would now, or at any time hereafter, go to Washington for me, where nothing he should ask, would be refused him.—In thanking him for the frankness and zeal with w.ch he cautioned me ag.t my friends, and a negligence of my safety, I assured him I was not afraid to meet the prosecution as I expected I should before my arrival here, without counsel or friends; but fr. present appearances, I was more curious than interested to learn, what were those means he said, Gov.t possessed of ensuring justice? Finding by his answer, he was now disposed to allure me into a confession of having written certain papers in the hands of the prosecutors. I told him, the warmth of his offers to serve me could not make me forget either his situation or my *own* with relation to the Gov.t; that I cared not, what writings should be charged upon me: that I should admit none, 'till fairly proved—w.ch if any *such* sh.d ever appear, I w.d justify, if necessary, on the scaffold.—He now summed up the objects of his mission whatever produced it, with abuse of Burr, Tyler & Smith, acknowledging, that he had been served, gratis, by the first, in the most handsome manner: that the others were more concerned against the Gov.^{t} than I was, but swearing that he believed, if I did not follow his advice, they would make a scape-goat sacrifice of me for their deliverance. Can I make no use then of this adventure? Yes—I will put this Interest in requisition, if I can't find a readier means, to abreviate the imprisonment of Vaun.—I have again laid by my brief which I shall not probably soon resume, till all my expectations of Burr's success & my own are reversed. In the mean time, I will attend to the adjustment of my private affairs.—Ellis called in today and seemed pleased with having it in his power to offer to spare some money to me, if I wanted it. I was very glad I said, to find Col: Burr was [*blot*] in cash. Not at all said he. I was w.th the Marshal and pretended a Subpoena had been served on me at Natchez and got 140 odd Dollars. This was all Col: B. could *yet* do for me. This is caution with a vengeance. See 6.th Inst. The Marshal's runners have these two nights past, been in busy search of Genl Dayton. If he is taken in this *way*, how will he appear to the multitude?—

Richm.^{d} Penit.^{y} Virg.^{a}
Mond. Augt 24. 07.—

My Diarrhea is removed, and the natural tone and habit of the bowels restored. Between 8 and 9 o'clock a.m. arrived Major Smith at this place. He has got the room under me to sleep in, and no reasons of state or measures of public safety appear at present, tho' they were obvious 3 weeks ago, to prevent our living together 'till bed time with the keepers or turnkeys i.e. 8 p.m. He has not heard fr. Burr, tho' Mr Martin has visited and offered him to be his Counsel gratis.—I was visited by de Pestre, whom I was obliged to send away to attend to Nicholas—who will probably do something definitive as to Sanders, with Alston to day or early tomorrow. For strange to tell, the latter de Pestre assured me, was going home to day, but Nicholas says, he will put it off till tomorrow—I apprehend, I shall be obliged to accept of that *friendly* invitation he gave me yesterday.

Smith has heard Burr has made financial arrang[ts] in Phila[da] to settle everything after his acquittal—midnight.

Richm[d] Penit[y] Virg[a]
Tuesd. Aug[t] 25. 07.—

The unexpected appearance of Alston on the stairs, before 8 o'clock this morning, whilst I was walking with Major Smith, in the passage, operated as a panic,—and soon inspired a conviction of the apprehensions I entertained yesterday, after having seen de Pestre, that he would be off, wth French leave. I composed myself, however, to receive him with an air of confidence, I have generally of late, dissembled towards him, affecting at the same time, a little surprise, at so early a visit. This he parried, with a whiff of his segar, which gave him time to think to say; the Court was to sit as early as 9, and he meant to lose nothing of all that was expected from Wirt, who would have the advantage of a good foil afforded him yesterday, by the wretched exhibition of M[c]Rae—which soon become so flat, that it nearly cleared the house. He affected, said he, to prance at starting, but could only crawl all day, over the ground; even Hay, confessing he did not understand the question, and Botts, who w[d] next have spoken, declaring he had heard nothing a reply fr. him required. Alston now called me into my apartment to dispatch the object of his early visit, which seemed to be to leave town, with[t] incurring any complaints of mine, for not concluding, before his departure, the so long expected arrangements with Nicholas. He therefore, objected to the difficulties that, he said, Nicholas and Randolph pretended to feel, in removing the attachment from my funds, in Phila[da] without particular orders from Sanders. I said I should expect or coerce, Sanders to do that, in virtue of the settlements I had made with him in Lexington, whether M[r] A. furthered that settle[t] or not. He then said Nicholas yesterday promised to have the necessary papers ready last evening; but he w[d] have me completely *exonerated* fr. the demand, before he did anything; to which I of course, assented.—But I asked what had occasioned the determ.n I heard he had formed of leaving town yesterday, or to day? Oh! the certainty of the trial's ending this week, had made him desirous to leave this place, of which he was heartily tired, as soon as possible, and his anxiety to try to raise even a part of the money for my *relief* would the more hurry him away. He forgot, I suppose, he yesterday told Nicholas, he had just receiv'd *letters* that *suddenly* called him home. A propensity to rely more on his witts than his memory, is a prominent trait in this character. It w.d then, have answered no purpose to have inquired into the fact of the letters being *concerned*, rather than my sufferings, with the period of his journey. He could easily say, 'twas true, he had letters—for he is very circumspect to avoid any charges upon his words, w.ch I took an occasion again, to day, to put to the test, by observing to him, that I supposed my Losses, by Miller's sales of my effects, w.ch had been sacrificed, in Wood C.o would not be much short of $15,000 which sum w.d not replace 2/3 of my Library, my furniture, instruments, House-Linen, etc., etc. with all my farming-stock and implements of husbandry, for all which I had no other hope of *indemnity*, but what I could derive fr. the honour and resources of Col: Burr and himself—to all which he was *silent*—But he might and did add—nothing more engaged his concern so much as his wishes to relieve my embarrassments.—He then told me Col: Burr wished me to be upon my guard, against spies—as he apprehended, some had lately been visiting me, under the mask of friendship—On asking him whether he alluded to any particular persons, I found he had heard of Duane's visit to me, on Sunday evening, which was, next day, in everybody's mouth, and may possibly have had some share in engendering a report, which as yet has been only whispered, tho' it may have stolen into some of A. Burr's private audiences. This report states, that I now see Burr in a different light, fr. that I first, regarded him; and that my fellow-prisoner, Major Smith, is come on, determined to denounce Burr, and turn an approver. Alston did not hint this rumour to me. But I thought it w.d be serviceable to the interest of my pecuniary expectations fr. him, to send him back to

Burr, satisfied of my vigilance, and perserverance in those duties of honour and good faith, which if they doubted in me, I should never forget, I always owed to myself. Ha! said I, you've heard of Duane's visit to me then—Would you wish to see my notes of what passed between us? Yes, said he, eagerly, very much indeed. I then read to him, the minutes I had taken, on Sunday morning, with wch he seemed highly pleased, and said, they ought to be published. To this I told him, I could not accede, tho' it might seem to him, the more necessary, fr. some observations made to me, by Duane, more than I thought necessary to enter in my notes, of which I recollected l. that concerned A. himself—who now seemed all anxiety for the disclosure he expected. But I affected to attach little importance to the thing, and said, after no small enjoyment of his solicitude about it;—'Twas only, that Govt had got possession of one of his letters to me.—One of my letters, said he—I never wrote to you, but two upon *business* of a *private* nature: and by God, any other letter they can have of mine, must be a forgery. To be sure, said I: or at all events, fr. the favourable course things are now likely to take, *such* a letter could do no harm. But what did the rascal, continued he, state to be the purport of the letter? Nothing more said I, than proving—that you and myself were equally involved in all Col: Burr's projects. He then abused Duane, repeated his wish my notes were published, and took leave.—I find I have omitted to observe, owing to the hurry and fatigue I suffered, the day I arrived in this prison, that Alston, on his 1st. visit to me that evening, acknowledged the receipt of the letter I had written him fr. Natchez, containing a reprobation of his public letter to Gov. Pinkney, when he said, he felt now, no uneasiness at certain reflections I had therein made use of, which he knew, proceded fr. a warmth of temper, natural to me, upon a misconception of his motives, which he had explained to the *satisfaction*, (is it possible?) of Col: Burr.—To which, I answered, that the letter itself would say, it was not designed to *excite* his *sensation*; tho' it was written under impressions that could not be obliterated; and that his not answering my letter, which was so incumbent on him, fr. the nature of that part of it relating to money matters, so irritated and convinced me that he disregarded my expectations fr. him arising fr. his guarantee for my losses, by my concern with Col: Burr and himself,—that I was further led to declare at Lexington, that he was as fully concerned with Col: B. as myself, stating at the same time to him, a further motive for such a declaration, which will be found in my Notes of the 6th Inst. All this he accepted very kindly—assuring me, he had written 2 letters to me. What? 2. Yes: he not only then, that is, on the 4th Inst. said 2. but he said so again: today. Now those who are blest with his correspondence, will find, he is not in the habit of bestowing 2 answers upon 1. letter, especially, when that 1. has chiefly for its object to bring a demand upon him, into action; much less, to grant a single reply to a letter, which, thro' respect to his wife, he might at least acknowledge.—I allude to our friend Harding's letter to him. That he confessed, he had recd but told me on his 1st. visit, it merely enclosed some *papers* to him, and required no answer. So, the generous labours of the head and heart of one of the best men living, did not deserve even the Thanks of this coxcomb. But it appears fr. all this, that, if his 2d letter was in answer to the only one I ever wrote him, his 1st. was occupied with some other subject. And the palpable interest, with which he listened to the late news Duane left wth me for him, joined with the motives that induced him to write the death warrant of his character to Pinkney; and some late rumours of designs in Govt to institute prosecution against him also,—all leave little room to doubt that the prosecutors have got hold of something, he would not like to see. But if this alarm will give me hold upon him, to keep him long enough here, to carry some of his sincere wishes for my relief into execution—I shall owe Duane more obligations *for* his visit than he is aware of. I recd soon after breakfast, a pettyfogging letter fr. Hen. Clay of Lexington, telling me, he wd accept of $20 as his fee, for telling the Court at Lexington, he spoke "there, as a citizen—and that I did not want him." Tho' I told him I had no money. But I will send him his fee, with a letter he will not show for twice the money, because, in settling the business between Sanders and me, he has, as S's att^{y} done every thing he could to embarrass my means of adjusting the demand of Miller also upon me, tho' I declared, I would not give one a preference over the other.—I also rec^{d} a note fr. Prichard, covering the bill, I had drawn on Phila^{da} in his fav^{r} which was returned, for—reasons already given in my Notes of last monday.—Behold me then; without a dollar, except the few that remain of 30 Prichard sent me, a fortnight since, on this very bill—I have got my coat repaired, my umbrella new covered, my hat dressed, and my boots new-topped. But this economy will not pay my tavern-bill, or those of my grocer and washer-woman. Nor will it restore to me, the only funds on which I depended—for my only *care*, the maintenance of my family. My own wants will never solicit the mantle of charity, to shelter them fr. the pinching blast of adversity, till death shall lay the storm. Till then, they cry, even to the heart of Mr Alston "pray spare a trifle from yr. stock to clothe my naked family, with that credit of which you've stripped it." In this spirit I wrote to him what follows—I have just rec^{d} the enclosed by wch you may convince Mr Nicholas of the unjust and absurd obstruction of my credit in Phila^{da} by the continuance of Mr Sanders' attachment—Having no other source of pecuniary *supply*, to which I can resort for *subsistence* of my *family*, 'till I can collect the wreck of their property. I await the accommodation of such credit or *remittances* as yr. dispositions may devise for the relief of my exigencies. —yrs etc. H.B.—

What sort of answer will the patience of a friend or a wretched wife, further travel thro these notes, to hear I received? The servant returned with a verbal answer in these 4. words "He will *see* him," importing, that Alston would see Nicholas, as if *seeing* N. will indemnify me for all I have suffered or support my family. Be these things only known to thee, my wife, hereafter. But let them SHOUT, and ever, be my first of cares, until I set them right, or perish.—Alston told me

Belknap has confessed, he rec^{d} fr. Smith, $700 for me, which he denied, the night he arrived on the Island fr. Kentucky,—the night I left it. midnight——

Richm^{d} Penit^{y} Virg^{a}
Wedn. Augt 26. 07.—

The Bird I believe, has not flown to day, but may take wing, I [*blot*] know not what moment. I have neither seen nor heard fr. him since his verbal answer to my letter of yesterday. The little animal has clapped its wings in screaming essays toward the Oaks but yet may it remain a little longer on that egg, it has not yet hatched, for the cuckoo that laid it. Duane's cuckoos may lose some eggs.—but they keep up the breed. Wirt raised his reputation yesterday, as high as McRae sunk his the day before. The former, I hear, paid me some compliments. We have many visitors as usual, of whom I shall only notice Kerr, who sat 1 hour here this ev^{g} Was cautioned by Dud^{y} W^{dge} to beware of Bennet. But I have him secured by Tupper, who tells me, he T. will support the declarations made by Bennet to him and me, on B's first visit to me here. Maj. Smith is suffering something of a seasoning. midnight.—

Richm^{d} Penit^{y} Virg^{a}
Thurs. Augt 27.-.—

Rose ¼ past 5 this morning, to walk [*blot*] in the yard, as I had agreed with Maj. Sm. last night. But he rested badly, and had a profuse perspiration, when I called upon him, which determined him, with my advice, to stay in bed. So I walked for an hour alone under a disagreeable fog—with a view to try, whether breathing, so long, another, if not a better air than that of my room, might not enable me to escape today, a periodical Head-ach, with some fever, we both complain of, about 2 o'clock, every day, since sunday, and of which we are not free, some nights, before we go to bed. Young Swartwout called upon us, with Alston. The latter called me out, to tell me, things will be completed to day wth Nicholas, fr. whom he will get the original bills, on which the attach^{t} was served on the House of J.S. Lewis & Co as my garnishees, by which I suppose [*blots*] I can again, open the chanel of my Credit, which the attach^{t} has so long shut up in Phila^{da} He assures me, Luckett's Acct. is not admitted to be correct by Burr, and that I shall not be liable for the Bill of 2500 Dolls. wth my endors^{t} in L.'s hands. He has also offered me, a Dft at Sight, in Charleston, for the Bill, returned to me by Prichard. He concluded his money-business with me this morning, by telling me, Col: Burr will soon be in Cash, having concluded some financial arrangem^{ts} with a Mr Pollock, who is very rich. I must not forget however, he also told me, his settling both Sanders' and Miller's claims if the latter will come into the arrange^{t} will, with the incidental charges, require payments by him to the am^{t} of $16,000, so that after settling Sanders' claim, if Miller won't settle in the same way, he has proposed to take up his present letter of guarantee, and give me another— [*Blots written around, both pages.*] to indemnify me, for which Miller may be entitled to recover of me, to which I have assented. Mr A. has found Wirt, tho' not without merit, so far as he was figurative,— monotonous, with bad or no action, and better recommended by the foil McRae afforded him, than any interest his late essay could inspire.—He seems, to day to partake of apprehensions, entertained by Col: Burr's friends—that the Ch. Justice may yield to want of energy, in ruling all the points now before him, as the able efforts of the Counsel for the defence can not fail to prove, the Law requires.—Surely, if the Law has not been mistaken on the side of the accused—the calumny which has been propagated through the crowd, of Burr's emissaries having made an attempt to take off Mr Duncan, by Laudanum— w^{d} tend to strengthen rather the energies of such a Head and Heart, as the Ch. Justice is probably blessed with.—This Duncan has been brought here I am told, to prove a negative; viz. that Wilkinson is not a Spanish Officer or pensioner.—Duane has kept his promise to abandon the field yesterday. I find to day, he is an expert angler, and adapts his flies and tackling not only to the waters and seasons of his choice, but to that kind of Fish that are the objects of his sport. At least the first cast of his line has caught that wary fish, the natural history of which has engrossed so much of these notes. I have been accordingly informed a formal demand has been made upon Hay, to declare whether the Gov^{t} or himself possess a certain letter of which a sketch has been given here the 25th Inst. The scene that this interview probably presented, will I know not how long, be reserved for recital in the secret mysteries of the prosecu^{n} A. on his part, gave me too sublime a rehearsal of the dignity and force with which he launched the bolts of his Defiance on all the Titans of Virginia, for me to presume to initiate it in these memoranda, without incurring the suspicion at least [*Large blots written around, both pages.*] of being disposed to burlesque it. The Titan Hay however, he assured me, he overwhelmed with mountains of consternation and dismay. In short, the fact was denied—and what was very extraordinary, as the like never happened before—imprecations of mendacity on the fame of Colonel Duane—were endured with patience by Jefferson's att^{y} The existence however, of the letter be it remembered, is as yet no more disproved than A's title to Agrestis, is established.—When A. observed to me today, he would give me a new guarantee ag^{t} the am^{t} of Miller's recovery, I said, that w^{d} be necessary for 2 purposes,—tho' not all so, as between him and me: 1st. for the purpose of transferring it, as I had the former one, to Sanders, or raising money on it, as I had nothing else left to pledge. 2dly for the benefit of my family, in the event of my death, which I tho't very probably, might soon happen. I could [*Large blot, written around.*] see well enough, to discern a pointed attention on his part to the last reason. He had on a former occasion, observed when I assured him I sh^{d} publicly expose the perfidy and dishonour of Graham and the Hendersons at all hazards-be the issue of these trials what it might,—"that my short sight w^{d} lay me under very unfair disadvantages": to which I answered I should know how to accommodate the distance to the extent of my sight. And to day, he hoped with *earnestness* that I w.^{d} not think on any gloomy subject, to cloud the prospect of many happy years I shall yet enjoy. This was not *his* language but his precise meaning;—how far it was sincere may be imagined fr. his talking in this way, after he returned me, what another man might have kept, my letter given here the 25.th without lisping a syllable on the exposure I made to him, in that letter of my 2.^{d} humiliation before his wealth, to solicit an atom fr. the heap, to assuage the distress he is bound to relieve. Be it remembered, [*blot*] he has never questioned demands I made upon him, independent of his first guarantee, for disbursements I have made for Col: Burr to between 4 and $5000, in a letter of which he acknowledged the receipt, on the 4th. Inst., any more than statements of other losses, indemnity for which, when ascertained, will be sought in the *honour* and resources of A. Burr and himself.——Tupper has promised me a copy of his song of the Battle of the Boats and tells me, the Hendersons now affect to regret that they are obliged to testify against me. When we recollect their menaces in Wood C.^{o} to denounce me after they had prostituted their honour to a spy—we must rather believe, they regret to testify against that letter, Sandy wrote his father, soliciting his consent to his sons' espousing the principles and conduct I confidentially recommended to them, which letter will show what treason I recommended or was engaged in.—Robinson and others tell us this evening, Hay had the insolence to insinuate to day, to the Chief Justice, an impeachment if he did not overrule all the points now before the Court. Does C. Justice want energy, at such crises, to declare the law? Surely this insult sh.^{d} give it to him.—Prichard assures me Burr, on his acquittal, will not soon, leave this town. Civil demands upon him, will gather round him, from all quarters, to a far greater amount, than he can find Bail for. If Pollock, or some other preserving Angel does not shield him from this new Host;—then indeed, will he fall more inglorious than fr. a gibbet.—I am very unwell this ev.^{g} suffering under a return of the like oppressive weather I endured during lst. fortnight of my impris[t] These Notes I will continue, whilst I have health, in a similar volume. They may hereafter, engage the interest of the best of wives. Midnight—

[*No entry for Friday, August 28, 1807.*]

[*Followed by a page inscribed only with* Notes, *top, center, book inverted; then four pages of writing and a blank page. For a transcription, see Textual Notes.*]

[*Top, center; rest of page blank.*]

Journal
commencing
Aug[t] 29. 1807.

Richm[d] Penit[y] Virg[a]
Sat[y] Aug[t] 29. 07.

[*Written in clear but faint hand.*]

I awoke yesterday morning with a continuance of the indisposition, under which I laboured on thursday evening. I was affected with much fever and racking head-ach, to a degree of severity that compelled me to return to bed, before breakfast, after taking 3 or 4 grs. of calomel. I took also, two small doses of Ipecach, at the distance of 2 hours apart, designing them to operate as cathartics;—but fr. the weakness of my stomach, they proved emetics, and I discharged much bile, after which I had some perspiration. But the fever and head-ach still raging, I had my back bathed in warm-water in the ev[g] when the fever abated a little. About 10. p.m. I determined upon a large opiate, to which my head-ach yielded in a 1½ hour; after which I enjoyed a refreshing night's rest, and complain to day, only of *weakness.* [*Script darkens after this point.*]—Dud[y] Woodbridge—called me aside this morning, to complain, that the Enquirer had misrepresented the evidence he gave last wedn[y] He said, he had been to the printer on the subject. I c[d] not understand distinctly however, what particular fact had been misstated.—He observed to me, that he was at a loss to conceive the object of the counsel on both sides, examining him upon matters altogether irrelevant to the questions before the court.—such as his opinion of my talents and studies; his knowledge of the am^{t} of my property, and particularly the value of my place on the Ohio. But he supposed, the drift of Col: Burr was to show, that I c^{d} in no sense, be regarded as a military character. He apologized for his having said, that I had "more other sense than common sense," an expression, which he said, escaped him in the hurry and warmth of his examination. I accepted this explanation; but wishing him to inform me, what motive the Counsel could have to exhibit me to the Jury as a character less skilled in the ordinary affairs of life than common men? He now stated to me, that Burr's special confidants, who formerly sought his company here, of late, seemed rather inclined to avoid him, for which he was at a loss to account, but that whilst he boarded in the same house with Bollman, this gent^{n} had devoted much pains to learn fr. him, all he could, of *my* character; by which, having extracted fr. him, an opinion—that I was *excentric*, Bollman, who was informed of the testimony he had given before the G. Jury—regretted very much, that he W^{dge} had not informed that body of the circumstance. All this is mysterious to me, and will remain so, 'till I can explore the matter by opportunities I shall not fail to seek.—I have had a large draught upon my little funds, of 255 cents for a large packet fr. Phila^{da} covering the following enclosures, viz. 2 letters fr. Elliott, and another, with the seal cut open, fr. his wife; 1 fr. the Knight of Kerry, recommendatory of Elliott 1. fr. my Sister McGilli[cuddy] and 2 fr. Tarbert, by Martin, of the 27th Feby and 16th May, the latter—seemingly written in some haste, to invite me to enquire after an Estate of £ 6000 a year, which Mr Martin supposes, must have fallen to me, by the death of Lord Ross, late Aymantoun, and Mr Jarvis who has died in the W. Indies, and next to whom, he says, I stand in the entail. The packet also brought me a friendly letter fr. Joe Lewis, saying he intends to have all my bills taken up, except 1 or 2 that have been returned.— Burr, yesterday informed me, by note, he had an *unsettled* account with Luckett, who holds 1 of his Drafts for $2500 with my endorsement, which it would gratify him, much, if I could discharge. But Alston 2. or 3 days ago, assured me L's Acc^{t} was not allowed, and I sh^{d} not be called upon to pay this Draft.— Will these adventurers never meet, but in duplicity? Mr A. has not appeared to me since thursday—He is probably engrossed to day, by Martin's concluding speech, in reply upon the points, now before the Court.—Wood, this morning gave me some information which if true, proves Burr—as bad a general out of the field, as I have no doubt, he would prove in it. Speaking of several characters that Burr had subpoena'd fr. Kentucky, I inquired, what benefit, he expected to derive fr. Jno. Brown, who I heard had arrived? He can expect none fr. him, said Wood. He will find Brown more Wilkinson's friend, than his. Brown is as truly pensioned as Sebastian was—by the Spa. Gov^{t} and Col: Burr must have strangely overrated his own powers, if he ever thought that these men would have joined him in any thing but words, against Spain,—whilst he might, with the greatest ease, when he was in Kentucky, have enlisted Daveiss, and the whole Marshall party, in his interest. Daveiss and Doctor Marshall, he added, would gladly have embarked in all or any of his speculations: they had no Spa. ties to break, and Daveiss instituted the first proceedings against him, partly from a sense of neglect, on the part of Burr, and thro' enmity to the President, who, he fully believed, was concerned with Burr, or conniving at his operations. Be these things as they may, true or false, as Wood is more or less deserving of credit; it should be remembered that Wood once, possessed the confidence of the Marshall-faction, by wch he had an opp^{y} of knowing their dispositions: that however unprincipled he may have proved, in other instances, he still adheres to the denunciations he published in the W^{n} World which have already ruined Sebastian, and may yet lead to the conviction of other culprits, and that as he has now abandoned all concern with politics and news-papers, save so far as he can be serviceable to Burr, he can have no calculable interest in depreciating the views or talents of any of the persons he has reflected upon.— But the present trial can not fail to furnish ample testimony if not to the guilt, at least to the defect of every talent, under the assumption of which, this giddy adventurer has seduced so many followers of riper experience and better judgment than myself. You were right therefore, honest Hay, in observing the other day to Wood^{ge} whilst expressing your humane concern for my situation, that I must now think Burr had duped me: but you were wrong in supposing I am indebted to you for the discovery. I am possessed of it these 9. months. I am still without relief of my anxiety for my poor family.—I pray the mercy of heaven to prepare me for the 1st news I shall hear of them. 11 o'clock p.m.

Richm^{d} Penit^{y} Virg^{a}
Sund. Augt 30. 07.

I have heard this morning fr. Ellis, that Genl Jackson is hourly expected in town, and Ashley's arrival also looked for, this ev^{g} or tomorrow. If by either of these chances I shall be blessed wth no disastrous news of my family, or even with a revival of those hopes that I have too long, brooded upon, of once more beholding the picture of my beloved wife—how great a load of care my hours of sorrow will throw off—I trust Almighty God will first ordain I shall behold with devout gratitude, before I bound in levity, to transports, to which I have so long been a stranger. Or if I idly dream, to wake perhaps, to realities of sad reverse—then, let me first, invoke the Divine Mercy, to enter and retain me, faithful to all my duties, in every task allotted to my destiny.—I had a very interesting conversation this morning, with Jno. Banks and Mercer, who both eagerly charged themselves with the care of sending me good soup, etc., as my late sickness induced me, at their desire, to complain of the quality of necessaries sent fr. the tavern; in pursuance of which, soon after, Mercer left me a present of refreshments, of fruit, good butter; and fine calf's feet jelly on

Ice was sent me by Mrs Gamble. The conversation of course, having none other object so natural to engage our Interest, as a comparison of the foundation of different conjectures respecting the Decision the Ch. Justice will deliver tomorrow, on these points wch have so long balanced this town, between Law and Faction—and will so much longer, poise the trembling passions of the distant multitude on the—same pivot;—each of us was not without an Innuendo or an Anecdote, of no small Interest to Major Smith, who, I was happy to find, continued of the party. *My* Hints were thrown—out, only in general terms, alluding to the inferences I had endeavoured to draw fr. the intelligence Wood—yesterday gave me, and the remarkable union between Chess and Criminal-Law, mentioned 23d Inst.—Mercer, who, it is said, is much enamoured of a very accomplished yg. lady, a relation of the Ch. Just. ably exerted his happy address for some time, not indeed to confirm the sense Banks and myself professed we so fully entertained of Genl Marshall's high talents, deep erudition, and amiable virtues,—but to discharge our apprehensions of some doubts, we said, we lamented they had imbibed, that The Ch. Just. would possess *all* the energy that wd be necessary to reconcile the opinion he had delivered on the part of the Sup. Ct in the case of Bollman & Swartwout,—with such another as would be required of him, to establish the most material of all the points, now before him. Mercer insinuated, that he had opportunities fr. whence he cd deduce a different anticipation. But as neither Banks nor myself could hereby, perceive his conjectures to be better warranted than our own—Banks was now led, after indulging himself with some general reflections on the difficulty and delicacy of the Ch. J.'s present dilemma—in which we all concurred—to tell us an anecdote, with which I was surprised to find Mercer unacquainted; fr. whence B. indeed did not infer, that the Ch. J. will on the prest occasion, shrink fr. his duty, as an able Judge, or a virtuous Patriot to avert the revenge of an unprincipled Govt or avoid other trials, menaced and preparing for himself, by its wretched partizans; —but he lamented, and certainly, our choicest sympathies harmonized with his feelings—that the facts he had mentioned, of which he vouched the verity, referring Mercer to the Office and File of the Argus—alas! unhappily in one instance, and that too, in the case of Burr—had already proved—that the Ch. J. had explained or accommodated his energies on the Bench in conformity to the views of his enemies—by ordering or permitting in his *private character*, something to be inserted in the Argus, in the form of an apology to, or exculpation of Wilkinson—purporting to contravene, but altogether inconsistent with, the tenor or expressions of declarations or opinions, he as a Judge had delivered on the Bench. This will no doubt, engage Mercer's interest and anxiety so much, that I will to day, add not a word to wh.t I have already said, on a discovery that has not a little depressed me: yet I am certain, whatever dust or insects may have sought the Judge's Robes—whilst off his back—none will venture to appear upon the ermine that bedecks his person.—Mercer and Banks gave me not less than 2 hours of their company, which, whether considered, with regard to elegance and interest of Mercer's conversation—or the friendly concern testified by B. for the issue of the trial, constituted 1. of the most agreeable visits I have rec.d since my Confinement. Mercer promised to bring me the earliest tidings of the decision tomorrow.—Alston is too much occupied to call upon me, when such an effort is not indispensible.—the Influenza has arrived here and found its way into half the families of the town. I am severely affected with it, afflicting me with head-ach, coryza, great defluition fr. the nose, and some fever. This is the 3.d sickness I have had here which has compelled me to resort to medicine.—As we were chatting over some of M.rs Gamble's fruit after dinner, in came the whole rear-guard of Burr's Forensic Army, I mean the celebrated Luther Martin, who, yesterday concluded his 14 hours' speech. His visit was to Major Smith, but he took me by the hand, saying there was no need of an introduction. I was too much interested by the little I had seen, and the great things I had heard of this man's powers and passions, not to improve the present opportunity to survey him in every light, the length of his visit w[d] permit.—I accordingly recommended our brandy as considered superior, placing a pint tumbler before him. No ceremonies retarded the libation,—no inquiries solicited him upon any subject, 'till apprehensions of his withdrawing, suggested some topic to quiet him, on his seat. Were I now to mention only the subjects of law, politics, news, etc. on which he descanted, I sh[d] not be believed when I had said, his visit did not exceed 35 minutes. Imagine a man, capable in that space of time to deliver some account of an entire week's proceedings in the trial, with extracts fr. memory, of several speeches on both sides, including long ones fr. his own—to recite half columns, verbatim, of a series of papers of which he said, he is the author, under the signature of Investigator; to caricature Jefferson; give the history of his acquaintance with Burr, expatiate on his *virtues* and sufferings, maintain his credit, embellish his fame;—and intersperse the whole with sententious reprobations and praises of several other characters.——Some estimate, with these preparations, may be formed of this man's powers, which are yet shackled by a preternatural secretion or excretion of *saliva*, which embarrasses his delivery. In this, his manner is rude, and his language ungrammatical which is cruelly aggravated upon his hearers, by the verbosity and repetitions of his style. With the warmest passions that hurry him like a torrent, over those characters or topics of his discourse, that lie most in the way of their course, he has by practice, acquired the faculty of curbing his feelings which he never suffers to charge the enemy, till broken by the superior number of his arguments and authorities, by which he always outflanks him—when he lets loose the reserve upon the centre with redoubled impetuosity.—Yet Fancy has been as much denied to his mind, as grace to his person or habits. These are gross and incapable of restraint, even upon the most solemn public occasions. That is at all times, awkward and disgusting.—Hence his invectives are rather coarse than pointed; his eulogiums more fulsome than pathetic.—In short, my amiable y[g] friend Mercer, in his accustomed classical neatness, gives me every trait of his portrait, when in one word, he calls him, the Thersites of the Law. Yet the *poor* man did not intend to sit here, to so bad an artist: he has literally promised me his portrait, by a better hand; and I believe he is not without many moral good qualities, not very inconsistent with the sketch I have attempted of his character. I have no doubt, he is unrivalled for zeal in the service of his friends, whilst he retains them; fr. the concern with w:ch he spoke of Burr's financial difficulties—declaring, his friend could find security in Baltimore, for $100,000—which I doubt, tho' I do not at all question M. as he said so, would be his bail for $10,000.—I regret to find Smith neglected not only by Burr—but Burr's satellites. I asked Martin, if the prosecutors won't succeed, as I predicted by letter to B. before I got here, to put him upon a defence, on the Treason bill, that will *nearly* am:t to a confession of the misdemeanour? I think this has actually happened. Mart. tho't, that because B. alledges he expected a war betw:n Sp. & U.St. his exped:n was lawful. But may not a Jury think B. did not expect the war, and find their Verdict *then* on the confession?—

Richm:d Penit:y Virg:a
Mond. Aug:t 31. 07.—

I suffered a total privation of sleep last night, by the unremitting severity of my cough. This is the most oppressive day I have yet endured in this place; and my lassitude was so great that after seeing Strickland, who I am glad to hear sets out for Natchez about saturday—I read for 2 hours, but was obliged to go to bed, where I slept, 'till awakened by Mercer, with a report of the Ch. Justice's opinion, stating in substance, that all the p:ts of so much expectation had been established, in fav:r of the accused—and my indict:t virtually got rid of by the Judge's opinion, that the evidence adduced to prove the overt act, did not prove *such* an assemblage as the Law required to constitute a traitorous one. Mercer took much pains to state every detail, his memory could suggest, but I was little revived with the news. I have yet, too many other trials to pass.—The Court ajourned to six o'clock this evening—when the prosecutors are to be prepared to state the course they will now pursue.—The result I shall learn tomorrow-morning, and be thereby probably enabled to look to the period of my imprisonm[t] When *I* shall have access to Burr and Alston it will be my fault if I do not see them when I ought.—My chest is very sore—I will take 1. of the pills before described, and endeavour to sleep, after first, offering up my cares and prayers to Heaven, for my wife and Boys.—[m]night—

Richm[d] Penit[y] Virg[a]
Tuesd. Sept[r] 1. 1807.—

This morning I find my Influenza much abated by the good effects of the pill I took last night.—Visited, as usual by a variety of persons before and after the adjournment of the Court—by whom we learn, Hay observed with an affection of terseness, that he had examined the opinion of the Court—and had no *further* arguments or evidence to offer; by which, I sh[d] understand, he meant to invelope in uncertainty, the course the prosecutors will now pursue, of which no conjecture can be formed, before tomorrow. A diversity of opinions however, seems already to dissect the speculations of the prosecutors: some supposing, all the indictments will be abandoned by nolle-prosequis; others, that Burr will be proceeded ag[t] immediately, on the misdemeanor, and some more, that a motion will be made to have him sent to the District of Kentucky, where things may work more favourably to convict him of overt acts, suggested to have been committed by him, at the mouth of Cumberland-river:—whilst, on the other hand, it is said Burr will tomorrow, move for nothing less than to be *discharged* fr. the Indictment for the misdemeanor. But this seems to me to be too bold a dash on the part of the accused. I should rather presume on the contrary, that the Judge would allow the prosecutors all the latitude of discretion they may desire in adducing evidence to prove that degree or probability of guilt, that may induce the Court to transmit the accused to another District,—fr. which they had precluded themselves by the form in which they had framed the Indictm.t for Treason. Yet I cannot believe—The Ch. Just. will ever say a man, once put in jeopardy of life, in one District, for treason, charged to have been therein committed, and acquitted thereof—may afterwards, be put to answer to *charges* of *other* overt acts of the *same* treason, in another district—Tho' a man may be responsible to the Law, in 12 Districts severally, for a distinct treason committed in each, provided, the animus or design-quo with w.ch he sought his *object* by the o-acts in each, be proven to have operated the overt-acts as their immediate preceding motive, within the district where they are laid in the Indict.t to have been committed. Thus, a man may successively mediate and *mentally* organize or arrange 11 separate Treasons in as many states, the execution of all w.ch he may abandon, but finally, in a 12.th he may attempt to reduce his project into action. But evidence of overt acts in the last State cannot borrow evidence of the design fr. any of the former, to complete his crime.—The Jury I hope, have to day, evinced more of caprice than party-spirit by affecting to bring in something like a special verdict of acquittal—It will however be entered general on the record.——Burr has written to me, to solicit Alston to assume the am.t of the Bill Luckett holds—and felicitates me on the events of yesterday. I have gratified [*blot*] Luckett with a letter to that effect to A. whom I have not seen since Thursday. m.night.

Richm.d Penit.y Virg.a
Wedn. Sept.r 2.07.—

My Cough still causing me some loss of rest. I had not risen this morning before 7, when I was visited by Wickham and Botts. They staid about 15 minutes—and called, to acquaint me, they meant, tomorrow, to offer the special plea to my Indict.t on which account they had come to invite me to visit the folks at the Capitol. They told me, Burr was not *solicitous* about his discharge, which they tho't w.d not take place for 3 or 4 days.—They apprehended, an attempt w.d be made to have us all transmitted to the Kentucky or other Districts,—which they did not appear to think would prevail.—After Breakfast, being very languid, we did nothing but read, 'till a little after noon, when a Dep. Marshal unexpectedly roused us into action [*blot*]—by a summons to attend the Court. We dressed in 5 minutes, and accompanied the Officer, in a distressing warm walk. We did not return 'till the Court adjourn'd about 45′ past 4. On our arrival, the C^{t} seemed disengaged, as if it had been waiting for us. During this pause, I c^{d} only collect fr. Botts—that some motion was before the C^{t} which he had not time to explain, before Hay rose, to observe, that as Maj. Sm. and myself were present, and as we were similarly circumstanced with A. Burr, the same course should be pursued with us all. This called up Botts, who was followed by Wickham; both in very able arguments, contending: that our cases were totally separate and distinct fr. Burr's, the latter not being now, on account of his acquittal of the Treason, legally present before the C^{t}, the only proper means to bring him there, to answer to the indict^{t} for the misdemeanor, being by summons, or venire facias, according to the Laws and practice of Virginia where process of capias is not allowed for any offence, less than capital.—Burr said he was ready to enter an appearance to the Indict^{t} for the misdemeanor, insisting, 'till he did so, He was not legally in Court, on that charge: fr. whence I inferred, that the motion made before my arrival, was probably for his discharge, under the proclamation, that should have ensued on recording the verdict for his acquittal yesterday. Wick. & Botts supported their arguments with not only English and Fed^{l} authorities, but with the doctrines of Hay himself, delivered by him in his evidence on Chase's trial, which they dressed up in such comments and strictures as exhibited Hay, the most bewildered spectacle of confusion and mortification I ever saw exposed to a public assembly. The Ch. Just. said he sh^{d} proceed to assign Counsel to Major Smith, for which purpose the latter got me to write a letter for him yesterday, if the Counsel for the U.St. meant to proceed ag^{t} him on his Treason-bill: to which Hay answered, he believed it w^{d} be unnecessary.

The Judge then observed, that the arguments w^{d} require his postponing his opinion till tomorrow morning.—After the C^{t} was adjourned—Burr and ourselves were detained about 10′ by the absence of the Marshal and his Deputies, who had stepped aside, somewhere out of my sight, I believe upon some consultation, respecting the expense of Burr's guard, 'till tomorrow; for I soon heard Burr tell Botts, he would pay the expense himself. The guard over him at his present quarters, has hitherto cost the U.St. $7. a day, which it is now understood he must pay, himself 'till discharged, since his life has been redeemed fr. the mortgage the Gov^{t} had on it.—Burr during this detention, said, he hoped he should be able to come to see us tomorrow or next day. But I fancy, we shall have the liberty of the town as soon as his Highness——And so, after *all* it is 100 to 1. I shall never be arraigned of Treason! On entering the dome of the Capitol—I was indemnified for the severity of my walk not merely by the pleasure of the transition fr. the heat abroad, to the shade lower temperature of that part of the building, but by the enjoy^{t} of beholding a face I had not seen yet in town. I passed close by Phelps, whose visage exhibited so high coloured a picture of the disap^{t} of his malice that I involuntarily smiled upon him—with such satisfaction as almost tempted me to wish him joy. My hurry however did not permit me to speak. I must reserve my words for something more human. Tupper expects letters this ev^{g} I have charged Billy to see him and be with me as early as he can. If I but wake to good tidings fr. Natchez, how shall I sacrifice to the God of Fathers for his preservation of my Harman, whom I have again dreamed, I have lost. midnight.

Richm^{d} Penit^{y} Virg^{a}
Thurs. Sept 3. 07.—

I opened my eyes first, this morning, in quest only of that object, in exclusion of all others, that occupied my heart last night. But instead of letters thro' Gen. Tupper, Billy bro't me early, a note fr. him, to announce that there were 3 letters fr.

my wife, not here arrived for me, but at Marietta. To Almighty God be first offered my humble and grateful thanksgiving;—then, I am hereby, enabled to conjecture, with much probability, my beloved wife at least, was well, about the middle of July. But I dare not so far presume upon the favor of Providence, as to conclude, my Boys, particularly my *Harman* was in health at that period, much less how long, they and their mother have since continued well. This note has given me, however, a vivacity to day, in spite of the oppressiveness of the weather, I have not before experienced in this prison: where it is true, my friends have sometimes made me bear a part, in the humour or interest of a story: but I have ever felt on such occasions, in the state Nicholas describes, when he gives us the account of that part of his life, during which he was conscious of being under the influence of two minds at the same instant. Or, at least, my heart, would pity the momentary fluttering of my spirits, which, on such occasions, could never soar above its trouble.—That truly worthy Irishman, Mr Hendren, has come again to town, apparently on purpose to see me. See notes of 8th ulto. If I shall be detained here, as is probable, for some time—after I shall be bailed or discharged, I have engaged to visit him at Shirley about 20 miles fr. hence.—Not having seen any one since the rising of the Court, this ev^{g} we are without any knowledge of the proceedings there to day.—Luckett called, this morning, to tell me Alston required me to write to him again, to desire he w^{d} settle or assume the am^{t} of the Bill L. holds with my endorsement: saying, my last letter to him to do so on monday did not express [2] my desire, with sufficient certainty. This is admirable. Major Smith has seen that letter and only wanted to hear this statement—by Luckett, which if true, settles Mr Alston's intentions and mine. The first to put off; the last to hasten.—If he leaves this town, without his having reasons I shall approve of for not making the settlements he has undertaken, my purpose is *fixed* to follow him to the Oaks, with a friend, very soon after my discharge—when it shall not exceed 48 hours to conclude all my business with him.—I have written to Wm Thompson, a long letter—accepting his tender of a correspondence, and returning him my sincere dispositions to improve our acquaintance into a friendship.—Recurring with Mr Smith, to some incidents that happened soon after our first arrival at Natchez, and speaking of Cowles Meade, I was much surprized to learn what I had never heard before, that Meade had seriously taken up an idea of Col: Burr's being then *deranged*, alledging that he could not be mistaken, as he Meade, had very long known him.—Be this as it may, Burr, yesterday, looked 50 per cent better than I have ever seen him; and displayed a command of tone and firmness of manner he did not appear to me to possess, before the verdict of tuesday. 11 o'clock p.m.—

Richm^{d} Penit^{y} Virg^{a}
Frid. Septr 4.07.—

Visited this morning, by Ellis and Doctor Monholland who informs us yesterday was spent in Court, in a desultory disputation on Hay's attempt moved or suggested to have Burr transmitted to the Kentucky District, on which the Ch. Justice has yet made no rule, as they understand, he conceives the Indict^{t} for the misdemeanor must be first got rid of here.—They also tell us Burr went out about 1 o'clock to procure Bail, which they suppose he did not effect, as his guard were in statu quo, this morning.—I have written a thankful letter to two. I have rec^{d} one fr. Jas. O'Hennessy, a Kerry Schoolmaster, who appears to be settled as a private Tutor in the family of Hudson Martin Esq. near York post-office, Albemarle C^{o} and is very solicitous to serve me. Read, the best part of this morning, as is generally my practice when not otherwise employed; and which will show, I have not been idle wherever it might appear by this diary, the minutes of any particular day are few or uninteresting.——Hay has made a special return instanter to a subpoena—duces tecum, ordering him to produce a letter fr. Jef. to Wilkinson, Hay did not wish made public, as parts of it were confidential. But his return was not accepted, and he has been coerced to produce the letter. The whole day has been spent in altercation on this subject; and the Question whether evidence should be gone into to determine upon the Transmissal of us all to another District before our Indictments for the misdemeanor are here disposed of. In Burr's case the Ch. Justice has determined his discharge fr. his Treason-bill, and ordered his trial for the misdemeanor to proceed directly.—My appetite is bad to day, and my chest yet very sore. 11. p.m.——.

Richm.[d] Penit.[y] Virg.[a]
Sat. Sept.[t] 5.07.—

Burr is to day, to give Bail, to the misdemeanor, the Ch. Justice having yesterday, determined, a capias is the proper process, and not a summons—on grounds I am ignorant of. The Sum was settled at $5,000—Burr having prayed, it might be reduced below what it had been formerly fixed at: since his acquittal, and his being in custody, on *civil process* altered his situation, and now, made it more difficult for him, to find Bail, than before. Strange! I should never before have heard of this arrest on civil process having been made upon him, and still being unremoved. I observed to Alston, who has just left us, that I found, by to day's papers, Col: B. and The Judge had both referred to this circumstance, as influential, in settling the quantum of the bail. He did not like it; and asked, peevishly, "What is it, the papers will not talk about?" This man, with his most active associates Bollman and Sam. Swartwout to whom probably, y.[g] Dayton may now be added, has I believe, been more active with every thing than his purse, to serve the interests of Burr. His industry enabled him, rather than his judgment, or knowledge of the subject, to anticipate the opinion of the Ch. Justice in the late arguments of an entire week, long before any body else scarcely w.[d] venture an opinion or conjecture about it. And if the *Coryphoei* of the prosecution, were solicitous to collect fr. every opportunity, they c.[d] derive fr. the Judge's conduct, materials to fabricate an impeachm.[t] against him; The Triumviri above mentioned, were not less busy, in their preparations, by rumours or publications, to arraign him of timidity, before the tribunal of public opinion, in case his judgments had been adverse to their wishes—Notwithstanding the dignity and independence of the Judge's mind, I suspect, fr. some hints dropped to me by Mercer, M[r] Marshall, early *perceived*, his course lay between Scylla and Charybdis, tho' he equally disregarded the dangers that menaced him on either side.—Again, Alston has detected, by his spies, some curious governmental manoeuvers, that have been going on in Kentucky. Nothing less than preparations by Bib, the District Att[y] there, for our prosecution in that State, to be instituted, if not already commenced—at the moment we are discharged here—provided only, the necessary witnesses can be trained and suborned, and a Gr. Jury packed for the purpose. A. assures me, the Gr. Jury was, actually to have been embodied yesterday, if the scheme has succeeded, of which he expects to be advised by monday. Hence, we learn to account for Hay's delays to dismiss the other Treason-bills here, which he may yet possibly, proceed upon, tho' he has declared, he w[d] enter nolle prosequis—if he find his speculations in Kentucky, likely to miscarry.—Why else, has Maj. Smith been served to day, with copies of his Indict[ts]?—Alston tells me, Duncan was yesterday evening, x-examined upon interrogatories by consent, by Burr and Botts, preparatory to Duncan's leaving town to day. The object was to obtain matter to discredit Wilkinson.—It is pretended D. has proved W. guilty of forgery, in erasing and altering the cipher letter. But I do not place implicit reliance on the full extent of this statement.—Burr's guard it is added, will be dismissed to day. But the business of bailing may undergo some procrastination, I suppose, if any part of it depends upon expectations fr. Alston, who has not to day, said a word to me, upon money-matters: fr. which I do by no means, conclude, he has yet, concluded anything with Nicholas or Luckett. I was not sorry, he did not call me out. I shall not forget to construe his silence upon my last note to him, to settle with L. for the Bill—as an acceptance of one demand at least, beyond the limits of his letters of guarantee.—

Tho' had he spoken to me in private, I was prepared, to express to him, my surprise at the freedom he used, in speaking of wh.^{t} passed, during my visit fr. Duane,—after I had apprized him, I did not wish it published: also, to warn him of my being acquainted with the *officious* inquiries his friend Bollman had been making about me; and to acquaint him, that tho' his agent in Phila.^{da} w.^{d} probably exonerate me fr. 1. of the attachm.^{ts} yet L. had not paid the Bills in the manner stated to me on a former occasion. See notes of 27 & 29 ulto. Since writing the above before dinner, of which meal I have little partaken these 3 days—my appetite again, totally failing, I tried this evening. I have been much mistaken, in my conjectures of the morning, respecting the Hero of these notes. Luckett has just stepped off with Alston's letter of guarantee to me, on which I have seen a special receipt fr. Nicholas to him, for a Bond and Mortgage. Luckett brought it to me to request I w.^{d} also, endorse on it, in order to settle his demand for the bill, wch I did very readily.—The news by this arrival, is, that Burr, besides his Bail already mentioned, procured security to day also, for $30,000 in civil suits, wch have been here commenced ag.^{t} him; that he enjoyed a long walk, this ev.^{g} with Mrs Alston, in which he exhibited his person thro' the greater part of the town, and will probably honour me with a visit tomorrow. It is again threatened that Alston will be off tomorrow—but not with.^{t} seeing me. I fancy he will in case he comes, pour prendre congé take away with him, from my valediction, more matter of reflection for him to ponder on at the Oaks, than has yet troubled him on my account. ½ past 10. p.m.

Richm.^{d} Penit.^{y} Virg.^{a}
Sund. Sept. 6.07—

As I learned yesterday, which I've omitted to mention, that Burr's trial for the misdemeanor, had been ordered by the Court, to commence tomorrow, the uncertainty of its duration has caused me no small uneasiness, lest it might prolong my imprison.^{t} 'till the period of its termination. This apprehension has led me this morning, to suggest, by note, to my Counsel, the expedient of my pleading in abatement, to both my indictments, tomorrow-morning, on the opening of the court, at once, before the trial begins. I have had a short line, in answer fr. Botts, saying, he will this ev^{g} confer wth Randolph and Wickham, and endeavour to have *me* bro't into Court, pursuant to my desire.—My speculation on the success of this manoeuver, opens to me, a prospect of no small interest and amusement; as it may effect the recovery of my liberty, at least for a time, and promises to occasion no little embarrassment to the prosecutors, who can not, I believe, support a demurer to the plea, which when established, will, of course, destroy both the present indictments ag^{t} me, and thereby, reduce Hay to the dilemma of seeing me fully discharged by the Court, or oblige him to apply for a recommitment, in order to have me transmitted to another District: but to open and examine the evidence fr. which alone, he could exhibit even the semblance of probable cause to induce the Court to grant such a motion—would occasion such an interference and obstruction of Burr's trial, now pending, that he must inevitably, be distanced—unless he can prevent my pleading 'till the present trial is at an End wch I also expect, he will fail in, because I conceive it a matter of right, that I sh^{d} plead when I am ready to do so: besides, the C^{t} will have sufficient leisure. For I understand fr. Mercer and Kerr, that B's trial will not in fact, commence before tuesday or perhaps, wed^{y} These Gent^{n} in giving me this intelligence this morning, acquaint me with some curious circumstances which have occasioned the expected suspension. It seems after Hay's special return to the subpoena duces tecum on friday, stating that he deemed certain parts of Wilkinson's letter of 12th Novr to Jefferson confidential, which he therefore could not part with etc—was held insufficient, after an animated discussion by the C^{t} wch threatened to enforce Mr Hay's compliance with its orders;—he then begged time to learn Wilkinson's pleasure as to his producing the letter.—Yesterday, however, he took new ground and prayed to amend his return, which now set forth "that on a further perusal and exam^{n} of the said letter, he discovered it contained some secrets of State, whereupon he prayed time to obtain Jefferson's consent or dissent to his producing it." Fourth day, I am told is the extent of the time allowed for his receiving an answer fr. Monticello. But it is a little curious that in order to learn his master's pleasure, he sh^{d} send the letter to him, which I am assured he has actually done; so that, we may, by possibility be gratified with the scene that may ensue on Jefferson's Heroism opposing his shield to the onset of the Ch. Justice upon his Att^{y} But the bewildered Hay, has in the mean time, let the Cat out of the Bag. For the great secret of State is now all over the town. It happened thus. Whilst the Guardian of State secrecy and private confidence was yesterday, descanting before the C^{t} on the sacred obligation of these duties—The Deities or Demons of Theft and Discord, combining with the Evil Genii of Jefferson and Hay, directed the keen scent and piercing eye of a vulture to that prey most natural to his appetite.—Jno. Graham whose name may find a place perhaps, in the history of the present admin^{n} fr. his exploits, as a spy and informer in their service,—politely stepped up to the table where the letter lay and whilst Hay was earnestly defending the inviolable secrecy of its contents—this Bird of Paradise was pecking at the forbidden fruit. The example was followed by other fowl, I know not how far of the same feather. But some magpies I find, were so delighted with the fruit of which they had eaten in the same manner, that they flew thro' the streets in the ev^{g} intoxicated with its flavour, and chattering, the words "Militia Traitors."—These fine birds could not speak in detail of all the sweets on which they had regaled themselves. Yet can they rival that celebrated parrot that detected a prince of Orange incog., and squall when a little man passes by them, "Great General." The oracles of intrigue however at the Capitol have been resorted to on this occasion—who have answered, "that a Great General expressed his opinion as a secret of State, that the Mississippi and Orleans Militias should not be trusted."—I am a little pleased with this anecdote, and have some thoughts of giving it to the Public.—I find Tupper and many other witnesses about to return home: some being discharged as they arrived i.e. unexamined: some having, by consent of parties, left their affidavits. I am inclined to infer fr. these appearances that poor Hay rather fills crawsick than that he is not yet fully gorged with the banquet of professional fame, at which he has made so long a sitting. As for M[c]Rae he is utterly chap-fallen, an object of disgust of his friends and the pity of his Enemies.—Luther Martin sat some time with us this morning.—He pretended he came to his client Maj. Smith. But his vanity as an Author and a Father led him to bring me his strictures on the barbarous and sanguinary toasts that were drunk on the 4th of July ag[t] Burr and himself at Elktown in Maryland: and also to read two letters fr. two of his daughters. His retort on the Toasters is a good Philippic on their *bloody* ignorance of the Law, but a mass of verbiage, engrossing more than 1. page of a paper, the point and arguments of which might all be neatly expressed in 1 half of a column. He improves in interest as I get a nearer view of his sensibilities thro' which he shines far brighter as a father or a friend, than he will ever appear thro his oratory or his writings as an Advocate or an Author. M[rs] Kean's and Maria's letters are pretty & somewhat interesting. 11 o'clock. p.m.

Richmond Virg[a]
Mond. Sept .7.07—

This day at 11 o'clock a.m. ended my captivity which has lasted 53 days.—I was taken down to Court about ten o'clock when M[r] Botts called upon Hay to know what he meant to do with my treason-bill, which Hay agreed to have discharged, but required my detention in custody, on the Indict[t] for the misdemeanor which produced a conversation on the subject of bail, during which D. Woodbridge offered me his services. After an exam[n] on the am[t] of his property, he was accepted as my Security in $5000 myself being bound in the same sum, on condition that I attend the Court on wednesday and not depart the same fr. day to day with[t] license 'till discharged. Jno.

Banks had come up also to Court to assist me in the way of bail. He afterwards accompanied me in quest of a lodging, w.ch I have found at a Mr. Walton's who seems a good sort of a man, and will, upon my solicitation, if necessary, come forward tomorrow, to bail Maj. Smith; tho' L. Martin will take that friendship on himself. We then repaired to the P-office, where I was made happy by a letter fr. my beloved wife, of the 3.d ulto., whom the favour of Almighty God permitted the blessing of her health and that of our boys.—I then visited A. Burr now settled in the house occupied lately by Alston, who has at last gone off this morning, in the way he has so long threatened, i.e. without taking leave.——In the ev.g I returned to the Penit.y to visit Maj. Smith and after acquainting him with my having provided more agreeable quarters for him, I came away with L. Martin, and took up my abode at my Lodgings, under a severe head-ach, the forerunner of another day's sickness which I shall probably undergo tomorrow. But it is just the happiness conferred by a letter fr. Natchez sh.d be tempered with an alloy.——

Richm.d Virg.a
Wedn. Sept. 9.07—

As I apprehended on monday night, I spent yesterday in bed, under much fever and sick-stomach. In the morning, I fortunately begged M.r Walton to take my cloak, as he was an Invalid, and it was very rainy, and step up to Court, in case of his assistance being wanted to bail Major Smith. M.r W. had on monday agreed, after much solicitation on my part, to come forward as the Major's bail, if necessary. But as I had some slight fears of Martin's forgetting engagements he had made whilst in his cups, thought it most prudent to have Walton on the spot: and the event justified my prudence; for tho' Martin had not forgotten his promise, he was incapable of executing it—thro' the effects of yesterday's morning potation. I was informed by Major S. that had not M.r Walton arrived when he did, the Court would very soon have remanded him for want of bail,—Martin having in vain, endeavoured to express his purpose, in which Burr interrupted him, not liking the statement he was trying to make to the Court; tho' Martin would gladly have entered bail to any amount, for he is, I am now convinced, 1. of the best hearted men alive.—I slept badly last night, and am very weak to day, tho' I have attended my place in Court, where the trial of Burr proceeded on the misdemeanor, Hay having presented fr. Jefferson, a mutilated copy of Wilkinson's letter, out of which Jefferson has reserved all the parts alledged to be confidential, in disregard of the opinion of the Court, rejecting the special return to the subpoena already offered to that effect, by Hay.—How far the Court will accept fr. Jefferson, what it has refused fr. Hay, will not appear, 'till the fate of 6 points made by Botts to day, to arrest all further evidence in this case, similar to w^{ht} was done in the Treason-case, shall be determined.—The arguments on this motion will not probably be closed, before the end of the week.—I had this evening, a pretty long tête à tête with Burr, during which, General Dayton was sequestered in another room. This Old sly-boots or Burr, who is often closeted with him, did not mention a hint of my seeing him, tho' Burr had the candour to tell me, when I was taking leave, he w^{d} return to Gen. Dayton in the next room. So that both were equally conscious, I sh^{d} despise the introduction. Our conversation turned altogether on the subject of my involvement in pecuniary claims upon him, in which I represented distinctly and with firmness, that I should expect indemnity fr. him, for every loss I might incur by his paper, or my disbursements for him, specifying to him, at the same time, many instances, in which my property on the Ohio, had already been sacrificed on these accounts; and adding that I particularly held Alston answerable to me for my bills with the charges upon them, which I might have endorsed beyond the amt. of Alston's guarantee to me, by letter; unless Burr would settle such claims.—He assured me, he would adjust all such demands whenever he can be freed fr. the present prosecutions, and can have reasonable time to collect his resources, 'till when, he expressed a desire, that I sh^{d} employ

Jacob Burnet now here, to procure as much procrastination of execution on Miller's attach[t] as he can—Alston having got Nicholas and Luckett to accept of his paper for their demands, to the amt. of $12,500 with charges. I will have one more consultation with Burr before I make my first demands upon Alston for the balance of his guarantee by letter which will be $2,500 at least. When that is disposed of, I shall meditate upon other demands on his verbal guarantee to me. 10.o'clock p.m.—

Richmond Virg[a]
Thurs. Sept. 10.07—

I have this morning conferred with J. Burnet, who tells me Miller may be delayed in effecting sales ag[t] me in Ohio for 12 m[os] to come.—I have also engaged him to act as my att[y] in Ohio Fed. Ct. ag[t] old Wood[ge] The Court heard Botts and Martin argue further on Botts' motion, and adjourned early, on account of the absence and indisposition of some of the other counsel.—I then enjoyed a further repast prepared for me, by my beloved wife, which had been withheld, I know not how long fr. my appetite. It was the letters she had addressed to me at Marietta, with others inclosed in them, to the am[t] of 9 Dolls. postage. These being with[t] dates I knew they must be old; and after that, I rec[d] on monday, could not be digested with the avidity, that was. But the profiles they covered of my dear Boys, were morsels of such exquisite and uncloying flavour that they have developed within me, sensations of delight I did not know I possessed. The fare besides, will always be equally plentiful and sufficient for my desires, 'till it suffer an exhaustion by theft, or loss, similar to that by which I lost the divine image of my adored wife. How many parts of all the lines and curves and prominences of these dear heads I shall scan and reflect upon, in many a precious reverie, it is given to few besides myself to care or comprehend. But did I truly *know* my piety and patience had obtained for me, any particular blessing, amongst the many I derive alone fr. a beneficient providence then how much better should I know the preeminent value of that blessing, and study the holy tenure, by which I could preserve it. I will never dare to ask, but will receive, fr. Divine dispensation, in this sense, its permission of the health and comfort of my little family, which I yet know not but beseech Almighty God to teach me, how I may deserve it.—I went this ev[g] to the Harmonic Society, at which I c[d] not assist for want of my spectacles. The Vice-president requested I w[d] consider myself an honourary member whilst in town. The Flutes are good, with four moderately good violins two tenors two bass players 1. tolerably good and three excellent singers who performed some charming trios of Doctor Calcott new to me, and composed for some affecting extracts fr. Ossian.—The Instrumental music was all old, and known to me. I passed a pleasant evening and came away at 12. Next thursday I shall take a part.—

Sept. 11. 07.—

Saw Burnet again this morning, and showed him Alston's letter of guarantee, which I assigned to Sanders, and is now returned to me, by his Agent Nicholas, with the latter's receipt endorsed upon it for Alston's paper, which he has taken in satisfaction of his principal's demand. I have written to Lewis to state this settle[t] and hope, it will restore my credit with his house, fr. whence, I have requested a remittance of $200 as I am in debt and without funds.—Court today was occupied with further argument on Botts's points. I heard Wirt for the 1st time. He is a handsome speaker, but faulty in his figures, rather thro' defect of study than genius. Ed. Randolph followed on the other side. He has suffered a depression in manner and matter of fully one half since I saw him display here in 1800. 11. o'clock. p.m.—

Richmond Virg[a]
Sat. Sept. 12.07.—

Randolph finished his argument this morning; and was as laboured, inanimate and uninteresting as on yesterday. He advanced nothing new, except an objection to the indictment's not setting forth with sufficient certainty that the expedition was carried on fr. the Unit^{d} States, pursuant to the manner in which the offence is described in the Statute: as he insisted, in the present Indict^{t} the words "fr. thence" referred to the Island—and not to the Unit^{d} States. The point seemed to me a good one—and the Ch. Just. took a note of it.—Martin followed for two hours, and was besides being clear in his positions, tho' as usual, totally regardless of arrangement, less cumbrous than in common with his *verbiage*. But Wickham, who closed on that side, exhibited a masterpiece of strong condensed argumentation followed with a severe but measured Philippic on the motives, ignorance, and misconduct of the prosecutors. This occasioned such agitation to Hay, who was alone, hardy enough, of the 3 on that side, to withstand its impression,—that he declared, his feelings ought not to be trusted with the duty imposed on him to offer remarks on expressions so unprovoked and unmerited wch Mr W. w^{d} *retract*. He therefore, requested to be heard on monday. The Court then immediately adjourned. But I trust, the Judge will not allow Hay to prove what he can alone do, viz that, Tutius est igitur, fictis contendere verbis quam pugnare manu—I have this evening, progressed with letters to A. Martin so long delayed. See notes of the 29th ulto. Should I ever succeed to the large estate which Martin supposes, now awaits me, who would imagine that did not know my indifference to wealth, I sh^{d} be so careless of it?

Rich^{d}—Virginia
Sund. Sept. 13.07.—

I was this morning informed by Mr Walton, a Gent^{n} had arrived in town, last night, fr. the Country who had come a considerable distance to see me and w^{d} call at 9 o'clock. I therefore staid within to receive him, certain it must be either Mr Hendren, or O'Hennessey; and was called upon to the minute, when a stranger appeared somewhat agitated. I inquired whether it was Mr O'Hennessey I had the pleasure to receive and being answered in the affirmative, I invited him up stairs. This Man I soon found, who had only seen me once or twice in Kerry when I was of the Counsel attending Jno. Crosbie's election I believe in 1793—who had never spoken a word to me in his life 'till this day,—this man I find has suffered many a sleepless night thro' his anxiety for me under the present prosecutions. And the first moment he learned, he could have a chance of seeing me—he has set out and rode 105 miles for the purpose. This is not all. He intreats me to suffer him to follow me to any indefinite distance declaring he regards it, as the first object of his heart to settle near me. He has no capital; but as a School-master and a skillful dealer in horses, can commend the means of a comfortable livelihood any where in America. At Natchez, he can soon get rich.—He will therefore accompany me with a Mr O'Connor, a Mathematician, who will follow his fortune; so that I have secured a good tuition for my boys in the dead languages, English, and, the elementary branches of the sciences, 'till a prospect of a better means for their advancement may be more *clearly* opened in Europe—the only contingency that can draw me from the Mississippi.—O'Hennessey has besought me to command a fine horse and what [*blot*] money he can raise. The latter I have thankfully declined and given him *hopes* as to the horse. I visited Burr this morning. He is gay as usual, and as busy in speculations on reorganizing his projects for action, as if he had never suffered the least interruption. He observed to Major Smith and me, that in 6 months, our schemes could be all remounted: that we could now, new-model them in a better mould than formerly; having a clearer view of the ground, and a more perfect knowledge of our men. We were silent—feeling the full force of his last remark on men, which however, we did not fail I believe, duly to apply both to him and ourselves.—It should yet be granted, that if Burr possessed the sensibilities of the right sort, with 100th part of the energies for which, with many, he has obtained such ill-grounded credit,—his first & last determination with the morning and the night, should be the destruction of those enemies who have so long and so cruelly reaked their malicious vengence upon him. But time will prove him, as incapable in all his future efforts as he has been in the past.—Honest Hennessy dined and spent the evening with me.——

Richmond Virginia
Mond. Sept. 14.07.—

[*Separation line blotted.*]

Major Smith soon after breakfast, brought me a letter, fr. the Office fr. my angelic wife, dated the 11th ulto. This letter too has announced to me, thro' the favour of a preserving Providence, the good health of my wife and boys, up to that date. I dare not then indulge a wish to lament the grief occasioned her by my arrest in Lexington, and the anguish that has festered in her breast from her reflections on the severity of my confinement in the Dog-days. I will preserve the letter however, as an unparalleled original model of sensibility and affections tho' the concluding sentence of it is so obscure as to alarm me with apprehensions for the effects of her gloomy reflections on my sufferings, which her vivid imagination seems to magnify, as much as, I have endeavoured to underrate them.—God grant she may seasonably receive the letter I wrote her last week, which I have forgotten to mention then, acquainting her with my discharge fr. confinement.—To day, the Ch. Just. has delivered as able, full, and luminous opinion, as ever did honour to a Judge, which has put an end to the present prosecution. But I have no doubt the prosecuting Counsel [*Ink through page from heavy line on reverse.*] will show their ignorant malevolence by carping at it as they did at the other in the Treason case.—The Jury must, tomorrow, deliver a verdict of acquittal: Hay, in the meantime, having prayed the C^{t} to adjourn, to give him time to study the op^{n} and thereby shape his future course. But in this he could not avoid showing his petulance, by pretending the prosecutors should exclusively be accommodated with the opinion, which he w^{d} not say, when he would return to the other side. An application however, from Botts, to have it left with the clerk, for the benefit of both parties, corrected this insolence, under which Mr Hay sunk as usual.—O'Hennessey could not leave town today, 'till he heard the opinion, and saw Burr, to whom I introduced him in Court. He was highly delighted with both. He again visited me after dinner, and will return to Amherst C^{ty} tomorrow: I mean as far towards it of his 105 miles as he can.—I have this ev^{g} progressed further in my letter to Martin—with^{t} yet having reached the subject of his last letter,—the news of the estate of \$ 6,000 a year he has talked of.—11. p.m.

Richmond Virginia
Tuesd. Sept. 15.07.—

Saw Burnet this morning, who tells me he has given such information to D. Woodbridge, as will probably induce him to become bail to the attach^{t} ag^{t} me at the suit of Miller, by wch I hope to procure time enough for Burr or Alston to settle that demand, and exonerate my property at Marietta fr. it.—The prosecutors, still true to evil purposes and malicious designs attempted to day, to get rid of the prosecution ag^{t} Burr, by a nolle prosequi. This produced an argument, in which they were overthrown having nothing to rely upon on their side, but a dictum, in Foster's treatise on Homicide.—The Jury were ordered out, and after an insidious attempt but which failed, with 1. of them, to bring in a special verdict, they returned into Court, in half an hour, with a general verdict of acquittal. Hay then said he would tomorrow, enter nolle pro^{is} on Smith's and my indict^{ts} and proceed with his motion to the Judge to commit and transmit us all, to some other District. All are busy in preparing for this new contest, in which I shall probably personally take a part, fr. want of instruction in my counsel, absence of witnesses, and other reasons which will appear hereafter.—midnight.——

Richmond Virginia
Wedn. Sept.r 16.07.—

On opening the Court this morning, Hay after some desultory conversation on both sides of the Bar, exhibited a general charge against us, in writing, of having levied War ag.t the U.d St.s at Cumberland Island in Kentucky, at Bayou Pierre, on the Mississippi or at some intermediate place.—We were all three i.e. Burr, Smith and myself proposed to be subjected together, to the inquiry, leaving it to the Judge to separate, and apply to each such evidence of overt-acts as the testimony might disclose. The Judge acquiesced in this proposition of Hay's, and one James McDowel was called, who proved nothing more at Cumberland than that Burr formed there a circle, and said he w.d not tell his secrets at that place. There are however a dozen other witnesses on the ground here, who were at Cumberland at that time and will swear that nothing of the sort took place there. Hay then attempted to examine as to the facts in the Mississippi Territory which called up after some conversation, an argument on four points made by Botts. viz. Want of power in the Judge to transmit under the Judicial act. Right of Burr to a bar by 2 acquittals here. His discharge by a Jury already in Mississippi Terr.y and all his acts, taken together, constituting but one offence for which he has already been tried and acquitted within a District, which the prosecutors have selected out of the whole for the purpose. Botts was very able and perspicuous in opening the argument, which Burr very neatly summed up and condensed before the Court adjourned about half past 3. I had no opportunity that presented the least necessity of my rising, and think that will probably be the case till the motion for our recommitment is disposed of and defeated altogether.—I was glad to find Burr had at *last* tho't of asking us to dine with him, as I was rather curious again [*blots*] to see him shine in a partie quarrie consisting of new characters.—We therefore walked with him fr. Court, Luther Martin who lives with him accompanying us.—We found but one other face that was strange to us and a foreigner, who, I hoped might turn out to be Bollman.—Martin by the way, told me he thanked his God, He sh[d] not now labour, under the Lock-jaw which had hitherto restrained him before democratic Juries. He should now be no longer tongue-tied. Our foreigner was very taciturn and reserved, and turned out to be a cousin of Judge Prevost's and of the same name. The Dinner was neat and followed by 3 or 4 sorts of wine—Splendid poverty! During the chit-chat after the cloth was removed, a letter was handed to Burr next to wh[m] I sat. I immediately smelt musk.—Burr broke the seal, put the cover to his nose, and then handed it to me, saying, "This amounts to a disclosure." I smelt the paper, and said, "indeed I think so." His whole physiognamy [*Cancellation blotted.*] now assumed an alteration and vivacity that to a stranger who had never seen him before, w[d] have sunk full 15 years off his age. "This," said he, "reminds one of a detection once very neatly practised upon me at N. York. One day, a Lady stepped into my library whilst I was reading, came softly behind my chair and, giving me a slap on the cheek said, 'come, tell me directly, what little French-Girl pray, have you had here?' The abruptness of the question and surprise left me little reason to doubt the discovery had been completely made. So I tho't it best to confess the whole fact, upon which the Inquisitress burst out into a loud laugh on the success of her artifice, which she was led to play off upon me fr. the mere circumstance of having smelt musk in the room." We all applauded this anecdote, as it deserved. But I have given it a place here, only to convey an idea of that temperament and address which enables this character on certain occasions, like the snake, to cast his slough, and thro' age and debauchery, seems to uphold his ascendancy over the sex in a country where sensuality is love, and sentiment but a name.—After some time Martin and Prevost withdrew—and we passed to the topics of our late *adventures* on the Mississippi—on which Burr said little, but declared he did not know of any reason to blame Jackson of Tennessee, for anything he had done or omitted. He has not heard of J's letter to Claiborne which Watkins talked so much about in the executive Council at Orleans, on the question respecting the legislative memorial to gov[t]—Such a General may well continue to sacrifice to Venus rather than to Mars.—But he declares he will not lose a day after the favourable issue of the present contest at the Capitol, of which he has no doubt, to devote his entire attention to setting up his projects which have only been suspended, on a better model, in which work, he says, he has even here, already made some progress.—Martin presented Smith and myself each, with his portrait tolerably engraved, as he had long since promised. I promised, to have it neatly framed by Prich[d]

Richmond Virg[a]
Thurs. Sept[r] 17.07.

This morning the Court heard a continuation of the arguments on both sides, which lasted till 5 o'clock this evening, when Randolph begged the Judge to indulge him with about an hour's hearing tomorrow morning, promising that he would show under the constitution and the spirit and genius of the Laws of this country, that the Court could not comply with Hay's present motion, to have us again committed and transmitted to another District.—Of the success of such an attempt I can see no prospect, even if the Judge sh[d] be of opinion contrary to what has been so ably contended, by Burr's Counsel, that the C[t] has a power to commit under the Judicial act; as a total failure of evidence to prove any overt-act upon us, must undermine the motion.—I spent the Evening at the Harmonic Society where I took a part in a symphony and a Quartet by Pleyel but with less effect than if I had been provided with my own spectacles. I had the pleasure of meeting there Neville, Spence and other visitors: besides hearing several good glees, in some of w[ch] a Miss Coniers took the upper part. She is a very pretty girl and is said by Neville to be accomplished. The society broke up, however early: the music not producing the best effect fr. the state of the weather and the room being to much crowded.—I found an old letter in the post office announcing protest of the bill held some time since by Luckett, with my endorsement of $2,500. so that every thing that little shopkeeper had told me of no proceedings having ever been taken against me as an endorser was utterly false.—I was called upon this evening by David Meade, who seriously assured me, that vicious partizan Scot the Marshal had been trying to make a bargain with him to undertake the Office of a Deputy for the purpose of reconducting us to Kentucky—anticipating the success of the present motion; tho' Hay has certainly said out of Court, this evening, he does not expect he shall succeed. Such are the tricks of these jugglers, in and out of Court. Midnight.

Richmond Virginia
Frid. Sept. 18.07.—

Randolph kept his promise this morning, so far as making out his hour; but did little more service, having offered nothing new, except one argument to show, that where a man had been charged for the same murder, in different states,—the law arising upon his acquittal in the first, was different fr. what it would be, in an acquittal of an overt-act of the same treason, in the first district where the Offender was tried.—Then the Judge delivered his opinion, condensing the 4 points made by Botts, within the observations he made on 2 of them—viz power of the Court, under the Constitution and the Laws of the Un^{d} St^{s} to arrest, and transmit to a *territory*—which he decided in the negative; and the effect of Burr's acquittal, which he hoped, it w^{d} not be necessary for him to decide upon, as he should prefer a decision by the Sup^{e} C^{t} of the U^{d} St^{s} It followed as he laid it down, fr. this adjudication, that the prosecutors might adduce any evidence in their power to prove any overt acts against us, Burr inclusive,—committed anywhere in the U^{d} St^{s} to authorize him to transmit us to any District thereof. But does it thence follow, that a persecuting and vindictive Gov^{t} may order its att^{y} to harrass an obnoxious but innocent victim of its wrath, by playing off the farce of prosecution ag[t] him, in a District of its own selection, without effect, and afterwards, ruin him, by dragging him thro' every other District in the Union? What better answer can be given to this supposition, than saying such a case is rendered improbable, by supposing no Gov[t] will be wicked enough to contrive such a villainy? But this is begging the Question. So that, at least, one Republic is established in the world, in which the life of a citizen is less secured against a possibility of hazard, thro' the machinations of the Gov[t] than is that of a subject under a British monarchy. I have here put a case which had not been supposed at the Bar. But with very little alteration, it is our own case. How long is it since the Gov[t] began to digest all the information it collected by the most illicit means from the most foul sources, not of our acts but of our designs, before we did any act? Did they not order prosecutions 1500 miles fr. the present? Did they not make two selections of their ground, besides an attempt at a third, by Graham their agent, or at his insistence, as a Spy and Informer, in the State of Ohio, which was only, avoided by my flight? and after having failed in all, of proof—do they not now, seek to drag us back again to the same Districts where they have already miscarried? and failed in every thing but the success of the plunder and outrage committed under authority of the President's proclamation, on my family and property, by informers and personal enemies the Dregs of all Human-Society, in my absence, when I had incurred no forfeiture? There may be little Law in this, but it shall serve to furnish some ingredients in the History of the pres[t] administration.—The Judge having further declared the prosecutors might now proceed with their evidence; they called up James McDowel, who swore to some unimportant statem[ts] which if necessary we can disprove by a dozen witnesses. But they attempted repeatedly to go into evidence, not only of alledged facts but even of declarations of 3[d] persons, whereof to prove overt-acts and designs—within the U[d] St[s] And the Judge, for reasons I cannot imagine, seemed disposed to countenance the proceeding—which is certainly in direct hostility with his own opinion this day delivered and, unless, as a *committing magistrate*; thinks he ought to indulge a greater latitude of investigation than he would permit on a trial. But tomorrow's proceedings will further elucidate these matters. 10 o'clock p.m.

Richmond Virginia
Sat. Sept 19.07.—

Strickland called upon me before the sitting of the Court this morning to say, he should in two hours, set off for Natchez. I wrote a short letter to Harding, to give him some account of my situation, and tell him, I hoped, the *present* demands of the Gov.t upon our persons, would be satisfied on Monday; after which I hoped to be at Marietta in 15 or 16 days, whence I sh.d proceed for Natchez as speedily as my affairs w.d permit.—But I since regret to find, fr. the complexion of affairs in Court to day, that our detention may yet extend even to a month; unless our Counsel shall succeed in efforts they will not cease to make, to confine the prosecutors within the limits of established rules of evidence, and the adjudications already pronounced by the C.t For this whole day was spent in arguments and altercations in violation of both. This was chiefly occasioned by the prosecutors persisting in the conduct they pursued yesterday, which produced a corresponding opposition, which I lamented to see the Judge not only—permit, but in some degree participate in. For instance, Dunbaugh was allowed to day to testify to facts at and below Bayou Pierre, whilst two or three witnesses yesterday, were always stopped, with the concurrence of the Court, so often as they offered to speak of any thing without the lines of the U.d St.s How this is reconcileable, with the opinion of the Court I have yet to learn. Altercations on points already settled,—or on a series of topics where the contest is a logomachy, have always a narcotic influence upon me. Nor could any sense of interest I had in the consequences, or any stimulus the ingenuity of Wickham or Botts could apply to all the intensity of my admiration of their talents, prevent my passing the day in a sort of dose.—Burr, I observed, seemed so irritated with the Judge's apparent inconsistence w.th himself, that he would not trust himself to rise to sum up and condense the forces displayed by his counsel into compact columns, after the engagement, towards the close of the day, as is generally his practice. He has no fear of the final result, but feels fr. a mortifying check he has rec.d m.night.

Richmond Virg.a
Sept.r 20.07.—

I proposed, this morning, to devote the entire day to writing; my attendance in C.t thro' the week totally preventing almost the whole of the labour demanded of my pen. But a solicitude to confer separately, with Burr and Mercer, on the course indulged to the prosecutors by the C.t the last two days, forced me to go in quest of those so oppositely interesting characters. And the debts yet unpaid, that laid so heavy a burthen on my reflections, which I wanted to discharge to M.rs Gamble, M.rs Chevalié and Col: de Pestre, who had long been confined with the Influenza,—hurried me out of doors immediately after breakfast.—I found Burr, just after a consultation with his Counsel, secretly writhing under much irritation at the conduct of the Judge, but affecting an air of contempt for his alledged inconsistency, as he asserted he did not for the last 2. days understand, either the questions, or himself; had wavered in his opinions, before yesterday's adjournment, and should in future be put right by strong language, I am afraid to say, abuse, tho' I think I could swear, he used that word—in the part of the defence. I observed, that tho' I believed the Judge's the purest amongst all human hearts, I could not in my best judgment, reconcile the latitude he permitted the prosecutors, either with the letter or spirit of his last opinion, delivered on friday. Burr replied nothing to my offer of tribute to the Judge's heart—but said his opinion should draw him back from his deviations fr. it; and he would hang him, not so facetiously indeed, as Eaton swore he would hang Miranda, but upon every comma of his opinion. He then inquired where Mercer was, and expressed a strong desire to know his thoughts on the Judge's late conduct. I answered that I had come out chiefly to gratify the same desire and should go directly to seek Mercer. I left Smith wth him and took leave.—I bent my way to Mr Chevalié's to see de Pestre, whom I found at home.—Mrs Chevalié received me very kindly, and prevailed on her husband, who was confined to his room, to come down stairs to see me, and beg of me to partake of a family dinner wth them which I accepted. After 1. hour's conversation I then made a visit to Mrs Gamble, who seems a most amiable old lady, and so fraught with the generous humanity characteristic of her sex as to suffer not the connexions of her fine daughters Mrs Cabell the Governor's wife and Mrs Wirt to prevent her expressing not merely a concern for the general hardships we have suffered; but even to censure the two last days' proceedings in Ct—I was not fortunate enough to find Mercer before I returned to Chevalié's to dinner, where I spent a pleasant evening, save so far as Mr C. was not of our company, being confined to his bed.—Mrs C. is as lively and agreeable as it is possible for any woman to be, with limited endowments and without beauty. I had 1. hour's interesting conversation by means of a walk before tea with de Pestre in the garden, which however, touched upon no new matters except his informing me that Mrs. Alston had expressed to him a wish that he would engage in nothing before next spring, that might prevent her father fr. having an opporty of forming another connection with him—conveying an intimation wch he avoided as delicately as he could. We again harmonized in reprobation of Alston in every point of view—when I hinted to the Col: some expectations and reasons I entertained for urging Burr or Alston to give me an obligation, if they can't raise money, for the amt of my losses by them, yet unsatisfied—which he approved of—He will spend 1. hour with me tomorrow evg when we will prosecute our thoughts.—I visited Mr Ch. after tea in his bed-room for ½ an hour, and on my return home, I learned fr. Smith a confirmation of what de Pestre had also mentioned to me, that Burr sets off immediately for England, after his liberation fr. the present motion before the C^{t}., to collect money for reorganizing his projects—wch I now have ascertained to be as baseless—as the interests of the parties or persons to whom he discloses them, are opposed or variant. For he assures *his* creditors here—at least he has done so, to Smith, that when he raises money in England, he will not be *strict* in questioning demands upon him in this country which he will fully discharge. In London no doubt he will pledge himself to appropriate every guinea they will advance him for the promotion of such operations on this continent, as will best serve the Interests of Britain: and if he had not already exposed his duplicity and incapacity in his favorite art of intrigue to Yrujo, he would *again* as readily promise to advance with Spanish dollars and Spanish arms, the fortunes of the Spanish minister and his master. But it is not a little strange that he should never have dropped even a hint to me of his projected trip to England. I have had more of his confidence than either Smith or de Pestre. For he has insinuated to me that the former was not disposed to fight on the Mississippi—when, I thought, he had the disposition not to do it himself,—and he has, during our embarrassments on that river, thro' Wilkinson—spoken in the presence of Major Smith, myself and others of the probability of de Pestre's being hanged thro' failure of an enterprise he had sent him on as an event, which he treated with the utmost indifference—Surely I may repeat, that whatever feeling this man possesses, is confined within the sensuality of his temperament, if indeed his conduct in the eyes of all who know him, does not warrant the suspicion of Cowles Mead, and fully prove, whilst his whole Bar as little knows him as Col: Swartwout, whose attach^{t}. is still unshaken, that there is at best but method in his madness.—midnight—

Richmond Virg^{a}.
Mond. Sept. 21.07.

Dunbaugh was reproduced to day with no other effect than to contradict himself, by saying Burr communicated to him in secret, his having been betrayed by Wilkinson, tho' he swore on Saturday, Burr imparted to him no secrets. The Judge has noted enough in this witness to destroy all credit in his testimony. The day passed in the examin^{n} of other witnesses called by the prosecutors, whose evidence was altogether favourable to us: tho' I was mortified to see the Judge, considering himself as an examining magistrate, open so wide the door to the wanton discretion of the prosecutors, as to allow them to offer testimony of any sort, which they alleged to be explanatory of the so called overt-acts on Cumberland Island at which place, it is confessed, the assemblage, at most, was doubtful or equivocal in its character. I can not comprehend the distinction taken by the C^{t} between admissible and operative evidence. Nor do any of the Bar here I believe, perceive how evidence that cannot operate upon the subject can be admissible.—It seems to me, that perhaps the Judge has at last tho't it necessary to sacrifice a little to the public prejudice, when the concession can not cause any serious consequences in the issue of this strange contest.—This evening de Pestre spent an hour with me, which was passed in a more dilated view of his past concerns with Burr. He gave me a description of the manners and character of Yrujo, who is reconfirmed in his embassy to this country in spite of all the efforts of this Gov^{t} for his removal. This Minister is according to de P.'s portrait of him a shrewd politician, who pierced the cobweb tissues of Burr's intrigues with him at a single glance. Tho' he assured de P. who was charged in Kentucky last Octr with a special mission to him, that had Burr opened his designs with frankness and really projected a severance of the Union, and nothing hostile to the Spa. provinces—He Burr—might have had an easy resort to the Spanish Treasury and its arsenals—whilst his confidence w^{d} have been safely lodged in the Honour of a *Spa. Nobleman*—But Yrujo laughed at the awkwardness with which Burr endeavoured to mask his designs on Mexico, and expressed his concern for de P.'s having lost his time in such service.—Burr I suppose, will henceforward learn to appreciate that honour in Foreigners of liberal education, which he will never find in the miserable shopkeepers of his own country, to whom he deals out his confidences by the smack, as they retail their goods by the y.[d], reserving the piece to themselves. But Burr if he had capacity or money for reanimating his projects has lost a season never to be recalled. He might, last winter have had the whole equipage of two French ships of war, who offered to bring their small arms with them into his services. If he had not talents or spirit to use them, he is where he sh.[d] be. m-night.

Richmond Virg.[a]
Tues. 7.[r] 22.07.—

A variety of witnesses examined to day,—by the prosecutors, seem to me, to advance their cause but little, tho' their newspapers pretend they throw great light on the mysterious proceedings of Burr. But his mysteriousness is surely an impenetrable shield to cover his treasonable designs if he had any. I have seen a complete file of all the Depositions made before the Gr. Jury, in Burr's possession. It must be confessed that few other men in his circumstances could have procured these documents out of the custody of offices filled by his inveterate enemies. I have long been at a loss to imagine the means he used, of which I am not yet full informed. But I have learned accidentally that Skelton Jones has become friendly to him. This Jones a noted Duelist & the Bro.[r] of the late Reviewer, that who formerly conducted the Examiner—an influential Democrat, I am told, received a letter some time since fr. Burr, covering a Bank-note with.[t] specifying, for what purpose the money was sent. Jones returned it, with civil remonstrance, which gave Burr an opp.[y] of requesting an interview which if it did not succeed in removing the easy scruples of this honourable Patriot, has however, since that event completely attached Mr. J's interest, as I have learned fr. a M.[r] Braxton a young lawyer here of some talents.—Burr has again asserted today in C.[t] that he expects, by the mail, documents to enable him, to show that Eaton must be an *incompetent* witness in any C.[t] This if established, will give the coup de grace to the fame of the Dernean Hero; who I am assured by Robinson, has sworn the peace against a M[r] Smith of Petersburg, who threatened to kick the General out of the room. And yet he appears every day in C[t] affecting by his looks an air of defiance. Wilkinson also exhibits his bloated arrogance sometimes in the same place. But his exam[n] cannot come on for some days. When it takes place, it must be of the highest interest in the eyes of those who knowing his character and the insidiously artful deposition he has made before the Gr. Jury—will contemplate a spectacle of depravity seldom equalled, whilst such a summons to the address, I will not yet add firmness, of Burr, will leave no nerve untouched. But *I* may venture to predict, that Burr will sink under it. For, apart fr. the merits or demerits of either, there are reasons why it should be so in this country, if not in any other upon Earth; which I will unfold at large, hereafter. I find by D. W[ge], many people have died at Marietta within 2 months past, of a malignant disease prevailing there. Did God's mercy place us elsewhere? midnight.

Richmond Virg[a]
Wedn. 7[r] 23.07.—

It chiefly engaged my attention in C[t] to day, to hear Burr contend that conversations by me with others, respecting him, whilst he was absent and prior to the period of any alledged acts should not affect him. This attempt was made to obviate the effect he apprehended fr. the testimony of the Hendersons—But the Judge was pleased to overrule it. Woodbridge has expressed some wish to be discharged and return with Belknap to Marietta but assures me he will still wait 'till the whole affair is finished, or whilst he can be of any service to me. I have begged he may not, observing, his being my bail need not detain him, have told him to take no trouble on my acc[t], etc. He seems satisfied, as I have referred him to the fact of Gen[l] Dayton having gone to Ohio, tho' not discharged fr. his recognizance.—½ p. 10 p.m.

Richmond Virg^{a}—
Thurs. 7^{r} 24.07.—

This morning I was treated to the narrative of Sandy Henderson wch is considered to bear more particularly on me than any other testimony. I had projected a long cross-examin^{n} of him which I sh^{d} have pursued with good effect in any other country.—But our Counsel feared it might operate quite contrary to my expectation fr. the uniform experience they have that within these virtuous States, when once witnesses determine to swear for a purpose—all attempts to involve them in inconsistency only tend to render them more desperate. I therefore agreed to postpone my cross-examination till the next day, that I might in the mean time confer with Mr Wickham on the subject, as he feared I suppose, that something might break out injurious to Burr thro' my pressing Henderson; and Mr Botts fr. his connection with the family, wished to be excused fr. taking any part in this examination: I had here another check from the obligations Mr Botts has already imposed upon me. But I assured him I had discovered his connection too late to prevent his having been concerned for me. It was yesterday I should have mentioned as having seen Henderson first called, and in consequence of the difficulties affecting Wickham on account of Burr, and myself on account of Botts, I last night drew up a series of interrogatories which I wished Henderson to answer upon affidavit by consent, with which I called upon Wickham in the ev^{g}—We also conferred with Burr upon them. All approved of the questions, but still feared the effect of them fr. the apprehended hostility, of the witness—so that we concluded upon one only of them which was put to him this morning in Court, viz. "Whether at the time of my alledged communications to him, he did not, and doth not yet entertain a strong prejudice ag^{t} Col: Burr?" which he answered in the affirmative.—I met this evening with an introduction at the Harmonic Society to a very handsome woman, a Mrs Meyio, who has been too many years[3] a widow, tho' I hear she is soon to be married.—I mention her, as being the Niece of the amiable and highly esteemed Mrs Carrington, whom I have not yet visited to thank her for her generous offer—more than once made thro' Mercer, to send me refreshments, to the Penity And also to implore from the best and most charming of wives, a pardon of my momentary admiration of this lady.—Mrs M. with her daughter, a girl of about 10 years of age, sat in a situation that received the light fr. the orchestra with every advantage to my view, of her engaging countenance and elegant figure. She appeared to me to be about 27 years old, with all the bloom of an European of that age.—Her face tho' not a perfect beauty, was of a character to inspire desire and admiration irresistibly, where *another* was not present. Her dress was elegant and contrived with taste. So that, to the face, person and drapery, nothing could be wanting to command the active homage of that accursed sensibility to wch I am a devoted victim, but an animation which I soon found to issue with dazzling radiance fr. *her* fine eyes. But I had a further summons fr. an invincible archness which alternately succeeded to those intervals of sensation in which the genius of Haydn seemed to enchain her Soul in unison with mine. In those pauses of our common fascination wch occurred between the pieces, a studied display of her figure, or a clear shot fr. her glances with the velocity of light, and reflected fr. mine with the fidelity of a mirror seemed, as it were in a moment, to dissipate all the stores of reflection my imagination has for so many years, been providing, for the incessant demands of my first *beloved* upon my heart.—

But as if all this were not enough for my conviction,—my guilt was soon further placed beyond all doubt by my participation in overt-act of pantomime entendue which was occasioned as follows. After the conclusion of a delightful symphony of Haydn, the singing party commenced the charming glee of "Here in cool grot and mossy cell"—which soon checked the gambols of the sportive little God on the opening of this chorus to the Muses during which he leant upon his bow in silent stillness 'till the harmonizing of the waterfall arrived, when the little urchin at the same Instant stole between us breathing, with the music, listen, listen, it is for our ears; and then tittering—"to the water-fall"— . . . Soon after this I sincerely complimented Mrs M. on her sensibility to the music, inquiring whether she performed? Now the chain by which I had been exorcised began to break.—She . . . "was indeed fond of music: but had been bro't up too *remote* fr. opp^{y} to learn, had come to the Society to form her daughter's taste, etc., etc. Her conversation on the whole comported rather with her opportunities than her figure; and I was released thus fr. the captivity in wch this Circe bound me for a moment, I hope not thereby degraded from the favour of a more amiable Penelope than ever really furnished a model to Homer. I last of all, observed the Orchestra was defective, but that c^{d} not be helped as I learned there was a great want of Horns in this town.—M^{rs} M's reply—"pray, what sort of Horns" confirmed my liberty, if not my absolution: and after she had heard me take a part in a Symphony of Vanhell—we parted probably never to meet again. I then took a part in the 2^{d} Quartet of Haydn's and in the glee of "How merrily we live"; returned home after midnight——

Richmond Virginia
Frid. 7^{r} 25.07.—

Yesterday Jno. Henderson gave his testimony to the same effect Sandy had done, and underwent little or no cross-examination. Jno. Graham also delivered his to the same purport with that he gave ag^{t} me before Toulmin and Rodney.—But in cross-examining him I asked him to say, "who was to pay the 1000 Dolls. for forfeiting his recognizance to appear to prosecute me in the Mississippi Territory?"; he applied to the C^{t} to be excused answering this question; denied he had applied to Col: Scott to invite A. Burr to his house, to dinner, to have him kidnapped, and said he has got his present office of Ch. Clerk in the Secretary of State's office lately.—Today after consultation with our Counsel, I agreed to waive objections I had offered against reading the Querist in print—on Henderson's evidence of my having shown him only, a manuscript of a composition by me, with such signature. The reading of the 4th no. by the prosecutors; with the exam^{n} of Dana & Gilmore finished the day.—9 o'clock p.m.

Richm^{d} Virg^{a}
Sat. 7^{r} 26.07.—

To day the long expected examination of Wilkinson came on, after that of Eaton to matter or conversations between him and Burr, which had been excluded as improper evidence on the Trial in chief, but was now, thought *admissible* before the Judge as an examining Magistrate. I have taken I fancy, faithful notes of everything that fell fr. both of these persons—by which it will appear, that Eaton's testimony is indefinite as to any bearing that it sh^{d} have upon Burr's *designs* without seeking for those inconsistencies with his former story before the Gr. Jury, and on the Trial in chief, which Martin—under the signature of Investigator is endeavouring to establish in the Virg^{a} Gazette here.—The General W^{n} exhibited the manner of a sergeant under a C^{t} Martial rather than the demeanor of an accusing Officer confronted with his Culprit. His perplexity and derangement, even upon his direct examination, was no unfaithful picture of the talents and resources under which the American army is marshaled and his cross-examination has placed beyond all doubt "his honour as a soldier and his fidelity as a citizen." It will appear fr. the gauntlet he has begun to run, which he will not finish before monday evening, that he has confessed,—he altered a duplicate of the original cypher letter, for the express purpose of erasing fr. it an acknowledgment by Burr, of B.'s having received a letter fr. him W^{n} of the 27th of Feby that this was done for the *avowed* purpose of concealing fr. the Legislature of Orleans, a part of that letter, fr. which that body might *infer* that he was privy to, or concerned in the projects of Burr; that he substituted other words in the room of the erasure as a translation of the erased cyphers, *afterwards*, but at what time he c^{d} not recollect: that the translation of the document sent to the Gov^{t} was from this mutilated original; and that he had sworn so by an affidavit, he produced himself in C^t^., that such translation, *faithfully* rendered the *substance* of the original.—On the other hand—Burr who was very unwell wth a Diarrhea, preserved a composure inspired by W.'s self condemnation and supported by his indisposition, contrary to the expectations I had formed a few days past. The cross-examination progressed but a little way, and was adjourned 'till monday.—Yesterday ev^g^ Wood^ge^ called upon me in the mo. abrupt manner to repeat to me, what he had before observed on wednesday evening, that he was very desirous to return home, and hoped I w^d^ that ev^g^ look for other Bail. But he hardly allowed me time to answer, that I sh^d^ and whether I succeeded or not, I wished him not to stay a moment on my account, before he had the unfeeling ingratitude to add, that if I did not, he should give me up—in the morning. I was accordingly prepared on the opening of the C^t^ this morning, to state to the Judge, "That Mr Woodbridge was about to be discharged; but previous to his leaving town he wished to be discharged fr. the recognizance he had entered into on my account, for reasons I did not inquire into: that it thence became necessary, I should find other securities or be recommitted, of which I sh^d^ prefer the latter, rather than solicit bail in a place, where I was almost an utter stranger. But I believed two citizens of this place, were voluntarily attending for the purpose of entering with me, into another recognizance. —Jno. Banks and a Mr A. Leach, a cabinet maker, then were called forward—and thus ended, I wish I could say, my last concern with the Woodbridge family; of Dudley it must not be concealed, fr. those who may have access to these notes, that altho' he is reputed to have given a fair candid and to us, an advantageous testimony—he has not yet told the *whole* truth—having suppressed my communication to him, of our Designs being unequivocally against Mexico—which I suppose he kept back because he embraced and embarked in the plan on the first mention of it to him.—Tho' he afterwards receded fr. it, upon his own reflections or the counsels of others. Such is the address with which ingratitude and dishonesty are made to pose in the garb of integrity, like tar-cloth, under fine muslin.—m.night.

Richm.[d] Virg.[a]
Sund. 7.[r] 27.07.—

Whilst at breakfast this morning I rec.[d] a verbal message fr. Burr, importing that he wanted to see me. On my arrival, soon after at his house, I found him in bed.—He informed me he wanted to see me to know what I w.[d] advise him to do in his complaint, observing, he had no confidence in the Physicians here. I suggested to him my being of the same opinion, unless I excepted McClurg, whom I believed to be a man of some genius and probably possessing some skill in his profession. Burr said he was a creature of rule—and calling again for my opinion, I said I would have some pills made up—for him which by taking them for 2 or 3 nights w.[d] gently carry off the complaint and restore the tone of his bowels.—I left him to go to the druggist's where I had the medicines carefully prepared which I sent him at 2 o'clock accompanied with a note conveying directions for his diet and the use of the medicine.—I called there again in the evening to see him. But whilst I was engaged in the parlour,—with several persons—where Martin was reading to us a heavy—manuscript of his next Investigator, I found on going into Burr's bedroom, soon after Martin had done,—Burr had just taken instead of my medicine, a dose of Laudanum.—He swore he felt so weak and was in such want of rest he tho't it best to take an opiate. I told him, he must then omit my pills for this night, wished him good rest and took leave. On my return to the parlour, Baker told me a M.[r] Smith who knew my family in Ireland and might possibly recognize myself, solicited him to bring us together: He sh.[d] accordingly bring M.[r] Smith with my leave to my lodgings. I assented and thanked him.—He also acquainted me that M.[rs] Broughenbrough, commonly called Brokenberry here who is regarded as the nearest approximation in this town, to a savante and bel-espirit, has expressed no small solicitude, and has insisted that Hay will enable her to read the Querist, which is much praised here. Martin boasts of the 4th No not a little as a piece of argumentation which the prosecutors had better conceal from the public, whilst they wish to keep them uninformed on the merits of the question respecting a severance of the union.—Martin has also assured me Judge Tucker, tho' a violent Democrat seriously contended at a party with Judge Marshall in this town since May last, that any State in the Union is at any time competent to secede fr. the same, tho' Marshall strongly opposed this doctrine.—I find Robinson the only correct stenographer who takes exact notes of all the proceedings at the Capitol, and is besides a Scholar who understands 5 or 6 languages will give the Querist a longer life by incorporating it in his book than it was likely to enjoy in the barren soil of the Ohio Gazette where it appeared to bloom but as a humble flower and trampled under the feet of the swinish multitude.—Baker is a young lawyer, whom Burr employs more for the benefit of his influence out of doors, than fr. the aid of talent or services in Ct where he is only of use thro' his humour and the freedom with which he lavishes his abuse. I believe he possesses as good a Heart as is permitted to a Democrat, and his spirit and popularity are perhaps in effect as valuable to Burr as the talents of Wickham or Botts.——

Monday 7r 28.—

I had this morning a long double letter from my adored wife. Its red seal was as welcome to my eyes as the evening star to a mariner after the agitation of a storm. For I had last week suffered no small anxiety from the want of a letter. But the seal notwithstanding its colour and every curve and turn of the letters in the superscription had long passed under jealous inspection to undergo every scrutiny fr. which I could augur the import of the intelligence within before I would venture to break it open. But I was assured by the seal there was no mortality at least on the 25th ulto., as by the postmark—I trust then the heartfelt offerings of thanksgiving I tried to breathe forth to Heaven were borne to Almighty God—before I consulted the contents of the letter. There I soon saw how industriously my beloved continues to practice the only fraud her pure soul is capable of conceiving—that of endeavouring to hide fr. me all she feels for me and has suffered for our dear boys. Her complaint in her chest is mentioned in a way to alarm me thro' the veil of disguise she has attempted to throw over it. But the weekly reports she will not fail to see of the criminal proceedings here, will I trust lighten much of the anxiety she labours under, which I know, much aggravates the affection of her breast. I next find my boys have, both of them, had fevers; and my dear Harman who has suffered most was perhaps at the height of the disease about the period, when I last dreamed I had lost him, and has perhaps been spared to us thro' the merits of his incomparable mother, which have not been upheld with the less favour of Providence whilst I was offering up my prayers in the Penitentiary for his preservation. I have, I find observed in concluding my notes of the 2^{d} Inst^{r} observed I had again dreamt I had lost my Harman. Did my first dream of his irrecoverable injury from a dog so long ago as when I lived near Duck-river in Innisfree, typify the disorder of which he was to suffer; and did my 2^{d} dream which was visited upon me in the Penitentiary a night or two before I noted it on the 2^{d} Inst. come upon me as another vision to announce, perhaps a relapse he has undergone since his mother's letter of the 25th ulto. was written? These things are only known to the Eternal and All-wise Dispenser of our mortality. But whilst reason shall continue my only guide to faith, I will yet wonder in mysterious awe of—such dreams as these, which my understanding cannot scan whilst they appall my heart.—I lamented the 1st. intelligence I rec^{d} of my Peggy's removal to Mr Moor's House; as it was in contradiction to the earnest solicitations I long since made to her by letter, I think from Nashville, or fr. the Chickasaw-Nation to take up her residence at least 5 or 6 miles fr. the Mississippi swamp, after the middle of July.—If I shall be blest with the sight of another red seal next monday—I shall put off a heavy burden of anxiety which now oppresses me.—The Court does not sit today, on account of Burr's illness. I find he is much worse than yesterday. He says he will take my medicine to night; he has rejected bleeding proposed to him by McClurg, in which I fully agree with him that he sh[d] not part wth his blood even at a Joe a drop.—I called upon de Pestre this morning at M[r] Chevallié's where M[r] C. kindly pressed me to dine en famille which I declined thro' a desire to write at home & attend a private Quartet-party at the Harmonic Society's room this ev[g] The invitation of Chev. was given in the most friendly manner with a reprobation of the restriction imposed on the hospitable dispositions of the families of this town by the effects of a system of espionage which is kept up by Gov[t] and its agents to a degree that has generally prevented here those attentions we sh[d] otherwise receive. This must be the case, as I have not received a visit fr. any family man much less an Invitation, since my release fr. confinement; tho' M[r] Pickett who lives in the 1st stile here informed my landlord, Walton, t'other day, he means to invite me to his house.—So that etiquette seems also to be totally disregarded: and, no doubt *here* as in many other parts of the country *a want* of better breeding is received by strangers as a proof of inhospitality not merited.——

Richmond Virg[a]
Tuesd. 7[r] 29.07.—

Burr took my medicine, last night as he promised, rested well, and is much better this morning: But he has prudently declined attending Court: tho' he is evidently mortified he is not able to witness the progress of his recrimination of Wilkinson, conducted by his counsel, in which he is so desirous to take a part, especially as Botts has retired to Fredericksburg, to attend to other professional calls upon him. I perused this morning at Burr's some interesting documents forwarded to him fr. N. Orleans, by Ed. Livingston & Alexander all, tending to overtake Wilkinson with a portion of that retributive justice he has so fairly earned. Of these papers I trust the Ch. Justice in the spirit of that latitude he has so liberally permitted to the prosecutors, will, as an examining magistrate allow the affidavits of Derbigney and Mercier to be read, as both go to prove the Brigadier's corruption in having rec^{d} fr. Carondelet, in 1796 a douceur of $9,000 at Cincinnati, wch added to every thing else that will appear against him, should surely settle his integrity and credit, if not his admissibility, as a witness.—On opening of the C^{t} Graham voluntarily came forward to explain a part of his testimony: and I know not why, was pleased to declare I had told him last 9^{r} at Marietta that both Burr and myself perceived the people were not ripe for a severance of the Union, that we should not hurry it as it would take place fr. natural causes, of itself, and we had no personal interest in the event.—Then came on the Little Upstart Brigadier—whose demeanor to day, was no doubt as opposite to that bloated arrogance in which he strutted at Orleans during the reign of his brief authority, as was the carriage of Dionysus at Corynth compared with his royal port before at Syracuse. But I should not have degraded the fortunes of that tyrant by a comparison with this Urchin.—I continue to take notes of his testimony to his own turpitude which I shall not transcribe as they may be seen amongst my papers, by my friends. But it is here I should observe that the address of Wickham in conducting the cross-examination to day, was masterly and ingenious, not only in regard to the witness but to the Admin^{n} which so embarrassed Hay as well as the General, that it would be impossible to say, which of them, most heartily welcomed a sudden adjournment in wch Hay hastily sought the only retreat that was left to his confusion. The Judge had hardly risen fr. the Bench, when a general buzz about the General's embarrassment ran thro' the crowd; and in five minutes every Democrat in the Capitol was expressing his surprise at the effect, with which we had so suddenly changed our characters & turned accusers.—I count the hours till Doctor Cummins arrives who has not yet appeared.—I sat this evening an hour with Burr. Bollman—and

Major Smith were the only other persons of the party. Here was an opp^{y} to confirm my conviction that neither Burr nor Boll^{n} desired I sh^{d} have any acquaintance with the latter, for neither solicited or proposed an introduction. Both no doubt have discovered long since, I am not of a temper to further their intrigues. But they are short-sighted in not perceiving how effectively I can and will assuredly frustrate them.—Well! we chatted nevertheless on the exclusive topics of our *present* concerns with the Gov^{t} amongst which it was observed by Burr that he sh^{d} not be surprised if the next Enquirer attributed his absence fr. C^{t} at this time to fear of confronting Wilkinson. I remarked that such misrepresentation could have no effect as the Virg^{a} Gazette w^{d} contradict it. Burr said this last paper had no circulation: and if $300 could be raised immediately the press of the Impartial Observer, which had been obliged to stop for want of funds, could be again set to work. The editor was bold and ingenious, passed for a good Democrat, w^{d} represent things right and print everything that was required of him—He then asked me if I could not raise even $120. with which a beginning could be made. Could not I get 20 subscribers even to advance $10. each? How sorry he was, Tupper and Mercer were gone away! They w^{d} readily contribute.—Would not I look about etc. etc. I said I knew not a man that would advance a Dollar.—Burr seemed surprized that I did not eagerly offer my services as a runner to beg for him, and said I *might* look out if I pleased, i.e. he added, if I felt any *interest* in the thing. Now I am at a loss to divine the drift of this set upon me. Was it to remind me to smother any rising thoughts within me, to renew my hints to him of other calls for money? Was it to exhibit me to Bollman in a character he would not appear to impose on him? I own I am at a loss for a solution—But certainly however solicitious he may be to revive the Imp. Obser^{r} he *was* not indifferent to making use of this occasion for some other purpose. Smith however said he would look about him and I abruptly took leave.—Bollman kept silent during the most of the visit. He is engaging in his appearance: but I have yet had no opportunity to catch any lines of his character, which I hope will not hereafter escape me.—Swartwout is dispatched to Washington on some secret mission w.ch is as mal-apropos, during Wilkinson's examination as Burr's disappearance fr. C.t Sw. it is said will be back on thursday.—Eaton has come forward today in C.t to say the toast was first given at a public dinner given to him and Decatur at Georgetown, w.ch being in or before 10.r 1805 contradicts wh.t he before swore to on that subject. I believe I am recovering flesh of which I lost much in my confinement.—m.night.

Richm.d Virginia
Wedn. 7.r 30.07.—

The C.t having been only opened to day for the purpose of adjourning 'till tomorrow to accommodate the Bar who are obliged to attend the C.t of Chancery—I spent an hour with Burr after breakfast in miscellaneous conversation during which Bob. Robinson and Smith were present. The arrival in town of Poindexter and Williams, fr. Natchez being mentioned and conjectures offered as to what Poin. could say, as a witness for the Govern.t, Robinson observed he was inclined to think Burr was fortunate in having made his escape when he did from that country, as, had he delayed it for another day, he w.d probably, have been seized and have fallen into the hands of Wilkinson. Rob.n seemed uninformed altogether of the nature of Meade's stipulations with Burr last February or January in what was called the *armistice*, at Natchez. Burr now entered into a train of statements to show to R.n how Meade had violated his engagements on that occasion. If he had made out such a story as he now told in the presence of Smith and myself when we were not by, it might perhaps pass like other representations which have, I know not in how many instances been received upon the credit of his word.—But that he sh.d tell any one in our hearing—that Meade pledged his honour to him that our people should all keep their arms when we knew the solicitude with which he afterwards had them all *hid* and sunk in the river; and say he was not taken a prisoner under guard to Washington in the Mississippi Territory fr. the interview he had, as it was called, with Meade, at Cole's Creek, in persuance, of his forebearing to prefer resistance which he might have made, to a surrender of his person—would indeed surpass all credibility—if he had not with the same temerity assured Wickham t'other day in Court, that the Mississippi Militia whilst ordered out ag^{t} him could hardly be kept by *him* fr. deserting to him by whole companies.—What they might have been disposed to do, had he shown himself worthy of their support, is, too far removed fr. wh^{t} they did, to need any attestation fr. us or our friends in that country. But young men, whom I can redeem fr. future connections with every incapacity but the talents for intrigue must not be entangled in those snares so imprudently or so rashly laid for their credulity.—Indeed, I am again disposed to recall to my aid Cowles Mead's impression last winter that Burr was at *times* deranged as the only means of accounting for his occasional rashness in his assertions. Certain I am he exhibited at that season every derangem^{t} but that of avoidable hazard. And as his memory is confessedly strong he can not now surely rely upon his facts with^{t} a similar, if not a worse, apology.—Saw today, a curious parallel of Burr's character and my own drawn by Wirt, in his speech reported in the Enquirer, on Wickham's motion to arrest the evidence in the Treason-case. I'll transcribe it hereafter, m.night.

Richm^{d} Virg^{a} 8^{r} 1.07.—

Wilkinson's cross-examination was continued this morning by Wickham with gr. ability, and suspended 'till tomorrow to give him time he desired, for reflection and further recurrence to his papers, and also to enable Burr to finish it tomorrow—as the latter is not well enough to attend to day.—Then came forward the ingenious Poindexter, who delivered a very petulant and dogmatical testimony in the course of which he had the effrontery to state the whole affair of the alledged recognizance of Burr taken by Old Rodney, in a manner to induce if he could a *belief*, that Rodney was perfectly correct that Burr had forfeited an original recognizance, and that Rodney was one of the best men living whilst no *honest* man in the Territory believed a word of the stories, that were told there of another recognizance or memorandum for one having been suppressed. He even went so far as to say he heard and believed that Harding had begun to write an original—but got *tired* before he finished it, and it was *thrown under* the *table*. O Harding, my estimable friend, may you soon be able to scourge this paltry, pettifogger, who further declared, on his oath, that the matter was now before the Sup. C^{t} of the Territ^{y} where the securities w^{d} get off, not upon the merits of the case, but because the Judge who bound them had not cognizance of the offence. I will look to it with you. 5 p.m.

Richm^{d} Virg^{a} Frid. 8^{r} 2.07.—

Burr attended to day in C^{t} and concluded the cross-examination of Wilkinson,—after which, Poindexter was again called for, and was if possible, a greater curiosity as a witness than he had been yesterday. His parade of his opinion, of the jurisdiction of the Courts in the Mississippi Territ^{y}—his strictures on the presentments by Burr's Gr. Jury there—his justification of his conduct as honorary Aid de camp, and Att^{y} General, and his insolence to Burr and his counsel—all exhibited him in a light, which introduced a character into the piece now performing at the Capitol, as novel as it was unexpected. Then succeeded a witness of a very opposite cast, a Mr Trisley, one of the late Gr. Jury here, who has riveted upon Wilkinson's character and credit, those fetters Jefferson and himself were so long forging together, for the fame and liberty of others. I presume my notes of the whole will be interesting.—After a close struggle between the opposite Counsel, Wickham succeeded by his usual address in wresting fr. the prosecutors a very curious letter by Jeff^{n} to W^{n} of the 3^{d} of last Jany wch I must if possible get a copy of. It will I am sure, prove a monument of Jeff^{n} malice and ascerbity which will long survive the fame of his philosophy. Martin was both yesterday and to day more in his cups than usual, and tho' he spared neither his prudence nor his feelings, he was happy in all his hits———11 o'clock p.m.

Richm^{d} Virginia
Sat^{y} 8^{r} 3.07.—

Wilkinson, tho' it was thought by many yesterday, that his cross-examination was concluded, was this morning again further interrogated as to the import of his instructions to Lieu^{t} Pike—and the nature of his confidential Intercourse with Tim Kibby.—But nothing could be got out of him as to the former, and as to any dealing with Kibby, of the sort alluded to in Kibby's published Affidavit.—he would no more confess it, than that he is said by the records of scandal and infamy to have had in his youth with Gen. Gates. He produced 2 copies of alledged instructions to Pike. These papers, being of his own manufacture, left his adversaries, of course to content themselves with whatever effect the suspicions arising fr. their questions might produce in the minds of the auditors if not of the Judge. But the publication in the Argus to day of no less than six documents, in the course of his exam^{n} offered by W^{n} and rejected by the Judge, as improper to be given in evidence, will operate a preponderating counterpoise in his favor.—Before he withdrew, he appealed to the C^{t} on the attempts that had been made, during his exam^{n} upon his honour and veracity: observed that it now w^{d} be easy for him to show his whole conduct in its true light freed fr. all manner of doubt or suspicion of his motives, if Burr would produce the letter of the 13th of May alluded to in the cyphered letter, which w^{d} enable him to expose other letters from Burr, which occasioned that letter. He then declared that Burr's opinion "that the letter of the 13th of May had been put out of Burr's power into the hands of a third person with W^{s} knowledge" was unfounded and destitute of all manner of truth: that B. knew the reverse was the fact, and he again challenged him to produce it, with warmth and asperity of language.—Burr with an air of dignity and composure, which I think he borrowed fr. an opinion that he is not bound to give W.[n] a meeting out of c.[t], demanded, whether this sort of language and such topics were giving testimony? and then observed that the Gen.[l] was there to tell the whole truth and nothing but the truth upon his Oath, and sh.[d] reserve other matters for another place.—W.[n] now withdrew. But who can not perceive, that in this scene, the craft of the advocate shrunk from the charge of his enemy?—I examined soon after this Gates, and Jones: the latter of whom fully proved the terms of a parole agree.[t] to go down the River with me, last winter, in a manner to defeat every effect the testimony of the Hendersons could possibly produce to my prejudice. I find Burr has a heavy Bill against the U.[d] States on account of advances, he says he has made to agents employed for summoning his witnesses. How many have undertaken this service for him I know not. Some I do know, who advanced their own money, in expectation of being refunded by Burr or the U.[d] St.[s] But how far Burr will be only indemnified for his *advances* in this business, may be guessed fr. the transaction already narrated of the manoeuvre by which he put Ellis, one of his creditors in cash. See conclusion to notes of 23.[d] of Aug.[t] But Ellis who was to day examined parried, some lounges made at him, during his cross-examination on this subject by saying it was a verbal summons he got at Natchez; the proper one was served here upon him.—I will now set down here, Wirt's parallel of Burr's character and my own. After having stated, that Burr was manoeuvering to escape fr. the prosecutions by having me sacrificed in his stead—he asks "By what sort of legerdemain is it, that Burr wants to shuffle himself down to the bottom of the pack, and turn me up, principal Traitor?" He then proceeds, as follows.—"Who then is Aaron Burr—and what the part which he has borne in this transaction? He is its author, its projector, its active executor. Bold, ardent, restless, and aspiring, his head conceived it, and his hand brought it into action. Beginning his aspirations in N. York, he associated with him men whose wealth is to supply the necessary funds. Possessed of the main-spring his personal labor contrives all the machinery. Pervading the continent from New York to N. Orleans, he draws, into his plan by every allurement he can contrive, men of all ranks and descriptions. To youthful ardour he presents danger and glory; to ambition, rank and titles and honour; to avarice,—the Mines of Mexico.— To each person whom he addresses, he presents the objects adapted to his taste; his recruiting officers are appointed; men are engaged throughout the Continent. Civil life is indeed quiet upon its surface; but in its bosom, this man had contrived to deposit the materials with which the slightest touch of his match produces an explosion to shake the continent. All this his restless ambition has contrived, and in the autumn of 1806 he goes forth for the last time, to apply his match. On this excursion, he meets with Blen^{tt}

Who is Blen^{tt}? A Native of Ireland—a man of letters who fled fr. the storms of his own country to find quiet in ours. His history shows, that war is not the *natural* element of his mind: if it had been, he never would have changed Ireland for America. So far is an Army fr. furnishing the society natural and proper to M^{r} B$^{tt's}$ character—that on his arrival in America he retired even fr. the population of the Atlantic States, and sought quiet and solitude in the bosom of our West^{n} Forests. But he carried with him taste, and science, and wealth: 'and lo the desert smiled.' Possessing himself of a beautiful island on the Ohio—he rears upon it a Palace, and decorates it with every romantic embellishm^{t} of fancy. A Shrubbery that Shenstone might have envied, blooms around him. Music that might have charmed Calypso and her Nymphs, is his—An extensive library spreads its treasures before him. A philosophical apparatus offers to him all the secrets and mysteries of nature. Peace tranquillity and innocence shed their mingled delights around him,—and to crown the enchantment of the scene,—a wife, who is said to be lovely even beyond her sex and graced with every accomplish^{t} that can render it irresistible, has blest him with her love and made him the father of her children.— The evidence would convince you sir that this is not a faint picture of the real life.—In the midst of all this peace, this innocence, and this tranquillity, this feast of the mind this banquet of the heart,—the destroyer comes—he comes to turn this paradise into a Hell.—Yet the flowers do not wither at his approach; and no monitory shudderings thro' the bosom of their unfortunate possessor warn him of the ruin that is coming upon them. A stranger presents himself. Introduced by the high rank which he had lately held in his country, to their civilities,—he soon finds his way into their hearts by the dignity and elegance of his demeanor, the delights and beauties of his conversation, and the seductive and fascinating powers of his address. The conquest was not a difficult one.—Innocence is ever simple and credulous: conscious of no designs itself, it suspects none in others; it wears no guards before its breast, every door, and port and avenue of the heart is thrown open to all who chuse to enter.—Such was the State of Eden, when the Serpent entered its bowers. The prisoner, in a more engaging form, winding himself into the heart of the unfortunate Bl.^{tt} found but little difficulty in changing the natural character of that heart, and the objects of its affect.^{n} By degrees, he infuses into it the poison of his ambition: he breathes into it the fire of his own courage, a daring and a desperate thirst for glory: an ardour panting for all the storms and bustle and hurricanes of life. In a short time, the whole man is changed, and every object of his former delight relinquished. No more he enjoys the tranquil—scene; it has become flat and insipid to his taste. His books are abandoned; his crucible and retort are thrown aside; his shrubbery blooms and breaths its fragrance on the air in vain; he likes it not. His ear no longer drinks the rich melody of music; he longs for the trumpet's clangor and the cannon's roar; even the prattle of his babes, once so sweet, no longer affects him; and the angel's smile of his wife, which hitherto touched his bosom with ecstacy so unspeakable,—is now unfelt and unseen.—Greater objects have taken possession of his soul;—his imagination has been dazzled with visions of Diadems, and stars and garters and titles of nobility: He has been taught to burn with restless emulation at the names of

Cromwell, Caesar, and Bonaparte.—His enchanted Island is destroyed soon to relapse into a Desert; and in a few months we find the tender and beautiful partner of his bosom—whom he long permitted not the winds of summer to visit too rudely,—we find her shivering at midnight on the winter Banks of the Ohio, and mingling her tears with the torrents that froze as they fell."—Whatever may be the defects of this performance, which I have no time at present to criticize—it is remarkable as containing far more real history than fiction, tho' wearing so much the face of the latter.—

Richm.[d] Virg.[a] Sund. 8.[r] 4.07.—

I called on Burr this morning-when he, at last, mentioned to me during a short tête à'tête that he was preparing to go to England, that the time was now auspicious for him and he wished to know whether I could give him letters. I answered that I supposed when he mentioned England, he meant London as his business would probably be with people in Office:—that I knew none of the present ministry, nor did I believe, I had a single acquaintance in London. He replied—he meant to visit every part of the country, and w.[d] be glad to get letters to any one. I said I w.[d] think of it that I might discover whether I had any friends there whom it w.[d] be an object worth his attention to know, and took leave.—Thus it is this strange man continues to expose his inconsistency with himself rather, than lay aside the mysterious mask with which he has ever sought and still continues to disguise his very hints—a practice, I believe, he has not departed fr. in every instance, fr. Wilkinson down to myself.—We can only conjecture therefore his designs. For my part, I am disposed to suspect, he has no serious purpose of reviving any of his speculations in America, or even of returning—fr. Europe, if he can get there. His anxiety to elude his creditors is I believe occupation enough for his energies which are little, except in his reveries. Out of them he tells different stories to different persons, enjoining confidence fr. all, but committing himself in nothing, to any one. I have suspected, for some time however, he really does dream of appearing in London, with something, according to his ideas, in the nature of a suite. Some weeks past, he consulted de Pestre, to learn fr. him, how much money would be wanted to enable him to go and return. He said he supposed that $10,000 might answer—de P. told him that w^{d} depend on the nature of his business and the time it w^{d} require to transact it—But he has more lately been engaged in endeavouring to attach to him some y^{ng} men, who may accompany him. I yet only know positively 2. Sam Swartwout was enraptured with the prospect, and still may feast his imagination upon it,—tho' I could not resist the propensity I felt to convey to this fine young man, without his suspecting fr. whence it came, a curb which may restrain his generous ardour and innocent credulity.—His relation Major Smith has endeavoured to apply it. Bob. Robinson was the other. And to save him, my breast heaved with indignation against his tempter, whilst my heart laboured for the danger of my young friend, when I found that his *property* was Mr Burr's object: for Burr it seems in the first-place certified himself by inquiries of Major Smith, that R's father was *wealthy* and R^{n} an *only child* before he proposed the voyage to him, which I find he had the insolence to introduce by telling him, R^{n} would be much pleased to accompany him, as M^{rs} B^{tt} had assured him, than which nothing is more false. But Burr is careless of his facts as of his religion where neither is exposed to scrutiny, and any liberty with them may advance his purpose for the moment. I had seasonably prepared this yg. man, who will tomorrow, make his escape to Pittsburgh, fr. the fascination of this serpent.—I was much entertained during 3½ hours by the performance on the Forte-piano of a young French-man with the name of Patricolas who is a fine performer, and made one acquainted with new music of Haydn, St[*****], & others, he executed with masterly skill & expression.

Mon.[d] 8.[r] 5.—

This day was chiefly consumed with hearing testimony adduced to prove Eaton's incompetency or discredit which failed according to the legal rules of Evidence, tho' Eaton himself has already fully anticipated the object of his adversaries.—I am very unhappy in failing to hear fr. Natchez to relieve my anxiety for Harman. But why should I presume to pray for the removal of my trouble, for him and his mother, when I know how unworthy I have been of the many blessings I have already enjoyed in them? If I have ever tho't too highly of my Dominic in prejudice to his brother, my late cares for the latter have equalized the account. 10. p.m.—

Richm.[d] Virg.[a] Tuesd. 8.[r] 6.07.—

Burr and Martin made a considerable blunder today by producing a Major Bruff to the discredit of Wilkinson as they thought. The Major it is true, told some curious stories to the Court and the General, as unexpected by the Judge probably as they were unpalatable to the Brigadier. But the effect only tended to show both equally rivals in treachery to the state, if not to themselves. Burr w.[d] gladly have pretermitted the exhibition of this scene. But it was too late: the curtain had risen and Peacham and Locket stood confessed in every line of their characters, except a compromise of their differences. But as in such cases "honest men come by their own." The public feelings on the Mississippi will necessarily be relieved by the disclosures of this witness fr. the insult and mortification of again seeing Wilkinson command in that country. It is in vain that W.[n] has promised to destroy the credit of this witness. The Major has brandished his sword with such effect and address on this occasion that he has not only cut down the General but even disarmed his auxiliaries Jefferson, Dearborn, and Rodney who have so long fought by his side, throughout this immoral warfare. In short unless this testimony which fr. its effect upon Jeff.[n], etc. I regard the most interesting that has occurred, can be totally obliterated fr. the reports of the present motley proceedings at the Capitol, and the Major be absolutely foxed, the execration of the administration will soon be sown on the Mississippi to produce a crop similar to that which sprung from the teeth of the Hydra.—I regret the whole narrative will not probably appear in full before Robertson's report of the whole proceedings.—This ev^{g} my friend Hendren who has again come up to town chiefly to see me has called to express his satisfaction at the near prospect of my restoration to my family, and to solicit my acceptance of a horse he has a long time destined for me together with whatever money I may have occasion for. He has duly tempered the frankness of these propositions with sentiments of corresponding delicacy.—I alas! have made no better return to this generosity than words that lightened not the burden he had laid upon my heart, which I hope God will give it strength to carry to my *grave.* How long have I sought thro' life—friends without my family, and where have I found any 'till the hand of Divine mercy pointed their regards to that piety that has supported the patience of my distress! I have declined H's favours and quieted his solicitude to serve me, by requesting him to look out for a few Negroes I want to purchase. He will see me again next monday. 11 p.m.

Richm^{d} V^{a} Wed. 8^{r} 7.07.—

Wilkinson was not ready to day to undertake his attack upon the credit of Major Bruff. He will attempt it tomorrow.—Nothing was done of any consequence in Court to day.—Soon after it adjourned I took a letter for my beloved wife, to the Eagle, to go by Col: McKee, who sets off for Natchez tomorrow. I had there, the happiness to see Doctor Cummins just arrived.—He made me happy, by assuring me, my boys were running about, on the 25th of Augt when he last saw them and has bro't me a packet which I shall receive in the morning.—I find I have omitted to note a very curious discovery in C^{t} made last saturday. Nothing less than letters of McKee's, some of them dated in Jany and Feby last, produced by Wilkinson proving the Col: to have been with us on the Mississippi far more as a spy, than a friend.—It seems the stream of turpitude is, unbroken in this country, fr. the Presid^{t} to his lowest retainers. The capillaries of the Col's physiognomy, during the reading of the said letters, were swoln to bursting. The man I believe would have hissed upon immersion in cold water. He was struck dumb and upon his release, went off in a tangent.—Burr can't endure a hint of this incident: and yet he has since been more than once closeted with the Colonel. Can he find no better friends? or is he really deranged?—midnight——

Richd Virg^{a} Thurs. 8^{r} 8.07—

Wilkinson has not kept his promise of to day, discrediting the testimony of Major Bruff. An unimportant witness or two were exam^{d} by way of killing time, which now seems to be the favourite object of the prosecutors. Afterward, Hay at last announced that the evidence was closed on the part of the prosecution, but reserved his right to examine with^{t} restriction all of those witnesses that may arrive according to his fancy, which was conceded to him.—He then entered upon his speech to comment on the evidence, which appeared to me the best effort I have yet heard fr. him. It was perspicuous and somewhat ingenious.—I have therefore taken pretty close notes of all such parts of it as appeared to me to be worthy of notice or particularly applicable to myself.—He spoke however to empty benches 'till the rising of the C^{t} wch was, for his accom^{n} protracted half an hour, longer than usual. A few minutes before he stopped I was much diverted, by a display of his irritability, which was excited by McRae's interrupting him with a whisper to stop at 4 o'clock. Upon this the Attorney fired with indignation and in his wrath plainly exhibited his contempt for his coajutor by telling him he would not be interrupted by him and then endeavouring fruitlessly to compose the trouble of his Ire—he lamented the condition of counsel that could neither agree with those on their own side or those who were opposed to them.—I sent to Dr Cummins, this morn^{g}

for the packet he bro't me fr. Natchez, but not having received it I called upon him this ev^{g} when he deliv^{d} it to me in a wretched state, having been taken fr. him in the Creek Nation of Indians by Col: Hawkins the Agent of that Tribe, who, after examining my letter-book and every original letter my wife had sent me except *perhaps* 2 sealed letters from herself, and after taking such extracts and copies of the whole, as he tho't proper, then, returned to Doctor C. as many as he tho't proper. This Outrage I shall have formally stated in an affidavit by the Doctor in order to procure an attachment ag^{t} the Colonel.—I spent a very pleasant evening at the Musical Society, where I met Mrs Chevallié and Mrs Wickham. The latter seemed highly delighted with some performances in which I took a part, particularly a Quartet of Pleyel's. M^{rs} Ch. gave me some hospitable reproaches for the scarcity of my visits.—I believe her husband a most generous and benevolent man, which his countenance fully bespeaks.——

Richm^{d} Virg^{a} Frid. 8^{r} 9.07.—

It is a little singular that my birthday sh^{d} yesterday, have passed by, without my having noticed it. But this has been the case for several of the last years of my life and the reason is, that my mind is hardly occupied once a year, in thinking of myself. I may have taken my height and weight, perhaps full 20 times in the course of my life; but I am certain I never remembered much less noted the am^{t} of either, so that I c^{d} remember it 1. hour, after trial.—Yesterday, then I completed my 42^{d} or 43^{d} year: for my father and mother were never agreed whether I was born in 1764 or 1765, tho' they coincided as to the day, fixing it on the 8th 8^{ber} But at such a distance fr. my suffering family I can not estimate how much happiness or misery they have been preparing for so much of my present year as it may be given me to count!—Hay finished his speech to day, of which I continued my notes partially as I did yesterday.—He was followed by Randolph in a style that will read much better than it was delivered. He relied chiefly on effect of Burr's acquittal and arguments drawn fr. the Constitution. As to me, he seemed to forget my case altogether, save so far as his concern for Burr, obliged him to mention my name and writings. This I suspect will be also the case with Wickham.—Nous verons.——m. night.—

Richm^{d} Virg^{a} Sat. 8^{r} 10.07.—

The C^{t} does not sit to day at the request of the prosecutors. They are yet eternally complaining of the tedious length of the trial, and their own confinement and sufferings by it. The accused have no sufferings it seems, worthy of their notice.—I have today spent much time in painful reflection on the state of my affairs with Burr. It appears by a state^{t} of my private account ag^{t} him so far as I can now collect here all my charges ag^{t} him (for he has but two credits,) he is indebted to me in a balance of $2864.96—independent of my account against him for what I have already paid and lost by my endorsement of the Bill held by Miller for $4,000. It will be useless or worse for me to attempt to appear at Marietta, without a sum of money if not sufficient to discharge Miller's claim, at least necessary to enable me to get my negros away fr. Ohio, if that is now possible, and to redeem some few valuable articles of my property that have been sacrificed at Sheriff's sales. I have therefore imagined [*Blotted line below, from facing page.*] a method of forcing Burr's exertions to raise money for me, which is the most likely to succeed. It is founded on the principle of effecting thro' his vanity and interest, what it is now evident I sh^{d} in vain, seek thro' his justice or generosity. My plan is to hint to him—my ability to introduce him into the first circles in England, by introductory letters, at the same time showing him my expectations of becoming soon possessed of a large fortune, in Europe: fr. which, I doubt not, I shall be enabled to engage his best endeavours if not his most warm interest. This plan I shall put in execution tomorrow, of which I will note the effect upon him. And leaving it to ripen in his meditations for a week, I shall, then open my present distresses to him in detail, and present him with his acct. It is a little painful, I own, to feel oneself obliged to bring, even a bad man, into the path of his duty, by artifice. But the details of the manoeuver when examined, & shall, I have trust, will do me no discredit, with my friends.—9. p.m.

Richm.d Virg.a Sund. 8.r 11.07.—

It being very warm and dusty this morning I sent to Jno. [*Separating line blotted.*] Banks's for a horse to visit his family and Chevallié's, they living 2 miles apart, and take the benefit of a short ride.—But I previously called upon Burr, whom I found alone and in good spirits. He attributed the removal of his diarrhea exclusively to the effect of my pills: his sore eye was nearly cured, and Dan.l Clark and M.r Powers had arrived fr. Orleans to support the depositions of Derbigny and the Younger Mercier to the confirmation of Wilkinson's character and ruin.—Availing myself of such a state of things, I entered into loose and desultory conversation affecting all freedom of thought fr. any particular object. The affair of the Leopard and the Chesapeake being mentioned, B. observed that tho' the difference between the U.d St.s and G.t Britain on that account might be expected to be soon settled, there were many other causes of dispute which would not soon be removed; that this was a most auspicious moment for his purposes to visit England, and he had no doubt, he could in serving himself and his friends there, show them (the Ministry) their best interests, in a manner that w.d convince their judgments. This was the best opportunity I could have desired for *my purpose.* I now told him, as he happened to be alone, I had been reflecting on the application he had lately made to me for letters to England, to assist the better means, he no doubt possessed, of establishing his intercourse with the best society in that country. I regretted that thro' the fluctuation of parties there, I had no acquaintance with any member of the administration. But I had thought of three Noblemen, with whom I had been at school at Westminster, and there intimate with them all; tho' I had never since met with any of them, except Lord Sackville, who had visited me in Ireland. To Lord S. therefore I c^{d} write, and also Lords Elgin and Courtenay. The latter I was very intimate with at school—and the former I presumed fr. the circumstance of his having been not long since Ambassador at the Courts of Petersburg and Constantinople, must be much respected by the present ministry if not in office with them. To all these personages I said I thought I could properly address a mere letter of introduction, which if it w^{d} not itself produce the end proposed, would not fail to do so when supported by the appearance he would make in London, the address with which he would be as impressive there as here, and the distinguished rank he lately occupied in the American Gov^{t} The effect of this communication was rapture. The whole man was changed. With all his studied reserve, he could not restrain his transports, which agitated his countenance and his movements far more than the news of a capital prize in the lottery could have done. I now after pausing a little, to give his reflections time to resume his usual composure, asked if he remembered a hint, I had sometime since given him that I entertained some expectations of hereafter becoming easy in my circumstances and perhaps wealthy? Yes! he hastily replied, very well.—I then alluded to a communication by letter from fr. a friend in Ireland, which I w^{d} now acquaint him with and fr. which I might expect if my prospects sh^{d} be realized possibly to meet him in those circles in Europe into which I proposed to introduce him: now drawing fr. my pocket A. Martin's letter of 16th of last May, which luckily contained no other matter than that I wished him to see and some political news,—I presented it to him. He read it deliberately over and over, and I now beheld myself established in an influence upon his *feelings* and a consideration fr. his notice, to which, I am persuaded, I had never before possessed the least title. Hey-day! Behold, the wretched and beggared Blennerhassett about to rise out of the misery in which I have plunged him and his unhappy family, into wealth and consequence! The Heir too, of a nobleman! His new wealth and his dignified connections must supply me with better materials for my projected speculations than all others I have hitherto collected.—His connections and his purse shall lay the foundation, under which I will *again* bury his credulity and rear upon it my own aggrandisement.—I am persuaded all this, and probably much more to the same purpose, entered and pervaded the mind of this arch-financier, with the velocity of light in an instant. Be it so. Let him outwit himself—He shall have my letters to the British Noblemen, and may make his own use of them, if he will first exonerate me fr. Miller's demand, and pay or secure the balance he owes me, before we part. Otherwise we break upon a *writt* and for everything else, I fear not his address in future.—Before I left him I look up a French heroic-poem, I observed lying on the windows. What do you think was the subject? La guerre des Dieux. A tale you suppose of Pagan warfare? Pshaw! Did you suppose the appetite of Burr have any relish for such fare as that? Not at all. This was a repast of blasphemy and obscenity, better suited to his vitiated palate. In an entertainment given to the gods of the Christians by the Pagan deities, The Father, Son and Holy Ghost, The Virgin Mary, Joseph and some others of the family of Mary's husband, are introduced in the 1st. Canto, as awkward, stupid, and astonished characters in beholding the magnificence and delightful variety of the Pagan abodes. Amongst the hosts, Apollo becomes enamoured of the Virgin M. and resolves upon possessing her. She is represented as a beautiful country girl, very awkward and ignorant. She passes thro' the boudoir of Venus where she finds the veil the dress and the other habiliments of that goddess. She puts them on, is astonished to behold in the surrounding mirrors, the hitherto unknown charms of her beauty. In the midst of her admiration some lovely little *boys* bring her the ambrosial perfumes of their mother: she caresses them and is charmed;—Apollo in the mean time, adjusts his toillette. He afterwards, on the meeting of the company in the grand sallon proposes the entertainment of his guests with his music. It is desired by all, particularly the V.M. But it no sooner begins, than it puts God the Father to sleep. Jesus pronounces it far inferior to what they had at the marriage of Canaan. Joseph with him and the Holy Ghost, are disgusted and all retire, declaring their preference of a Jig.—The sequel is invisible.—Such is the occupation of this vitiated and superannuated immoralist. He is delighted with the performance which has broken in upon his cares and his projects, only to salve the one and sharpen the other. The poem has the recommendation of originality carried by much classical management and I shall read it if I can obtain it, with[t] prejudice to that piety which is my firmest support and greatest comfort.—Burr did not say fr. whence he procured the book. But the musk it was impregnated with proved it came thro' the same hand by which he had the letter mentioned in these notes of the 15th ulto.—Cummins dined with me to day and appeared more occupied with the care of his parson than other concern; whilst Jourdan is eternally engaged in his libations, lost to the concerns of his family, etc.—I have rec[d] a note fr. Hendren to apprize me there will be a Sheriff's sale of Negroes at New Kent 30 miles hence on wedn. which Cummins I expect will attend on my account and his own.—I have compensated for my sins in looking into La Guerre des Dieux to-day, by afterwards taking a part in some sacred music with the parson at Jno. Banks's.—Chevallié as usual pressed me to dinner.—I have such full confidence in his goodness that I believe I shall venture to request him to endorse or negotiate a Bill on Philadelphia for me.—m.night—

Richm[d] Virg[a] Mond. 8[r] 12th 07.—

I am miserable this morning by being denied a letter fr. Natchez. The season advances and witnesses continue to arrive so constantly that I am filled with apprehensions of being unable to descend the Ohio before the breaking up of that river.—Martin commenced his speech on the evidence this morning and only reached his first full stop at the hour of adjournment. He will probably hold out full two days more.——

Tuesd. 13.—

Martin kept on his feet to day 'till the adj[t] He has only come to the second period.—I had this morning an extremely friendly note fr. Chevallié telling me he never lends his name to anybody—but has 1,000 Dollars at my service which I have accepted to send to the sale by Cummins.—I have spent a pleasant ev[g] at Banks's, where I often take Smith with me, as the poor fellow knows no one here. B. has given me some lines he made on the late Miss Gray, which I will here transcribe, as they deserve preservation.——

Sweet Shade:
Within our hearts, thy mem'ry is embalmed.
Beyond the usual gifts that grace thy sex,
Thy various virtues and acquirements shone;
The dignity of worth, (like thine) it would
Degrade, to blazon each peculiar claim
That mark'd thy value here; for all who knew
Thee, felt its force, and every tongue seem'd
Emulous to praise. The young enraptured,
Hung upon thy name; With equal rev'rance
And grateful love, hail'd the bright Exemplar
That adorned the sex.—pleas'd with the theme
The aged matron too, for this laid by
The frigid caution of maturer years,
With joy exulting, join'd the general praise,
And wish'd (a pious wish) her offspring might
Thro' life's alluring scenes, tread the chaste path
That mark'd Eliza's step.—
One kindred trait that mark'd thy latest hour,
Unknown to all but to thy weeping friends.
Who clung around the sable couch of Death;
T'were impious not to note.—The God who smote
Still bless'd thee to the last. Its pow'rs thy mind
Retain'd:—whilst conscious of the approaching call,
Thy steadfast Soul still stood serene and firm!

No tumult there, no dread, no terror cou'd
Disturb the heart, which purity inspired:—
Twas Resignation's calm! Thy closing eyes
T'is true, a transient tremor felt, and o'er
The fever'd cheek a Drop let fall. Oh! Twas
A sacred gem, incalculably rich!
A legacy divine!—for others' woes
It fell!— Twas filial sympathy, which like
A shock electric, struck the palsy'd nerve,
Impervious but to this.—Dim tho' thy sight
Yet still thou saw'st a parent's pungent
Agonizing pangs: a precious pearl
Thou gav'st,—and with the boon expir'd.—
Sweet Shade! This tribute is not half thy due!
Alas! too soon we pay the solemn meed.
Yet bear it on thy wing 'twill pleasing prove
A passport to the skies:—and when, blest Shade!
Thy Sister-spirits, who, thy flight await,
At Heav'n's portal shall peruse the Scroll,
In strains celestial, (not unknown to thee)
They'll chaunt the theme divine, until it reach
The Throne of Grace.—There in regal State,
The King of Kings, in all the Majesty
Of Heav'n array'd, with sweet solacing smile.
Shall hail thy welcome to the Realms above,
Whilst myriads of the Just around him Sing
"This the reward of virtuous—acts below
External life—and Bliss for Ever more."——

[*Except for last two lines, poem is copied bottom-to-top on three pages.*]

Richm^{d} Virg^{a} Wedn. 8^{r} 14.07.—

Martin at last concluded at 4 o'clock with the adjourn^{t} this evg. Martin bears everything to an extreme. Want of arrangement, verbosity, and eternal repetitions have more than sated the malice of his enemies.

Thursd. 15.

M[c]Rae consumed this whole day with somewhat less discredit to himself than might have been expected. It appears that he is now the only 1. of the 3 prosecuting Counsel that labours to bolster up the credit and consistency of Wilkinson. Hay has declared, out of court, he has washed his hands of him. Look you, Jefferson. One of my Quartettes was tried this evening at the music society and reorder'd minds.—I had a friendly letter fr. Devereux, announcing his being about to return to Ireland, where he expects to recover his estate, and assuring me with much concern for my present sufferings, his actions shall prove his friendship, whenever his means can give it that operation he now so generously laments he cannot direct to my succour. He assures me however Pierce Butler Esquire of Philad[a] has directed him without solicitation to invite me to call upon him for any precuniary aid I may need. M[r] B. Dev. assures me is a noble minded Irishman th[t] I hear is very wealthy.—m.night.

Friday Oct. 16.1807.—

Wickham followed Martin instead of M[c]Rae yesterday, and was I think far below his former efforts. He occupied the day nearly—It was to day, M[c]Rae exhibited as I have just mentioned, not having had time to set down yesterday's notes 'till this ev.[g]—

Satur. 17——

Wirt spoke very much to engage the fancy of his hearers to day with[t] affecting their understanding. For he can not reason upon the facts before him, and can no more conduct Law-argument than I could raise a mountain. As Junius says of the King—"The feather that adorns him, supports his flight: strip him of his plumage, and you fix him to the Earth."—He attempted to be sarcastic on all his opponents. Randolph he charged with a decay of professional and oratorical powers which kept pace with the march of his years. Martin he upbraided with ill earned and unmerited fame which had disappointed the expectations of the Virginia bar, before which he had shone thro' so many moons but had never yet appeared in any phases of the law. I mention this as a specimen of his efforts in the figurative style, to show how unhappy he is in his researches into those mines of taste and study which the fancy of an Orator never explores in vain. Wickham he bluntly accused of unadorned plagiarism, in appropriating to himself the arguments of Dallas and Lewis in the case of Fries, and even expressing their ideas with inferior elegance. I took some notes of this Orator's performance which Wickham was very glad to get as he was absent during the delivery of what was so pointedly applied to himself—"Oh! that mine enemy would write a Book!" Wilkinson is writing one which some say is to ruin not only Burr, but Jefferson, too——

Sunday 8r. 18.07.—

I staid at home 'till evening, owing to the high wind and dust that annoyed everyone who ventured abroad. But I drank tea and spent the evg 'till 10 o'clock at Mrs Chevallié's. I there met Mrs David Randolph, who is about 50 but very accomplished, of charming manners, and possessing a masculine mind. Fr. this lady, the near relation of the President, and whose brother is married to his daughter, I heard more pungent strictures upon Jefferson's head and heart, because they were better founded, than any I had ever heard before: and she certainly uttered more treason than *my wife* ever dreamed of; for she ridiculed the experiment of a republic in this country, which the vices and inconsistency of the parties and the people, had too long shown to be nothing more than annual series of essays to complete a work ill begun, and which appeared to be nearly worn out before it was half finished.—But she always was disgusted with the fairest ideas she could ever imagine of a modern Republic, however she might respect those of antiquity. And as for the Treason—she cordially hoped, whenever Burr or anyone else, again attempted to do anything, the Atlantic States would be comprised in the plan.—She talked much of Thomas Moore, with whom she was highly pleased here, and recited some favourite extracts fr. him: but she is very much mortified by the indiscriminate censure of Virginia with which he has requited the hospitality and consideration with which he was universally treated in this State. His only two exceptions fr. his strictures being Wickham and the Ch. Justice. But in the former he could discover no accomplishment beyond professional skill and a slight knowledge of French with a talent for repartee, and an imagination denied all favours which it would, in vain, solicit fr. nature and the sciences. Of the Ch. Justice I can not speak out of the precincts of the law, or his politics, which I already begin to fear will exhibit his heart as unlike as those of Hardwick or Cambden, as his mind may resemble theirs.——I also obtained fr. that interesting lady, some sketches of the characters of General Dayton and Bollman with both of whom her acute penetration seems to have had sufficient opportunities of informing her judgment. The sentence of my moral craniology on these heads, thus presented to me, was, this, that the one is that of an unprincipled speculator, and crafty politician, who never appeals to his reason, but to deceive, and never departs fr. it, but to be sensual.—The other is that of an individual possessing similar talents more highly refined by nature but less consolidated by experience, with syren-faculties of speech and manner never exerted to captivate but to destroy their victim, and a temperament of antipathy rather than of inclination to the sex.—I this morning, closed long letters to A. Martin, for Ireland, after I believe full 2. months' neglect of no less an object offered to my inquiries than the claim of the large fortune he announced as having probably, descended to me fr. Lord Ross. I have so long been dosed with the incessant vexations of my prosecution, that I sometimes imagine, my apathy is better lent me, to befit me for the future frowns of unsteady fortune, than to prepare me for her insidious smiles.—I am already her puppet.

Monday 19.—

Wirt concluded with perhaps a better 2. hours' display of his powers than he has yet exhibited.—Lieutenant Jackson at last made his appearance; but fell very short of what the prosecutors expected of him fr. the purport of his affidavits which they have published in the Argus, and of every thing else but his own infamy: tho' he made out enough of treachery and perjury probably to swell the current of suspicion against Burr's treasonable designs.—Swartwout has sent Wilkinson a challenge with^{t} effect.

Tuesday.—

I have said nothing of my relief yesterday by a letter fr. my beloved bearing the intelligence of her recovery fr. a fever. Who w^{d} not think I was glad to receive this letter? I had been miserable for 3 weeks in apprehension for Harman. This new calamity has affected me with a kind of lethargic absence fr. which I awake often in surprize to wonder that we are all four alive; as if life upon any terms, was unnatural in our present prospects! Oh! Melancholy, how long wilt thou brood upon me? I have begun a letter to my Angel to dissemble with her. How earnest our contest of skills and the chess that cheats away our respective cares! Sustain her strength, O God, who approvest her, virtue and can best assuage her sufferings!— [*Indented nearly half a line.*] Tuesd^{y} Mr Marshall, at length, has delivered an elaborate opinion purporting that he cannot commit any of us for treason, not because we had none in our hearts; but because we did none with our hands or Corn meal. But the last article has determined him to commit me for trial to Ohio for a misdemeanor. Burr is of course ordered on this new dance. I shall however, I fancy, leave the little Emperor to exhibit it alone. For it is now time I sh^{d} withdraw behind [*Blot to word below.*] the scenes, even tho' I should employ Duane to shift them. I shall therefore set out to Phila^{da} first for this object, and next to close my pecuniary affairs with Burr there, which I could not do, here. I have given bail for my appearance at Chilicothe the 4th of Jany Bondsmen Smith & Cummins.—

Richd Virg^{a} Wedn. 8^{r} 21.07.—

Burr is in a sort of keeping at his own house endeavouring to get all his bail renewed in the civil suits here depending against him. Martin has become his security I believe to the am^{t} of $15,000. How much of this he may eventually sink in the purchase of the old staple of experience, he will ascertain in about 6 months.

Thursday 22.

Wrote to my beloved again a letter to go by Ashley which I will not close 'till the moment before I leave this town. It will reach her and I trust, tend to support her 'till I can escape to her and into Florida with her if necessary—which I am determined to attempt rather than play a part in a second farce, wch w^{d} separate me fr. my family, probably, for not less than a year fr. hence.—Was I criminal in seeking some little refuge fr. my trouble, this ev^{g} at the Musical Society?—I met there Mesdames Wickham, Chevallié and the Misses Marks. I only took a part in 1. Quartet by particular desire of the ladies. I affected an air of contentment; but my lovely wife well knows how fully my countenance w^{d} bespeak my feelings—midnight—

Richd Virg^{a} Frid. 8^{r} 23.07.—

Breakfasted at Mrs Chevallié's, where I met a pleasant party. At 10 o'clock I rode to visit Banks and prescribe for dissentery with which he is affected. Smith being finally discharged by the Ch. Justice—left me yesterday for N. York. I am endeavouring to obtain a lot of negroes in partnership with Doctor Cummins, tho' I fear we shall not succeed.—This ev^{g} visited Wickham to fee him with a few—words. He thinks in case gov^{t} sh^{d} be disposed to desire my conviction at Chilicothe, Woodbridge's evidence will enable them easily to effect it.—

Another call to Florida.—Revisited and spent the evening with Banks. He has offered to lend me $100. which I shall probably accept to enable me to return Chevallié's money. I take a horse and gig fr. B. as there is no conveyance fr. hence, in any public or private carriage for 10 days to come. Burr, Martin, Cummins & myself with two servants will probably form a cavalcade, to move tomorrow or next day. I must raise money in Phila^{da}, on chances—and even strain a point with Cummins there, to aid me, whatever success I may have with Burr—m. night.

Richd V^{a} Sat. Octr 24.07——

I have been all day too ambulatory to spend a moment with these notes, before this moment 11 o'clock p.m.—I am just returned fr. a 2.mile walk in the dark—to take leave of the family of my friend Jno. Banks, who has kindly pressed me to borrow of him the largest sum I believe he could spare. And before I lie down to take 2 hours' rest, before I am called up to set off in the stage for the Fed. city—I must note my having closed a letter I began several days ago to my adored and incomparable wife, to go by Ashley, who will commence his journey tomorrow or the next day—My excellent friend Joe Lewis I find by letter fr. him this evening has removed my fears for my credit and honour by remitting to Mr Chevallié $1000 to replace that sum lately lent me by Mr C. The house it seems, in Phila^{da} must still suspend my credit on account of the nonremoval of Sanders' attach^{t} But J. L. will lend his generous friendship to succour the honour of a friend in distress, who is not I trust, unworthy of the sympathies of his liberal heart. His counsel will soon direct my distracted cares to peace——

Washing^{n} City Tues. 8^{r} 27.07.—

Luther Martin just made his final immersion into the daily bath of his faculties, after a series of apparitions in all the phases of his accustomed orbit.—Whether in a stage-coach or a tavern he is indefatigable under the united stimulus of egotism and benevolence to harass the gratitude or try the patience of his friends. At 3 o'clock a.m. on Saturday morning at Richmond, he joined us in the coach: and neither the privation of sleep nor the fatigue of the journey—have in the least checked his loquacity or lessened his good humour. He read to me an able pamphlet on the subject of Jefferson's rejection of the new British Treaty, whilst we were jolting and jarring over as bad a road as any country can lament, with more dispatch than I could peruse it in my chair. His strong memory made him interesting all the way, in his anecdotes and his stories: and he is not unhappy in his powers of ridicule, which is well pointed, 'till it soon becomes blunted by the suggestions of his benevolence and the abrasions of his verbosity which like the revolutions of a grindstone soon wear away the subject applied to it, without undergoing in itself any sensible diminution.—We spent last night in Alexandria, where we recruited our strength by a good night's rest and reached this nominal city, to day by a packet-boat about 1. p.m. Here, at Stell's Hotel, Martin has kept up an incessant fire ag^t the Democrats and the Adm^n for he has had no want of that ammunition with which he always primes and loads for such duty. In our own room, occupied by Cummins, M. and myself, he is not content to confine his feats, for the gratification of ourselves and a few occasional visitors. He has several times, carried his arms into the enemies' country, I mean to the public room, occupied chiefly by members of Congress, with many of whom, he has no acquaintance, whilst all admire and acknowledge him privileged.—I had the satisfaction of reading the President's message in half an hour after it was communicated to day to Congress.—I have nothing to do with its pouting fretfulness ag^t Gr. Britain, its abject humiliation of this country to Spain, thro' the frowns of those in the Fr. Ministry, or the insidious misrepresentation of the financial prosperity of the U^d States. But the clause relating to the issue of the judicial proceedings against us at Richmond, w^d alone establish the fame of the philosophic author and ch. magistrate, if his labours had never erected any other monument of his literature, his justice or his policy.—He finds it seems—it will become his duty, to lay before Congress, the whole proceedings, for their wisdom to judge whether "*the defect*" has been in the testimony, the law, or in the administration of the law. There is a new sort of grammar in this performance, which has hitherto been concealed fr. the learned.—But the whole piece is replete w.th all the ambiguity and duplicity which have ever characterized the pen of this timid but crafty statesman. The news is, here, that he will yet support Wilkinson, tho' he may not find a more respectable Democrat than M.cRae to back him. Yet, he says nothing in the message, of the General's honour, as a soldier, or his fidelity as a citizen. He now speaks only of his *energy*, which—in conjunction with the exertions of the army and the *patriotism* of the militia, dissipated the plots that were—formed on the Mississippi. Here is a fine preparation after all, for abandoning his friend, which he fears, and with reason, he will be forced to do, but he has been too long identified with him in other more near plots, to attempt it 'till it becomes inevitable. The same paragraph of the message opens by implication, a contingency, that may induce the Gov.t party in Congress, to impeach M.r Marshall: by signifying a doubt—whether we have not still the use of our necks, thro' the misconduct of the Judge.—Should the latter suffer as 't were penance for that timidity of conduct which was probably as instrumental in keeping him fr. imbruing his hands in our blood,—as it was operative in inducing him to continue my vexations, to pacify the menaces and clamourous yells of the Cerberus of Democracy—with a sop which he would moisten at least, with the tears of my family;—should this be well founded what pity w.d sacrifice to his sufferings? And if it is undoubtedly true, that in a private conversation he had with Martin, soon after the latter first arrived in Richmond he observed to him—"that it w.d be difficult or dangerous for a jury to venture to acquit Burr, however innocent they might think him"—who hence, will believe, that the greatest talents lodged in such nerves, are not, when exercised in the judgment-seat rather a public curse executed on a nation, than a natural blessing conferred upon the individual?—Besides, the seasonable appearance at this crisis of a pamphlet by J. Daveiss, the Judge's Bro$^{r.}$ in Law, and late District Fed. Att$^{y.}$ for Kentucky, removed fr. his office, for his premature and unsuccessful prosecution of Burr; the indiscriminate censure in this pamphlet of Jefferson, Wilkinson and Burr; the probable information the Judge must have had of this intended publication, when he opened to the prosecutors, as wide a field of investigation as they desired on their motion for our recommitment; and in short, the well-known spirit of clanship and cooperation with which the Marshalls and all their connections—are so uniformly animated;—all these motives will readily explain how readily the Judge must be disposed to favour alike the ruin of Burr, W$^{n.}$ & Jeff$^{n.}$ in everything short of murder. Ah! generous and accomplished Mercer, how will yr. virtues hereafter receive my devotions, if you sh$^{d.}$ think them polluted with these blasphemies ag$^{t.}$ the admired relative of yr. adored!—But as my reflections are penned for no eye but that of my wife and 2 or 3 confidential friends—it will not be suspected by those who know my heart, that whatever share of further sufferings may result to me fr. the conduct of the Judge, can in the least, generate my suspicions of his integrity or warp my Judgment of his behavior.—Cummins leaves this early tomorrow morning for Baltimore, where I expect to join him the day after tomorrow. I entertain strong hopes of being able to obtain some negros in partnership with him.—Burr did not come along with us fr. Richmond, but will, we all believe, be through here in a day or two. I am enabled to say fr. separate information I have obtained fr. Martin and Cummins, he has made use of all the confidence he could inspire them with, to the utmost extent at Richmond, where he has induced them to become his securities in all the civil suits instituted there ag$^{t.}$ him to amount of $36,000. I have no doubt he has set every engine of his ingenuity at work to effect this object.—The credulity and good nature of Martin, who worships even his vices, and is as assiduous in enlarging upon his looks and sayings as ever Boswell delighted in such drudgery for Johnson; and the vanity of Cummins to purchase the interest of a man whose resources appear to his understanding, inexhaustible—both needed but little, the collateral security of Pollock, which however Burr has not only exhibited to them, but he has besides, laid before them, my expectations, I find, of succeeding to a large fortune in Europe, thereby meaning to persuade them also, no doubt, that he will then control my finances, altho' he had promised me, he w^{d} not communicate my prospects of the probability of that event to anyone. Such is his honour; such his unerring purpose to take every chance of converting even the hopes of his acquaintances, to his own interest—On the whole I should be well pleased with this last liberty he has taken with me, if it should hereafter make a part of that basis, on which I shall endeavour to ground his efforts to arrange my present pecuniary demands upon him.—It is quite unaccountable how he has disposed of all the cash he raised in Kentucky, last year: Jourdan has convinced me, that he B. received thro' his hands, at Lexington, not less than $40,000 of which he never advanced more than—$15,000 to all his agents and associates: to say nothing of all the property he has procured upon his Dfts. He could since have spent but little money; having received much fr. the U^{d} St^{s} and having been in custody till very lately.—I shall tomorrow, endeavour to investigate the further intents of Gov^{t} upon me.——

Wash^{n} City. Wedn. 8^{r} 28.07.—

I have this morning written by Martin to Rodney the U^{d} States Att^{y} General to request him to inform me officially whether Gov^{t} is *now* disposed to prosecute me any further in conformity with the late adjudication of the Ch. Justice, or will finally discharge me as has been done I hear, in the case of Tyler, or will dispense with my personal appearance at Chillicothe 'till the Septr session of the C^{t} there, as Gov^{t} cannot probably be prepared to prosecute at the next January term, and in the mean time the occasions of my family, and the serious demands of my private affairs demand my presence at

Natchez. I am very anxious to receive an answer before dinner, —in which I much fear I shall not be gratified, thro' my friend M.'s more indispensible devotion to his libations. I shall however note the result, I hope, to night.—But I can not; for I have been disappointed; tho' I spent a dollar in coach-hire to go with Martin this evening in quest of Rodney, we c.d not see him, as he was not returned fr. the President's where he dined.—Poor Martin I find is very incontinent of every thing w.ch ordinary discretion should not disclose, where there is no injunction in terms of secrecy.—He assured me to day, he is prepared to sacrifice $10,000 for Burr, if the collateral security of Pollock sh.d fail; that it will be nothing more than diminishing a provision of so much he had made by will, for his 3 daughters; which he had originally destined for a Miss Thompson, now M.rs Livingston to whom he gave an allowance of $600. a year for 6 or 7 years, and whom he saved fr. the arts of a seducer. But her husband is now, richer than himself.—However let the worst happen, he added, he had signed blank bonds which he left to be—filled up by the Attorneys employed ag.t Burr, and such bonds, he says are void by late decisions of the English courts adopted by the Courts here.—This w.d seem inconsistent with the warm spirit of integrity which seems to breathe [*Blot*] in all his thoughts and actions. And he declared accordingly, he would not take advantage of the circumstance.—I also find his idolatrous adoration of M.rs Alston is almost as excessive as my own but far more beneficial to his interest and injurious to his judgment as it is the medium of his blind attachment to her father whose secrets and views past, present, or to come, he is, and wishes to remain ignorant of. Nor can he see a speck in the character or conduct of Alston, for the best of all reasons with him, namely that Alston has such a wife.—This misled city, has certainly no resemblance to any other upon earth. Its extent as originally laid out has been known for some years past upon paper. But a few of its singular features, as they now smile or frown upon the Potowmac are remarkable. As to streets literally speaking there is not 1. yet in existence, unless the few wide paths and half-made roads that intersect each other can be called streets. On a Hill at the head of 1. of these about a mile fr. the river, stand the 2 wings without the body, of what is to constitute, but is already called the Capitol—they are cumbrous, ill-proportioned piles of buildings to my eyes with too small a space for the central building if it shall ever be reared. About another mile's distance to the westward stands the President's House with a low dead-wall in front and an ordinary post and rail fence, in the rear of it. On either side of it stands what are called its wings, which any person would require to be told were such, before he could believe it: for they are of brick and at too great a distance to appear to belong to the large white house between them any more than to the Capitol. They are each a row of ordinary brick houses. In those to the west is kept the post-Office. In those to the East, the Secretary of State's Office, etc. And both it is said are to be connected with the centre by a *garden*. But this last feature of American architecture has not yet—made its appearance. From what I suppose might be called the mons Capitolinus you behold, in four or five different directions at the distance of fr. 1 to 4 miles apart rows of houses each of 5. or 6 together: so that the whole appears like a grotesque jumble of fragments of villages, except that part being about 1½ mile N.E. of the Capitol where the Navy yard is *said* to stand, which is more built than any other quarter of the city. But after all every foreigner after his arrival here will inquire for 50 years to come, as is now very common "where is the City of Washington?"—Martin visited Rob. Smith this ev^{g} where he heard Wilk^{n} extolled and Burr as heavily denounced, as if he had not yet been tried. M^{r} & M^{rs} Sm. declared Gov^{t} had abundant proofs ag^{t} B^{r} which they c^{d} not produce fr. confidential restrictions. Martin before he left them convinced himself they w^{d} gladly dispense wth his visit.—

Wash^{n} City Thurs. 8^{r} 29.07—

I went this morning, with Martin in a carriage to visit Rodney before breakfast. R. is a trifling negative character from whose manner I c^{d} at once perceive he had yesterday, spoken to Jefferson of my arrival here. He abruptly told us Gov^{t}— meant to proceed ag^{t} us; on which he was received with a volley of abuse by Martin, who thanked his God for the news, as Gov^{t} w^{d} thereby hasten the consummation of their own infamy. R. seemed surprised to learn fr. us that not a single witness had as yet been bound or summoned to appear in Ohio. I told him as my call upon him was in his official character—I w^{d} leave him the letter I had yesterday written to him, which he promised he w^{d} and did answer, this ev^{g} by three or four lines—saying "he could only observe, *at present* that I w^{d} be bound to attend, persuant to the recognizance I entered into at Richmond." So this fellow is also trained to tease if he cannot injure, the infidels who worship not the Divinity of the immortal Jefferson. But this sniveller shall not have even a nitch amongst the worthies of the present admin^{n}——Martin has solemnly pledged himself to meet Gov^{t} at the sitting of the C^{t} in Jany in Ohio to see things are conducted regularly so far as may concern Burr and me, whether we personally appear there or not. He has found out fr. Robt Smith that Jefferson has no thoughts of war with Britain of which he has so much affected the contrary. For he will never act as he speaks or writes: he will always counteract his political professions by his back-stairs committees 'till Jack Randolph shall finally severe him fr. them. Burr I hear, is arrived at Georgetown 3 miles fr. hence, up the river. If so he will probably be of our party, in the stage tomorrow to Balt^{o} We set off at 5. in the morning. Several Northern members of Congress whose names I know not have had the curiosity or politeness to visit us. Fr. 1. of them I was truly concerned to learn the death of Mr Hunt, which happened last July, as he himself predicted, on his new purchase at French-Grant on Ohio. This place has been extremely tiresome to me. The Taverns are very dear, and badly kept. So that I shall leave it with pleasure.—I wrote to day to my Landlord Walton, Jno. Banks & my wife, to gratify as far as I could, all their cares and solicitude for my fortune and destinies. To all I acknowledged that tribute I so justly owe to Martin, who with better breeding and a redemption fr. his habits of inebriety, w^{d} be a perfect character. His heart is truly overflowing with the purest milk of benevolence. His potations may sometimes coagulate but they will never acidify the fluid with which it is so well replenished. May it never be wasted on the unworthy.—m. night.—

Wash^{n} City 8^{r} 30.07—

Rose before 5 this morning, but as the coach then drove up with a cargo of 11 passengers—I have been detained here another day. I have borne the ennui with which I have spent it with such patience that I w^{d} not walk 50 yards fr. the Tavern to visit the Hall of Congress or observe how they ballot there for their officers or their committees. Tho' I certainly should have gone so far to hear a debate, had there been any.-The election of officers reminds me of a curious Republican caper at Richmond last winter, which as it was of a negative nature, cannot be recorded in that State, but should be known every where else, to convict it of indecent conduct if not of impiety. It was nothing more than a "remembering to forget," on the part of the Legislature, I beg pardon, I mean the House of Delegates, during the whole Session, of the immemorial custom to appoint—a chaplain.—Burr I hear again is somewhere in this city. But I no more depend upon his appearance than on that of a new Comet. We start tomorrow. m. night.

Baltimore Sund^{y} Novr 1st. 07.—

Before I mention my having arrived here at last, I shall note the generosity of my Barber at Washington who reluctantly received 3/4 of a dollar fr. me, because I observed to him I sh^{d} give him more than his charge, if I was not rather poor at present. And he evinced his sincerity by assuring me he had $100 at my service, which he requested me to accept—How is this to be accounted for? Devereux, Hendren, O'Hennessy and Butler will all exclaim, he was an Irish-man. He is so: his name is Dixon, and it shall ever remain recorded in the duties of my gratitude.

Yesterday Martin and myself were wedged in amongst 10 other passengers in the coach. A Mr. Blount, brother of the late Governor of Tennessee was of the number. He is an infuriated Democrat, was at the Battle of German-town, and ordered the aim of the Rifleman who shot General Agnew in that affair.—I saw Tyler on alighting from the coach, who showed me his discharge in the hand-writing of Rodney, whom he declares he has not seen, having received it fr. Captain Pike, who escorted him to Washington City. T. denies his having made any deposition agt. me anywhere; and *professes* his friendship and attachment to Burr, whom he is very anxious to see before he sets out for N. York with Sam. Swartwout. To day I left my cards at Pringle's and the Gilmore's. Of these families I only saw Mrs. Wm. G. who seemed glad to see me. I have a little curiosity to collect in my fallen fortune as many exceptions as I can establish to the general condemnation of mankind pronounced upon them by the adversity of individuals. I breakfasted with Martin and shall dine with him tomorrow, as well as all the Burrites in town. Burr, I hear, again was last night, at Georgetown. His appearance here is a matter of curiosity with his enemies, as of interest with his friends.—But the elements of his orbit, I repeat are as unsettled as those of a new Comet. Martin thinks he might have been detained to raise money enough to pay his tavern bills, etc. whilst Cummins says Burr assured him he shd. suffer no detention on that account. So it uniformly turns out, that no 2 persons of his acquaintance will ever understand him alike, and yet all who still adhere to him, profess a unity of confidence in him.—Cummins has bro't on a fever by his debaucheries. I shall stay here at least 'till Wednesday. 11 p.m.—

Baltimore Mond. Nov. 2. 1807.—

I spent the principal part of the morning with Martin, reading the papers and conversing with various visitors he received.—The news we deemed worthy of most notice before dinner was that of two arrivals in town viz Wilkinson's baggage preparatory to his taking up his quarters at Fort Mc Henry near this city; and Burr's appearance at the French Hotel in Gay-Street. So the Brigadier as I expected, will probably never revisit the Mississippi in his present command; nor probably long retain it here, notwithstanding all the control he may possess over the imbecile heart of Jefferson, and tho' he boasted not long since at Richmond that he w^{d} be at Natchez in 30 D^{ys}—Burr will probably show himself as little as possible to the public. He has therefore sneaked into obscure quarters; tho' Steward, who now manages this house, since Evans's death, declared he w^{d} accommodate Col: Burr and his friends, with as much attention in their adversity, as he could have done in the days of their better fortune. The expression of this sentiment was drawn fr. him on the occasion of some liberal Democrats threatening to quit the house if we were received into it. I dined with Martin who had a select party, tho' he left out 2 Burrites—viz Tyler and Luckett—Burr called upon Martin for a few moments, before dinner. He returned in the evening, and had a long conference with Tyler, in an adjoining room during which the attention of our party in the dining-room was called forth to receive at the windows, some public honour offered us fr. the street. A desperate democratic printer commanding a company of one of the city regiments: whose name is Frailey, drew up his men under the windows, and there halted, whilst his fife and drum played the Rogue's march for us, then gave 3 cheers and marched off.—This salutation has proposed fresh fuel to keep up the blaze of Martin's wrath against all his opponents.—Burr, on his return with Tyler, to us, said, these excesses of indecency always recoil on those who enter into them; and he soon after withdrew—not evidently indifferent to such manifestation of the public regards; which however I am sure Martin will make his own use of with good effect ag^{t} Wright the Govr of Maryland whom M. first brought into notice, which the Governor no longer remembers. I left soon after, that is about 8. p.m. but did not go to bed till

11. o'clock, after I had a long conversation with Tyler who I find has long since taken up all my impressions of Burr, and will spare no labour to infuse his opinions into the prejudices of Colonel Swartwout, whom he has no doubt he will induce to adopt his sentiments.—

Tuesday Novr 3.07.—

Having accidently met Hayden the Dentist this morning who mentioned to me the late arrival, at the Academy, of a grand Electrical machine—I could not suppress my wishes to see it.—Hayden obligingly offered to walk there with me which I accepted. He introduced me to the Principal of the Seminary, a Mr du Barry, who received me very politely, and presented to me a Mr Paguet who took upon him the exhibition of the powers of the machine.—This was a superb plate of 46. French Inches diameter with a conductor forming three sides of a parallelogram, one of them in front of and parallel to the plate; the 2 others perpendicular to it. The machine with 2 turns of the plate gave sparks 12 inches long, and charged a Battery about 15 feet of coated glas in 10 turns which killed a duck.—On my return fr. the Seminary I repaired to Martin's; where 1. of his students informed me he expected a mob would this evening attack the house and offer violence to Mr Martin, Col: Burr & myself of which notice had been given by hand-bills which had been circulated thro' the town. Martin was not at home. I eagerly caught a view of one of the bills which is in these words.—

[*centered*] "Awful!!!—

The public are hereby, notified that four 'choice spirits,' are this afternoon, at 3 o'clock to be marshalled for execution by the Hang-man, on Gallows-hill, in consequence of the sentence pronounced against them by the unanimous voice of every honest man in the community.—The respective crimes for which they suffer, are thus stated on the record.—1st Ch. Justice M....... for a repetition of his X.Y.Z. Tricks: which are said to be much aggravated by his *felonious* capers, in open C^t on the plea of irrelevancy. 2d His Quid Majesty, charged with the trifling fault of wishing to divide the Union, and farm *Baron* Bastrop's grant. 3d Blennerhasset the Chemist, convicted of conspiring to destroy the tone of the public Fiddle.—4th and last, but not least in crime, *Lawyer* Brandy-bottle, for a false scandalous, malicious Prophecy, that, before 6 months, 'Aaron Burr would divide the Union.'—N.B. The execution of accomplices is postponed to a future day."—My first inquiries of the few acquaintances I met in the streets, who *now* know me, were directed by a desire to acquire some estimate of what we might expect in the evening; but I obtained little satisfaction. I then thought Burr might be best informed, as his vigilance I had before proved, tho' lively at all times, was most sharp on the approach of danger. I know not whether Tyler had smelt out what was brewing, before I had heard anything about it.—But I found, on my return fr. the seminary, before I had heard the news—he had fled, rather precipitately: for he had declared to me, not two hours before I last went to seek him that he shd not go away 'till tomorrow. I therefore bent my course straight to Burr at his shabby quarters in *Gay Street*; where I waited full 15 minutes before I could see him. I afterwards found he was packing up his things to escape in the Mail, which was to leave in 10 minutes. He laboured hard within, I could plainly see, to exhibit that composure of manner, to wch he has devoted so much of his life, to form his exterior by. He would not wait to write the superscription of a letter, which he requested me to direct for him to David M. Randolph. I bid him adieu, with an assurance that I wd follow him tomorrow. And he said I shd find him at Gardetter in Philada On my return to Evans's, I found Martin, Luckett and Cummins in my bed-room. M. defied the menaces of the mob, but he assured me he had just left the Mayor, who had promised him to make all necessary arrangements to secure the peace of the city, and protect everyone fr. personal injury.—Luckett, having come by a different *way* fr. that I took, tho' I was walking the streets in every direction all the morning—told me Burr and Swartwout had been escorted by a guard sent them, by the Mayor, fr. their lodgings to the Stage-Office, fr. whence he had seen them *start* under the good wishes of many spectators.—Cummins denounced the Gov.t and its rabble, and said it was impossible anything sh.d be attempted ag.t us. But I thought otherwise.—I deliberated a little on the various reports I had heard, however differing in particulars, yet all agreeing, that Martin and myself should at least receive an addition to our wardrobes of a suit of tar and feathers. I thought it w.d not be improper to leave town or at least change my lodgings forthwith. But I soon reflected how naturally Burr might expect to receive unwelcome obliquy for his flight, and I at once determin.d to *keep my* ground. At dinner therefore, I took my seat amidst a very large company at the long table, and remained there conversing a long time, with a French-man who sat next to me; at least half an hour after 3 o'clock, the time designated in the hand-bill, for the *spectacle* that was to take place in the evening.—I should have sat I know not how much longer, had not Steward, who manages the house, brought a man up to me, who inquired my name.—On giving it to him, he said he belonged to the police of the city, and had been sent with several others of that body to watch and give notice of any attempt upon, the public peace, or on the persons of individuals: that the mayor had particularly mentioned me to him by name, which I believed as he said M.r Thoroughgood Smith observed to him, that he had *formerly* known me and my lady here.—I took this man out. His name is Goldsmith; I then ordered liquor for him and his companions in another room—where I thanked them for the service they, in the way of their duty, were come to render me. They informed me, 2 troops of Horse were ordered out, and I had nothing to fear. The time passed away in conversation with these men, about 12 in number, 'till near 5 o'clock—when I sent Goldsmith to request Martin to come to me, as I wished to share his fate, having understood fr. them—that I ought not to go out of the house, which I interpreted into something like a wish, on the p.t of the Mayor. Soon after I returned to my room to write, Goldsmith returned to me with intelligence that Martin could not be seen at his house: that his students and some friends were armed and well prepared to repel an expected assault on the house: but that the mob (I beg pardon) he said the people, were in motion in gr^{t} force, had everything prepared for tarring and feathering, and would he believed, if disappointed or opposed, tear Martin and myself to pieces. He then begged of me not to leave the room I was in, adding, that his companions would drown him, if they could, in a basin of water, for his attention to me, tho' he was as good a *republican* as any of them.—etc. I now suspected that this man might possibly direct the drunken desperadoes of an enraged multitude to my apartment. I therefore determined to change it for another, the moment he left me. In a few minutes Steward came up stairs, and told me to go up into the garret, which I soon did, under an apprehension, that I was betrayed or sought-after. In the garret I observed 2 trap-doors opening thro' the roof of the house, on which I resolved to take my station, fr. whence I might contemplate at my leisure, if I could not distinctly see the scene that might shortly pass in the streets below. Both the trap doors were open. I shut down 1. of them; and intended to cut off my return into the house, by shutting the other when it sh^{d} become necessary.—But an uproar soon rose to my ears fr. below, and fr. 1. of the garret-windows, I saw the mob pass by the house, to the amount of about 1500 as well as I c^{d} estimate, in full huzza, with fife and drum-playing the rogue's march. I have since heard they drew along with them in two carts, the representatives, habited for execution, of the Ch. Just., Burr, Martin and myself. They passed on to Martin's house in Charles St. where they broke some of his windows, and performed some other feats of which I have not yet learned the particulars. In the mean time the troops of cavalry patroled the streets, not to disperse the mob, but to follow—and behold their conduct. But an American mob is as tame as it is unwieldy or immaleable. The mob made as much noise as if they were about to destroy the city—and returned about 7 o'clock, to the Point, fr. whence they came, headed I hear, by one Patterson who lives there, whilst the cavalry have I suppose, been long dismissed, in full confidence in the honour of the Mob-ility; I have been down stairs to supper at the long-table. It is now 10 o'clock, and I have not these 2 hours, heard any more of either of them.—How far the respectable part of the city will think it worth their while to show they had no participation in this frolic, which I am informed, was chiefly made up at the Point—we shall hereafter learn. I believe it altogether originated with the Democratic printers here, who are but little controlled by one spiritless federal paper, which is all there is at present on that side; whilst there are 3 or more federal prints supported in Phila.[da] where I have no expectation of receiving similar public honours to those conferred upon me here. Wrote to Natchez to counteract by anticipation the alarms my friends there, might take up for my safety fr. the rapid circulation of rumours, etc. then went to bed.

Wednesday 4.th Nov.[r]

Went early this morning to Martin's, where I saw M.[r] Ray, a warm friend to him, who had taken last night, the direction of the Gentlemen who had volunteered to defend the house. M. and his property I found were untouched last night, the sovereign people having contented themselves with menaces and abuse, offering a defiance to the party within and the cavalry without. Fr. whence I conclude that the Mayor was intimidated by them, and a large majority of the 2 Troops of Horse, well disposed to their views of their leaders, viz one Biays and others fr. the Point. Martin did not appear to his friends, 'till this morning. I took leave of him, on my way to the Packet, by which I set out for Phila.[da], where I arrived with no occurence during the journey, on Thursday the 5.th of Nov.[r] at 3 o'clock. p.m. Put up at the mansion-house late Bingham's kept by an Englishman in the best stile I ever saw in America. Dined, dressed and visited Burr and my worthy friends M.[r] & M.[rs] Jos. I. Lewis. Burr pretended he sh.[d] have waited if he had not believed everything at Baltimore w.[d] have ended with the Handbills. He was very glad to hear of Martin's having so well escaped, and said he w^{d} give Bollman, who boarded where I did, a letter of introduction to me. I observed to him that probably Doct^{r} B. did not wish my acquaintance, as he had never called upon me in Richmond.—B. tried to excuse this but failed.—He is trying to live here in cog., but every one knows he is in town. I supped with M^{r} & Mrs Lewis, en famille where my friendly reception, kind inquires and the interesting conversation of my amiable friends agreeably detained me 'till midnight, when I took leave with a promise to dine with them to morrow——(continued in another book).—[*No entry for Thursday, Nov. 5*]

[*Blank page*]
[*Top center of following page:*]

Journal commencing
Friday Novr 6th
1807—

[*Blank page*]
[*Begins top of following page:*]
Phila^{da} Frid^{y} Novr 6. 1807.—

Spent the morning chiefly in examining the News-papers and visits to the Lewises, Conrad, Caldeburgh and Turnbull's; as my friend Joe Lewis's family dinner hour is 3 o'clock.—Before I went there I had a call fr. Reeve Lewis to bring me a letter fr. Walton of no importance and engage me to dinner with him tomorrow.—Passed the evening sociably têt à tête with Joe. during which I was chiefly occupied in conversation with him on the subject of Burr's trials and adventures, and also that of my present financial derangements. About 7 p.m. we were called to the street by an alarm of fire, which turned out to be groundless, and I saw him back to his own house, where I then left him to return to my lodgings, as I had a severe head-ach.—Before I went to bed I observed that the American, a democrat paper of Balt^{o} contained an insidious paragraph approving of the insults offered to us there last tuesday ev^{g}—Bollman has left his card for me with a letter of introduc^{n} fr. Burr.

Phila^{da} Sat^{y} Novr 7.07.—

At Breakfast, this morning, Bollman presented himself to me upon his credentials, and I received him into my acquaintance in all the ease of courtly-etiquette I am master of—I invited him to take a seat by me, and entered into a conversation with him on general topics which was sustained for half an hour, and succeeded by his obliging one with his view of the Mississippi country, and particularly, the environs of N. Orleans, for which he entertains a decided preference to any other quarter—and projects—probably without the command of a dollar nothing less than the purchase of an estate at $60,000 within five miles of that city. Dan. Clark has assured him it is a great bargain, as it will yield a revenue of $15,000 a year by adding a few slaves to those already on it: and Boll^{n} wants a friend or two to join with $10,000 each, and he can effect the rest.—I have little doubt B^{n} has conceived I may be of use to him in this affair. But I am certain, he can not serve me in it—Mrs Dav. Randolph had no small trial of her skill in detecting this man's character, if her judgment has not erred in the attempt. For his countenance, manner, and address possess every qualification to engage the warmest interest in his favour as a scholar and a gentleman or perhaps a gallant. Yet has he formerly failed in this town as a merchant, rather thro' his excesses in speculation and intrigue than fr. any natural ineptitude to that sort of life. And his late wife's family discovered enough in him to determine them to oppose his connection with the N[*****] family as far as was possible. But I will, at present let him rest.—I dined and spent the early part of the evening with Reeve Lewis, in the same way I did yesterday with his brother, i.e. in the enjoyment of good wines and friendly conversation. I must however partake of no more of these early dinners, as the long sittings that succeed them, leave no time these short days to transact whatever business may yet detain me here.—Duane has announced the arrival of "Admiral" Blennerhassett at the Mansion-house and republished fr. the Balt^{o} Whig, its invitation to invest us with a suit of "Yankee Ermine," as well as the process-verbal of the Mobility of that city. But I shall visit this Apostle of Democracy on monday.—

Phila^{da} Sund. 9^{r} 8.07.—

Visited this morning by Tom. Butler who made me very happy by learning fr. him my beloved wife had quite recovered fr. her fever and she and the Boys were well after the middle of last 7^{ber} when he saw them; that is fr. 10 to 15 days after the date of her last letter to me of the 11th of 7^{ber} Whilst I was attending the service at the Roman Catholic, chapel in 4th Str. I had the honour of morning visits from sundry great personages who left their cards for me. viz. Burr, Bollman, & George Pollock reputed to be very rich—whose education I have heard, Burr has had some concern with, and at whose house here, he has taken up his quarters. After my return fr. Mass, I was visited by a Mr Reckless of New Jersey, who seems a warm partizan of Burr, and is engaged in endeavouring to do away an Indict^{t} pending in that State ag^{t} Burr for the killing of Genl Hamilton.—Upon the removal of this impediment, I find Burr means to try the effect of requisitions upon a considerable party, he considers attached to him in that quarter.—Mr. R. treated me with much consideration—and said, whilst I was abroad some members of the Jersey Legislature had come with him to wait upon me.—I find indeed the greater part of the numerous strangers, who frequent the mansion house regard me with no common attention.—I form acquaintances amongst them without previous introductions, whilst in the house, I am thus distinguished, I am not less recognized or respected thro' the streets and in the shops.—But this is more to be attributed to the sinking of democracy here into the coalition of Feds. and Quids, which has nearly annihilated the faction of Duane, than to any claim I could have upon public favour, fr. the merit of my acts or the singularity of my fortune.—I have, amongst others, met here with a Mr Bee fr. Charleston S.Ca who has travelled much and has embellished good talents with much accomplishment.

Philada Mond. 9ber 9.07.—

Conversed for half an hour after breakfast with Bollman, chiefly upon medical and physiological subjects, in which I was much pleased with some novelty of fancy, recommended by that suavity of manner and easy address which endanger the judgment of those who [*Blot at rt. edge.*] listen to him.—On generation, however, whilst he invaded the systems of others I found his own altogether unsupported by a sufficient basis of anatomical knowledge. I had invitations from Pollock and Joe Lewis for dinner tomorrow—Dined with Turnbull, spent part of the evening with Tom. Butler and supped with Joe Lewis en famille where I sat 'till midnight.

Tues. Novr 10.07.—

Soon after breakfast visited Burr and Pollock. Burr has again opened an audience chamber, which is much occupied.—Altho' I found 2. or 3 friends with him at breakfast; he was called out the moment he had breakfasted, and was absent about 1 3/4 hour; during which interval Mr Pollock gave me his company.—I find him a very well bred man, who has had advantages in Europe.—He spoke less of Mrs Alston than I expected—and has never seen her husband whose various talents however, he does not the less correctly estimate. With respect to Burr, whatever may have been the ground of his present intimacy with Mr P. I can venture to affirm, it has already been abused, on the part of the former, altho' the latter as yet, is evidently unaware of it.—Upon B's return P. withdrew, and I entered upon the objects of my visit—After informing Burr that Martin was resolved to appear for us at Chilicothe, he seemed all surprise and nothing could be more natural than the collision of such generosity with his own ingratitude. [*Blotted at rt. edge.*] For he fled fr. Balt^{o} with^{t} waiting even to thank his friend for the long and various services he had rendered him. Further he had not yet written to him from hence. On recovering fr. this new charge of Martin's benevolence upon his feelings, he exclaimed, "what a man," but told me I must write to him not to think of the journey 'till he should hear fr. him: that I sh^{d} direct him in the mean time to write to Burnet and Michael Baldwin the late Marshal of Ohio, to *retain* both, no doubt with Martin's advance of their fees, & that he still had no thoughts of going to Ohio, tho' he had given Notice to Scott, the Virginia Marshal to be prepared with a guard of gentlemen, by the 10th of Decr at Richmond, to conduct him fr. thence to Chilicothe. He added that Martin's too gr. zeal and indiscretion w^{d} do us great mischief in Ohio and, the skill of Burnet with the influence of Baldwin, who was popular with the blackguards, & exasperated ag^{t} the Adm^{n} since the loss of his office—were the best means to frustrate the efforts of Gov^{t} to have bills found ag^{t} us—which they w^{d} exert themselves to effect to divert his attention fr. other objects.—He now again assured me he w^{d} be glad if I could extricate myself fr. the Gov^{t} upon any terms agreeable to my own feelings: and fully approved of my effecting that object thro' Duane, in any way my judgm^{t} might suggest.—This business being thus dispatched I next solicited him on the subject of his finances, on which indeed, he had partly anticipated me, by inquiring "what were my prospects thro' my friends, the Lewises?" I informed him I had no expectations in that quarter, and sh^{d} absolutely starve whilst I was possessed of such splendid hopes in Europe if I was not relieved in the mean time. He regretted much the absence fr. town, of 2 persons with whom he expected to do something; but he had he said, negotiations on foot, the success of which he c^{d} not answer for, but sh^{d} know in 2 or 3 days. I now represented to him the probable necessity I c^{d} not resist, of urging Alston; but hoped such a measure w^{d} not be displeasing to him or to Mrs Alst. Upon this suggestion he was less reserved than he had been with me at Rich^{d} before he was acquainted with my pecuniary views and my means of advancing him in Europe; and freely declared, neither Mrs Alst. nor himself would be displeased with any steps I might take ag^{t} Alst. who had treated him in a manner I could well enough judge of, to save him the mortification of expressing his opinion of it. He even assured me he had demanded fr. Alston an explanation of his conduct in addressing the letter to Pinkney, immediately on his arrival in custody at Richmond—observing "that no humiliation of his condition could make him forget what he owed to his own dignity": that Alst. had shown much contrition, and made every possible concession, including even an offer of a public recantation in print. But Burr said he thought it w^{d} be prudent to spare him this extreme of humiliation (I suppose for his daughter's sake).—By the bye, it is remarkable that many persons of penetration and intelligence who have indulged an eager interest in investigating every thing during the last year, relating to Burr, within the reach of their inquiries, should have pretermitted that irredeemable passage of Alston's letter imputing to Burr a design to deprive his infant grandson of his patrimony.—Before B^{r} returned fr. the audience chamber, I found that Mr. P. had made a like omission, and upon my acquainting him with the circumstances—he expressed his feelings suitably, of the confounded folly and turpitude of the writer who had long before repeated to me assurances he had given his father-in law, that his property—was worth 100,000 guineas and he would, if necessary, embark the whole of it in the furtherance of Col: Burr's plans.—I did not leave B. 'till he had again reminded me of his hopes of my forwarding his views in England. To which I answered I could only lend my endeavours to serve him by the letters I had already offered him. He said it was to those only, he alluded.—So the baits I have thrown out to him, do not yet glitter in vain, which further appeared, by his observing to the party present, when I first called upon him, that he supposed, I had not yet taken the trouble to find out whether a certain man was dead or alive upon whose death I sh^{d} be entitled to a fortune worth at least 100,000 guineas, adding I had always a strange kind of indifference to objects few other men could resist. This was truly well thrown out for Pollock, etc.—But I was not a little amused to observe that he had been calculating how many yrs. purchase my expected estate of £6,000 a year w.[d] sell for. So that whilst this bait glitters, he will not lightly break fr. me.—Dined and spent the evening with a set party, at Joe Lewis's. I have found it due to so worthy a friend to offer him perusal of these notes, as I hope they will more fully devellope to him my character and necessities, than he could otherwise be acquainted with either; and I look to his aid and counsel rather than to any other present means, to lighten the actual burdens that bear so heavily upon my family. He has perused the first vol. with so much interest and satisfaction, that he has given it a second reading. This alone w.[d] be ample compensation for the little labour I have spent upon it. I feel I have penned many reflections, and passed many characters with my own, in review, in a light which should be admitted to few eyes, besides those of my wife. But I fully rely upon the safe-keeping of the confidence I have ventured with my friend, who will therefrom be enabled to take a better view of my sufferings and necessities.—I have lost some time in visiting Duane, which I shall not effect before thursday.—There are 2 excellent papers here lately set up ag.[t] him, viz the Spirit of the Press, and the Tickler, which would be perfect, if they were not too local.—

Phila.[da] Wedn. Nov. 11.07.—

Soon after Breakfast I was called by Note to Lewis's Counting house to meet Bartlet, the partner of Tom. Hart of Lexington, who kept me waiting there for him the best part of the morning,—but at last arrived and paid me $832. being so much saved out of my losses by Hart in 1805.—Dined with a formal party at my friend Reeve Lewis's; where I sat with a pleasant set after dinner 'till 11 o'clock, and rec'd an invitation to dinner fr. M.[r] Tightman, an amiable and convivial y.[g] merchant of this city and son of the Judge of that name. Reeve let freely loose the flow of soul and of wine. He is an excellent mimic and truly comic character, and might, if he had not a far better calling, easily[4] excell upon the stage.

Phila.[da] Thurs. Nov. 12.07.—

Occupied this morning chiefly by reading the papers, particularly a London Courier containing an excellent speech of Sheridan or rather only a skeleton of it on Irish affairs. This paper, Mr. Bee was kind enough to procure for me without solicitation on my part.—Till Dinner time I passed the remr. of the morning in walking, and buying a few articles for my wife.—Burr has taken an excursion of about 20 miles up the Delawar to return—I expect, on Saturday, when I propose, in the event of his being still out of cash, to make my last demand upon him so long projected: viz a requisition to him, to procure security to which my family can resort, in this country, for my claims upon him, to the amount of about $9,000. made up by my acct. already presented to him, and the debt and charges arising fr. Miller's demand—The mercantile folks, (that is, everybody) are much alarmed with the news of to day, threatening a speedy war with Britain. And I have heard it said, that shares in some of the Insurance stocks have fallen to day 10 p.ct But I observe the successful energies of my native country agt. Copenhagen, have petrifying effect upon the Democrats, whilst 19/20 of the merchants who are federal awfully contemplate the approaching crisis with England.—This evening I conceived a novel remedy for a sharp tooth-ach with which I was affected. It was grounded on the principle, that great mental engagement and exertion would operate a diversion of inordinate action expended upon a small diseased portion of the body. I attempted to put this fancy to the test, by effecting my too long neglected interview with Duane.—After tea, I set out upon this adventure, and arrived at his dwelling in much pain, 8. p.m. I think it deserves notice that I sh.d mention—because my feelings were singularly affected by, the preparation I found I had to undergo, to obtain not only an audience of this high priest of Jacobinism, but even admission within the walls that contained his Holiness. I had pulled the Bell three times—with[t] producing the common effect of bringing any one to the door fr. within-and was in the act of applying my hand to a fourth experiment when a man answered fr. without (an Irishman). He inquired my name, in a full Cork accent but very low voice: and on hearing it, said M[r] D. was not at home, but if I w[d] leave my name and business he w[d] mention it to him. I said I sh[d] suppose my name was now become familiar enough with everyone in the employment of M[r] D. to render my leaving it in writing, unnecessary. The printer's devil replied "to be sure every one knew M[r] *Hassett*, and M[r] D. w[d] be glad to see him." Whilst this conversation was passing, Duane, who had been listening in the alley, adjoining the house came forward, without his hat on: for he had passed fr. the rear of the house, into the alley to spy secretly the chances of safety as he could ascertain them by observing what he could see or hear between me and his scout. The Colonel has been further—seasoned [5] to the service of his party, of which he now begins to feel a little tired by two drubbings, since his return fr. Richmond. And as he rises in military rank and suffers in service, he grows more wary in caution, and has learned fr. experience the folly of exposing his person by night, without full assurance of the peaceful intentions of his visitor. All scruples of this sort, being removed up on the present occasion, I apologised for the unusual hour, I had fallen upon for my visit, which had seemingly broken in upon the Col: whilst he was engaged with business or with company, as he had been denied to me tho' I was fortunate enough to find him at home: To this I received some blundering answer; the scout withdrew, and I was invited into the house; where I was introduced to M[rs] Duane. In a few minutes I signified a desire to speak with the Colonel in private; upon this suggestion he took up a candle, and I followed him up stairs. I opened the interview, by informing him that I could not leave town without calling to thank him for the visit and friendly offers I had received fr. him, during my imprisonment in Richmond: that I felt disposed to regard his motives to that visit as distinct fr. considerations of party or politics, the mere dictates of national feelings, and the natural impulse of an Irishman to serve a suffering country-man, in distress: that besides this motive to my visit, I felt much curiosity and some personal interest to learn, how far he approved of the determination of Gov^{t} to pursue me with further indefinite prosecutions, which could add nothing in their result to the public interest or the credit of the admin^{n} however they might diminish or ruin my fortune: that altho' it might be deemed politic to keep Col. Burr busy by such vexations, Gov^{t} could apprehend nothing fr. me; and at all events I was sure he Col: D. could not approve of the vindictive spirit that had even refused to dispense, with my personal appearance, at Chilicothe next January, when Gov^{t} can not be prepared to go to trial—much less shall I. Then reminding him of the offers he had made me, at Richmond—I said my situation at present was very different as it regarded my connection with Col: Burr fr. what it was at that time. For I now regarded myself as cleared fr. all charge that the Gov^{t} had failed to establish against me; and no longer felt it incumbent upon me to undergo endless prosecutions to vindicate whatever concern I had in Col: B's speculations, especially, as he probably, will never renew them; and if he could, I sh^{d} have no further concern in them—I had no need to sound any deeper in the shallow waters of my research wch by no means possess that depth that is commonly supposed. Burr had advised me that this fellow loved wonderfully to hear himself talk, and that the best way was to let him run on 'till he was out of breath, and afterwards, to take him back to those points on which he had stumbled and on which I wished to fasten his attention. The hint was serviceable and I made more use of it than I might have done if I had depended upon the reserve Duane affected on his visit to me in the Penitentiary, which I now see arose fr. a discovery he soon made, on that occasion—tho' he durst not broach the unhallowed purpose for which he then visited me, which was a bargain, to induce me to betray my engagements or connexions.—Whilst on the present occasion, he considered me, rather as a politician assailing his interest underhand, than suitor soliciting his good offices.—I concluded my observations with stating, that I had understood Col: Burr meant again to surrender himself into custody of the Marshal of Virginia, with intent to be conveyed fr. Richmond, about the 10th of next month, to Chilicothe, at the public expense; and if I sh^{d} not soon discover that Gov^{t} w^{d} decline further proceedings ag^{t} me, I sh^{d} immediately commence the expenditure of so much of the public money as the law w^{d} allow me towards the charges of my defence, which had not hitherto cost the U.St^{s} a dollar.—But I wished him to be assured it was not my purpose to ask any favours fr. Gov^{t} at any time or thro' any quarters whatever: my chief object in making him this present visit, being to learn as far as I could thro' him whether the Adm^{n} preserved still a spirit of hostility to me personally?—He now launched out into abuse of Burr and Marshall and said the Gov^{t} were committed with the sentiments of the majority of the people, who would never be satisfied without our conviction on such full evidence as had come out, particularly that of Wilkinson, Dunbaugh and the Hendersons.—That it would look like *persecution* of Burr to grant me any forbearance; and that the ch. Justice must attone for his conduct, to the country. Luther Martin he declared had lately done Burr more harm than his enemies could have wished in the public sentiment by his silly and intemperate publications. Wilkinson, he acknowledged was as much concerned in Burr's schemes as Burr himself, but his exculpation was not only due to him fr. his seasonable discovery and overthrow of the plot, but his country should canonize him for it, and the Gov^{t} could never sufficiently requite him—He declared, he had a regular correspondence with Hay, who, he w^{d} not believe had ever censured or neglected to vindicate the *General*. I expressed my surprise at his entertaining such sentiments seriously, however he might advance them in his paper; but he was frank enough to protest to me that he considered Gallatin, *now* the most dangerous man in the country. Randolph was mad; Burr might still play the part of Coriolanus or Alcibiades; but Jeffersn and Madison were the only men on whom the country could depend—tho' he had no doubt Monroe would have been Presidt had it not been for the interference of Randolph wch had ruined his prospects. As for himself he had been proposed as Senator during his attendance at Richmond, without his knowledge, which was the reason he had lost his election: Mr Erskines dispatches, which had been used as a trap to ensnare him, only contained some *newspapers* and he had defeated the scheme, by *forwarding* them *after* the mail.—It appears plainly fr. this sketch, that we have authority for knowing the present party in power are divided amongst themselves: that the chief of the nation is still afraid of Burr which is further proved by his own indiscretion—for Jeff. has lately said that whenever B. cd get to the Netherlands he could command $400,000. Yet Duane continues his daily attacks upon Burrism, and complains a great deal of Burr being in town, tho' his bothered runners can not find out where he lives. Before I left him he affected to disapprove of the late rising in Balto no doubt because he can't excite the good people of this town to another, here. He seemed surprised to learn I had the hardihood to dine and sup in public on the day my effigy was executed; and when I told him I was always provided with a brace of pistols—he twirled on his seat. Having given him this impression for the benefit of himself and his friends I left him, in perfect freedom fr. my tooth-ach.—I returned to the Mansion-house where I passed the remr of the evg in miscellaneous conversation with several agreeable men.—

Friday 13.—

I have nothing material to note today except my dining and spending the evg with Mr Edwd Tightman whose hospitality but too successfully seduces the prudence of his guests, which he generally drowns in the best of wines.———

Phila.da Sat. Nov. 14.07.—

Took a family-dinner to day with Joe Lewis, who had yesterday appointed to take me this evening to see a fine grazing farm about 6 miles fr. town belonging to a man of the name of Sickel at the confluence of the Delaware and Schuylkil.—We set out in Lewis's carriage in company with a Mr. Hamilton a very amiable Englishman who formerly belonged to the Navy, is curious in paintings, of which he has a handsome collection that I have not yet seen, and keeps a small and well regulated academy with much credit.—We reached the place early enough to see it and the fine cattle belonging to it, together with a remarkably—beautiful heifer at a neighboring plantation of Sickles' on our way homeward. This heifer about 3 yrs old besides her fine make would weigh, it is said 1,500 lb. The farm was remarkable for its banks faced with stone, and luxuriant pastures of which however a great deal is wasted for want of better care, not withg. the crops of hay taken off every spring and summer.——

Phila.da Sund. Nov. 15.07.—

I am much mortified by my detention here—thro' the probably delusive hopes Burr has held out to me of the possible success of his efforts to raise money. I have almost let slip the season for descending the Ohio, for there is much appearance of an early winter: and thus will another item be probably added to the long account of my sufferings [6] by this man.—Wrote to my wife; read and dined at home with a company of about thirty—amongst whom were counted individuals of 13 different nations and General Moreau, who sets out tomorrow for N. Orleans, with a single companion in the stage by the way of Pittsburg.—The General spoke to nobody but his companion.—Bollman assures me, he is a man of little speech and no ideas, except on military affairs.—So that I had no loss in dining with a conversable party, at a distant part of the table. Wrote this evening to Luther Martin & Doctor Cummins to put the former off his design of going to Chilicothe for Burr *and* myself and remind the latter of my intention to travel with him & have a concern in his Negro-purchases.—

Monday Novr 16. 1807.—

Bollman to day handed me a printed estimate of the value and yearly profits of the sugar estates in the Orleans Territory furnished him by Danl Clark now here, who will decline visiting me I apprehend 'till I shall have extinguished the last spark of Burrism, within me, with which I suspect he has been sufficiently singed to dread the fire. Spent the best part of the morning shopping, after some conversation with Bollman, who further recommends himself by a disclosure of his family affairs and narrow circumstances, unsought altogether on my part. The result of Clark's state^{t} is a yearly return in Acadia County of 28½ per cent on the capital invested, and 22 1/10 in the vicinity of Orleans,—which is represented, superior to anything farming can produce anywhere else because, no more in fact than 1/3 of the capital is advanced for the first installment, the produce of the estate clearing itself in 4 years.—But tho' examples are given of what has been done by 2 or 3 planters for as many successive years, in the *vicinity of Orleans*, the counties of Acadia and La Fourche as yet, do not furnish *experience* of what might be expected in these situations, and the best *management* and no accidents are presumed.—Supped this evening en famille with Joe Lewis, and on my return home was blest with a letter fr. my beloved, which I found on my bed-room table, and probably was forwarded under cover fr. Balt^{o} to Burr, as it had no p^{t} mark, and did not reach me thro' Lewis. This letter is of the 20th 7^{ber} at which time, all was well at Natchez.—

Tuesday Novr 17.07.—

Had a note fr. Burr this morning, to dine wth him tomorrow, at 4 o'clock, which invitation I have accepted, in anticipation of mixing probably for the last time with a few of his choice spirits.—Spent the evening and supped en famille agreeably with Joe Lewis.—There was a great fall of snow since yesterday.—Reeve Lewis has solicited to see my notes which I could not refuse. He pledges his discretion in which I fully confide.—

Wednesday Nov[r] 18.07.

So much of these short mornings is consumed, with visits, the papers and the unavoidable waste of time that cannot be denied to acquaintances only that little business can be dispatched by me before dinner, when that call must be answered at 2 or even 3 o'clock.—To day however I did a little shopping, before I came home to dress for Burr's party, which I joined at half past 4 consisting only of M[r] Biddle one of his most attached friends and bro[r] to the Notary public here, Dav[d] Randolph, Tom. Butler, Doctor Cummins, Mr. Pollock, Burr and myself. The party was as insipid as possible. Burr is evidently dejected, and tho' he often affected to urge and enliven the conversation it languished—thro' the stupidity of Randolph, the unconcern of Pollock, the vacant reserve of Cummins, the incapacity of Butler, the nothingness of Biddle and the aversion of myself to keep it up 'till 8 o'clock—when it expired and I took leave soon after the entrance of a General Nichol who seemed another of Burr's gaping admirers and much resembles in manner breeding and intellect General Russell of Kentucky.[7] Thus ended the last invitation I shall ever probably receive fr. this American Chesterfield, who is fast approaching the limits of that career he has so long run thro' the absurd confidence of so many dupes and swindlers.—I had yesterday put into my hands for the first time Joe Daveiss' pamphlet, by Dav. Randolph. It is a hasty passionate performance seldom alluding particularly to me by name, but bearing hard upon Jefferson's hypocrisy and neglect of the author and the early information he gave him of Burr's designs and first movements. The book will with all its defects mortify Jefferson,[8] by proving to all the world, that he would, at no time, open his eyes or ears to Wilkinson's intrigues with the Spa. Govt. and therefore, to use an expression of the author's, the

President is as much espanishized as the Brigadier.—It has also great merit in its comments, and the parody it contains on Jefferson's communication of last January to Congress on Burr's operations last winter on the Ohio and the Mississippi, which has very much diverted me.—This performance together with Judge Marshall's last vol. of the life of Washington, exposing the origin and views of the present Democratic party in power, have by this time no doubt inspired Jefferson with a more deadly hatred of the Marshall faction than he has ever conceived of all the Burrites he ever heard of.—I was presented to day by a M[r] Nolte a young Italian, who has often met Wilkinson at parties in N. Orleans, with a caricature of that General a'la Falstaff. It is a good resemblance and pleased me, tho' it is not thought as well done as another he has made of John Livingston as a companion to the first, under the title of Lawyer Greyhound.—I have paid my 2[d] week's bill here amounting in the whole, to about $30 and for this tho' I do not dine at home half my time I cannot have a fire in my room. O caupones maligni!—

Phila[da] Thurs. Nov[r] 19.07.—

Visited this morning, the infant Academy of the Arts lately established here, with Joe Lewis who is a subscriber to the Institution, and showed me the way fr. his Compting-house, where I pass half an hour every morning.—The present collection in a well contrived building at the upper end of Chestnut Street is slender in paintings all of which however I did not stay long enough to examine. Two fine large ones by West of scenes fr. Lear and Hamlet are lent for exhibition by their owner M[r] Fulton: and there are few other originals of much value: for painters will for at least a century yet, find too much encouragement in Europe to permit the establishment of an American-School. But the many fine casts taken by permission of Bonaparte and now exhibited here offer a feast to better connoiseurs than myself, of high relish. During the little time I spent there however, I was highly pleased; amongst a great number my notice was directed by Lewis, to contemplate particularly a large and a small Venus de Medicis of which I did not like the line of straight continuation between the nose and the forehead, so justly condemned by Lavater,—and a want of embonpoint below the navel which is rendered more objective, where it stands, by the shade thrown on that part from the bright sun. I speak of the larger of the two, which in all its other parts is exquisite. The other one is a copy in marble of Venus coming out of the bath, has a better face and is extremely beautiful. The group of Laocoon and the Apollo of Belvidere are perfect to my admiration which would not be exhausted upon them for hours: and the Farnesian Hercules is as well copied in our Lavater as ever an engraving represented a piece of sculpture.—But Lewis's early dinner hour-was at hand; and my appetite for these morceaux was obliged to give way to his for his Beef-stakes—So I made only a first offering, on this occasion, of my admiration to the artists of antiquity, with a devout hope of discharging the full debt of my homage hereafter to them: when I shall speak more of this Institution.—Dined, en famille with Lewis, very agreeably as usual: and in the evening young Mr Cotes, son of Samuel Cotes whom we knew here in '96, stopped in and invited me to dinner, for next monday at his country-place on the Skuylkill to join a small party. Staid at Lewises 'till midnight.—

Phila^da^ Frid. Novr 20.07.—

Having determined last wednesday, I w^d^ not see two days more pass away, without leaving my ultimatim with Burr, I set out this morning for his quarters, resolved to burst the cobweb of duplicity of all his evasions with me upon money-matters. It will be seen every where in these notes, how long and how insidiously he has trifled with my claims upon him, fr. the time, when he assured Barton, I was a bankrupt, and denied to him, my possessing any legal claims upon Alston or himself, whilst at the distance of 1,500 miles he was writing most affectionately to me, 'till the last *interview* I have this day, had with him, in which, he treated me, not as a faithful associate ruined by my past connection with him, but rather as an importunate creditor invading his leisure or his purse with a questionable account. The time therefore was fully arrived, at which I sh[d] determine, whether I should attempt to secure upwards of $7,000 for my family, or sacrifice it to an absurd and amphibious character of an associate and confident in his views, to future projects without principle or object, and destitute of all means to promote them?—Under these reflections, patience now became exhausted and to procrastinate any longer now appeared treason to my family. I therefore set seriously about the task I had allotted myself for this morning.—I found him alone; and had not been 10 minutes with him, after he had discharged a shop-boy, with whom he had been trifling I know not how long, about some article of dress, before he asked me, if I had heard of M[r] Luckett's treatm[t] of him. On my answering in the negative, he informed me that L. had sent a Marshal to him, yesterday and obliged him to give bail to the amount of about $16,000 L's claim I supposed, being half that sum. This intelligence mortified me, as it convinced me I had lost time. I expressed my concern for this new embarrassment he had experienced, as it might narrow his means to satisfy other claims which he did not consider questionable like Luckett's.—He asked me upon this what claims I alluded to? I said it was with great regret I sh[d] mention my own namely the am[t] of the account I had furnished him with in Richmond, and my claim for his protested, draft held by—Miller with my endorsem[t] for $4,000, on account of which my property on the Ohio had been sacrificed to 4 times that amount.—Now had you seen how "that eye of his" (I can not add "whose bend doth awe the world) did from its lustre fly" you would have beheld a little man indeed. He was dumb, and motionless. Vox faucibus haesit. But he soon recovered his accustomed affectation, and asked the am[t] of my account, declaring he had never looked into it since I had handed him it. I said it was a small one, obviously meaning by comparison with most others he had settled or secured. A *pretty small* one, he replied, of only about $3,000, and said he had not *yet examined* it. This sneer at the amount, of my account, and the questioning of its fairness by referring it to examination, which he falsely said he had not yet given it—for he looked it over the evening I presented it at Richmond asked a question or two on some of the Items which I answered informing him I had vouchers for most of them, which he said he did not want to see, and was satisfied it was correct.—Such a diminution of that suavity of address with which he had already too often diverted me from my purpose now exhibited him a heartless swindler in the last swoon of his disorder, and determined me to hasten my departure fr. this disgusting spectacle of a quibbling pettifogger who will never have a friend but amongst idiots swindlers or bankrupts. I suppose I testified my feelings sufficiently by my looks and manner without removing his doubts of the impression this treatm[t] made upon me, by now telling him, as I did, that my time and expectations were exhausted and I sh[d] stay in Phila[da] no longer: that I perceived he could give me no hopes of money, which I did not expect, but that tho' I was contented to starve myself I must secure something for my family, since I had found he had found means in that way to accommodate every other creditor, which was all that sh[d] detain me in town. He now pretended he had no body he could call upon. I observed—I thought it very possible he might never return fr. Europe in which case my family must have a security to resort to in this country. To this remark, he had the kindness to reply, that when I said my family I meant myself, and that I knew all his friends—you do said he M[r] Blen*nahassett* (so he has frequently pronounced my name before, when he has got beyond selfmanagement.) Sir said I, I must insist upon it I do not know all your friends—Upon this contradiction passed between us, he begged my pardon and said he really thought he had informed me of all who were his friends in that city.—

[*Breaks off at middle of page. Rest of page and following pages are blank.*]

APPENDIX A

[These first loose pages of Blennerhassett's Journal were kept in the slip-pocket of the cover of the first of the three pocket note-books he used. These entries, like those for July 20–August 3, do not appear in W. H. Safford's edition and have been transcribed from the MS in the Library of Congress.]

Lexington Jail Kentucky July 14. 1807

H. Blennerhassett

Tuesday
Evg. 1/4 past
6 o'clock

Was ordered into the custody of The Marshal of the Un. St. Col. Crocket, on motion of Mr Bib made in the C^t^ House to Judge Todd until The Att^y^ should apply to the Circuit Judge to transmit me to Richmond grounded on the affidavit of which a copy is annexed—I was allowed pen ink and paper but told by the Jailor I must not send a sealed letter to any one without its first undergoing his perusal, unless it was to my wife. He accordingly read in presence of Mr Lewis Sanders of Lexington a letter I had written to a Mr Robert Alleson of Nashville on private business—Mr Prentis The Jailor also informed me I must converse with nobody, save in his presence.—he accordingly attended whilst I spoke to some persons who came to visit me.—I observed to him that I presumed he acted under the orders of Col. Crocket The Federal Marshal. He said he did, and under those of Mr. Bib, The United States Attorney for The Kentucky District, and agreed, on my requisition to sign such minutes as I should correctly take of his orders and the treatment I received during my confinement—

Wednesday July 15

I was conducted at 10 o'clock A.M. to Court. Judge Todd [,] on objections made by my Counsel Mr. Clay to my committment without other grounds than the affidavit of Mr. Meade [,] took time to consider them till evening. The objections of Mr Clay however were waived by me, and He stated they were not made for my benefit, or by my desire to procure my discharge. On the contrary I read to the Ct an affidavit I afterwards made before a magistrate deposing that I believed the fact of an Indictment for Treason having been found agt me at Richmond fr. the public papers, however insufficient such evidence be to warrant a committ by the Ct [,] that I should however never impeach that Ct or its officers for transmitting me to Richmond, and further solemnly pledged myself in the face of the Audience voluntarily to proceed hither with Mr. Meade, even if Court, in consideration of Mr. Clay's objections should not continue my committment and order my transmissal.—My Affidavit after stating the nature and term of my detention and discharge in the Mississippi Territory as well as the time and place where I was first informed of the findings of The Gr. Jury of Richd agt me, deposed to my having made immediate and several declarations of my decided purpose on my arrival at Lexington to offer up to the U. St. Attorney or Fed. Judge for the Ky Distt a surrender of my person which I was prevented fr. doing by the interference of arrest on a civil process till I was again arrested by the Deputy Marshal, on the part of The Un. States.—I left the Court in custody of the Deputy Marshal, and was reconducted thither in the evening about half past four o'clock—when the Judge delivered his opinion in favor of committing me, grounded on reasons he stated at some length amongst which he seemd much to rely upon my own belief of the fact of the finding of the Gr. Jury at Richmnd as stated in my Affidavit.—I was some time afterwards delivered up to the Jailor to reoccupy the quarters I had left in the morning—Mr Meade having first kindly accompanied me to make a visit of acknowledgment to Mrs Jordan for some conveniences she had obligingly sent me to the prison.—Mr Prentis, the Jailor, is assiduous as much as possible, but, in no instance, transgresses the line running between his duty and my situation, in rendering my confinement not only easy but comfortable.

Thursday 16. July—

Last evening, and this morning I have received several visitors accompanied with proffers of service and accommodation fr. many respectable friends. Friday, Saturday & Sunday passed without any occurrence worthy of notice, till the evening of the last day, when I went out into town, under charge of the Jailor about 6 o'clock in the evening to take the benefit of the fresh air and make a visit of leave and acknowledgment of Mrs Sanders and Mrs Jourdan for the kind attention they had shown me in my confinement. This liberty was taken by the jailor in pursuance of leave obtained for the purpose the day preceding fr. Mr Meade.—Mr Prentiss next ventured to leave me in the care of Major Boyd and Mr Wm Jourdan taking fr. them a joint receipt and an engagement to return me into prison before 10 o'clock, which they accordingly did, after I had also made visit of leave to Mrs Bodley.

For continuance of this journal, see my pocket book[.]

APPENDIX B

[This journal of the voyage of the Burr expedition's flotilla down the Ohio and Mississippi kept between December 16 and February 3, 1806–7, is not written in Blennerhassett's hand until December 20. This text is reprinted from W. H. Safford's *The Blennerhassett Papers* (1864), pp. 184–192; a comparison of it with the MS shows that in this case, unlike that of the longer journal, Safford made few substantive changes or omissions; these, particularly the letters added to the entries for 10/24 and 10/27, have been identified by square brackets.]

Account of a Voyage Down the Ohio and Mississippi

16th December.—Tuesday, we left Jeffersonville; crossed the falls; nothing extra; all our boats crossed safe.

17th.—Pursued our journey at twelve o'clock at night; landed at Salt river; took in seven hands; stopped some time; and started again at four o'clock in the morning. About ten o'clock, A.M., parted with Colonel Tyler, and four keel-boats left us. We had a very bad night, occasioned by heavy rain, which continued until morning.

18th.—Nothing remarkable; passed Anderson's river at thirty-five minutes past two o'clock, A.M.; passed one of the keel-boats at twelve o'clock at night.

19th.—Passed French Island at half-past nine, A.M.; passed Green river at half-past eleven, A.M. About one, P.M., had some trouble about a canoe, which some of our hands, being ashore after wood, had taken away. The owner followed; we had to pay him two dollars, and give up the canoe. Nothing [more] worth notice, until we arrived at Red Bank, then about sundown; found it to be a place of small note; there we remained.

two hours, and proceeding, passed Diamond Island about twelve o'clock at night.

20th.—About five, P.M., met with some difficulties among some sawyers, which is a term given by boatmen to old trees, which settle in the river, and which rise and fall by the rapidity of the current. They are often dangerous, and sometimes fatal. Immediately after disengaging our boats from the difficulty, we were prevented from proceeding by a ledge of rocks; with much hazard we cleared ourselves about seven; passed Highland Creek, where stands a town of small note, entirely inhabited by Roman Catholics. At half-past nine passed the Wabash river, came up with Colonel Tyler and his boats. In the forks of the Ohio and Wabash, stand a few houses, but of no consequence. The latter river here is of considerable magnitude, and runs into the Ohio, opposite the center of an island, which takes its name from the river. The Ohio, here, has a beautiful appearance, interspersed with handsome plantations along its banks. Four miles below the mouth of the Wabash, there is a large island, the name unknown to us. At half-past twelve, P.M., arrived at Shawneetown: this is a place of deposit for the salt, made at the saline, but of no other importance, being a place of no trade.

21st.—Nothing remarkable.

22d.—Nothing in the course of the day, but had a very wet night.

23d.—A beautiful day; nothing extra.

24th.—Very windy; repaired our boats, they being very leaky in the roofs. At eleven o'clock, P.M., an express arrived from Colonel Burr informing us of his intentions to meet us at Cumberland river; likewise orders for us to proceed; but we were prevented by high winds, so remained that night.

[Burr to Blennerhassett

NEAR NASHVILLE, Dec. 20, 1806.

My young friend Stokely Hays, the son of a respectable old

revolutionary officer, will hand you this, and will bring me your reply. I have experienced distressing delays; but shall be at the mouth of the Cumberland on the 23d, Sunday. Please to repair thither. Enter on the east (upper) side of the island, which lies in the mouth of the river.

I anticipate impatiently the pleasure of meeting you.

A. BURR

H. BLENNERHASSETT, ESQ.]

25th.—Left Shawneetown at eight o'clock A.M.; the wind fresh and ahead. Passed an island, name unknown to us. This day the wind blew so hard, that our boats were totally separated; with much difficulty our boat reached the Kentucky shore, after riding a tremendous swell; remained until sundown, and then proceeded on to join the rest of our company, who were in the same dilemma, being obliged to put in on the Indiana shore.

26th.—About five o'clock, one of Mr. Blennerhassett's boats joined us, being one of fifteen that were stopped at Marietta. At half-past seven o'clock passed the Rock and Cave; went ashore and viewed it; found no curiosities, more than a hollow cavern. Passed Hurricane Island and Creek at half-past ten o'clock; passed Clover Creek, eleven o'clock, on the Indiana side; passed the Copperas Banks at half-past three, P.M., Indiana shore.

27th.—Arrived at Cumberland river, at half-past—, A.M.; joined Col. Burr, at the above place. The day was very stormy, and put our little fleet to considerable trouble.

[Burr to Blennerhassett.

SUNDAY EVENING.

It is said that you have landed a mile below. We must all be stationary till morning. Send to me by return of this boat, Mr.

Hays, with five hundred in twenty post notes, and fifty dollars in silver.

We will endeavor to start all the heavy boats at an early hour in the morning: those below are to wait till those above shall come down. A gun will be fired as a signal for moving.

All is well, very well, at this garrison.

Your friend,

A. BURR

P.S.—Mr. Elliot has handed me some money. The silver is necessary, if it can be come at, and about three hundred dollars of paper. Hays need not come.]

28th.—This day a boat joined us from Cumberland river, with Cols. Burr, Harris, etc., on board. Pushed off on our journey, and landed on the Kentucky shore eight miles distant from the above place. In consequence of high winds, we landed about eight o'clock, P.M.

29th.—This day pushed off at eight o'clock, A.M.; wind ahead and strong; obliged to land immediately opposite the mouth of Tennessee river, where we lay by for several hours; pushed off again at sundown, and passed Fort Massac at half-past eleven, P.M., and landed one mile below.

30th.—Pushed off at five o'clock, A.M.; pleasant weather; came into the Mississippi at half-past three o'clock; passed the Iron Banks at half-past eight o'clock, and passed the Chalk Banks at half-past nine, A.M.

31st.—Pleasant weather; nothing happened worth notice. Landed, at sundown, on the Louisiana shore.

January 1st.—This day landed at New Madrid, at nine o'clock, A.M.; remained about three hours, and left one of our hands, Major G. Wood, behind with a canoe, in order to engage some men that purposed coming on with us. This evening on coming ashore, owing to our being in rear of the fleet, and going after dark, our boat ran aground, but got off with some difficulty, and effected a good landing in a short time.

2d.—Pushed off this day at four o'clock, A.M.; passed the little prairie at eight o'clock; fine weather; landed at five o'clock at the Little Horse-shoe.

3d.—Pushed off this day about five, A.M.; passed a number of islands; saw no inhabitants. I believe the whole of the fleet, our boat only excepted, got into an eddy; we escaped only, and by our timely exertions gained the opposite side of the island and river, say the right hand side; the rest put ashore. Although contrary to Colonel Burr's orders, we alone pushed on.

4th.—This day at seven, A.M., we landed at the Chickasaw Bluff, where there is an American garrison, commanded by Lieut. Jackson.

5th.—This day at six o'clock, A.M., left this place, and floated all day, and landed at nine, P.M., on an island, in consequence of a very high wind; pushed of again at eleven o'clock.

6th.—Floated all day; nothing extra.

7th.—Do.

8th.—Do.

9th.—Floated all day, until two o'clock, P.M.; landed to wait for Col. Burr; got some wood; perceived the sign of horses, but no inhabitants any where to be found; pushed off again at three o'clock, being joined by the Colonel and his boats; floated all night through a very dangerous navigation; about eight o'clock one of Col. Tyler's boats being lashed to a flat, and striking against a sawyer, was broken loose, in consequence of which Capt. Dean's boat stopped and dispatched a keel-boat in search of the one lost. Major Floyd's boat put ashore, in consequence of being deterred by a sudden squall of wind, which arose about eight o'clock; the rest of the boats proceeded.

10th.—At four o'clock, A.M., got into an eddy; could not get out, the night being very dark; stayed until daylight appeared; then got out, and came up with Col. Burr's two boats, namely, the boat he lived in, and one that had horses; they gave us a signal for landing, with which we complied, and effected a landing in the Mississippi Territory. About twelve o'clock this day, Col. Burr pushed down the river with a bateau and twelve men, and appointed to meet us again at Bayou Pierre; passed Palmyra at half-past one o'clock'; passed several islands, and landed about fifteen miles below.

11th.—This day pushed off at eight, A.M., and landed at Bayou Pierre at four o'clock, P.M.; joined Col. Burr and party; had some intention of staying at this place some time, but were prevented by a rumor spreading in the country of our intentions being hostile, in consequence of which a part of militia came and stationed themselves in the woods, some distance from our boats, with an intention to stop us the next morning. We being apprised of their intentions, pushed off in the night, and landed four miles below, on the Louisiana shore.

12th.—This day were visited by Col.—— and some of his dragoons; talked with Col. Burr respecting his business, and went away well satisfied. This day Major Floyd joined us from Natchez.

13th.—This day were visited by Col. Fitzpatrick and some of his dragoons; we brought them over the river; talked with Col. Burr, and seemed well pleased. Col. Fitzpatrick brought with him about sixty men, all armed, in order to stop us; but on hearing our business, he sent the men home, and left us quietly.

14th.—Visited by several militia officers.

16th.—Visited by Col. Shields, Gov. Williams's aide-de-camp, who conversed with [Col. Burr], and appointed a meeting between him and the Governor, and then departed.

17th.—This day Col. Burr started, agreeably to his appointment, to meet the Governor at the mouth of Cole's Creek, with several gentlemen with him. This day was remarkable for a heavy fall of snow, perhaps four inches deep.

18th.—The water falling rapidly, we thought it prudent to remove from our situation; and, agreeably to the orders of Mr. [Blennerhassett], two of our boats moved down the river about a mile, being afraid of being blocked in by a bar that was outside of the creek, where we then lay.

19th.—This day Col. Fitzpatrick, with some other officers, came on board, and took an inventory of all the stores and property we had on board; we then pushed off, but were immediately challenged by a Major Flaharty, with about thirty armed men, in a keel-boat, [who] ordered us to put on shore. Being told that his Colonel was in the rear, and that it was by his sanction we put off, he left, and troubled us no more. That night we put on shore at the Petit Gulf, on the Louisiana side; Major Flaharty and party immediately opposite, on the other side.

20th.—This day, about ten o'clock, in consequence of a very bad landing, we thought proper to remove our boats up the river, which we effected. This day several boats trading to New Orleans were stopped by Major Flaharty and party, examined, and permitted to proceed.

[*The rest of this Journal is in the handwriting of Harman Blennerhassett.*]

In the evening the Major visited H.B.; professed friendly intentions, and a determination to join us, with the greater part of his regiment.

21st.—We received news of the approach of a Capt. Davison, with a party of horse, coming, under the orders of Col. Fitzpatrick, to search for concealed arms, supposed to have been secreted in the brush; during the night a party was sent out by——to obviate *effectually* the success of the design.

22d.—This morning an altercation took place between Majors Floyd and Flaharty, which induced the former to address a letter to the latter in a sort of defiance. This measure having been taken without my approbation, I informed Major Floyd I would not co-operate with him in any acts he should enter into upon his letter or motives, but should, by myself and my party, resist such conduct on the part of Major Flaharty as I should deem improper, or as occasion required. Major Floyd, I believe, apprehending no attack or removal of our boats from their present station, seemed to yield to my observation, and in the morning made a visit to Major Flaharty, to engage with him in a shooting-match. On his return to the boats, he informed me that Major Flaharty, this evening, expected fresh orders from the Government, to enable him to move our boats down to Cole's Creek. Eleven o'clock at night, [there were] several shot fired from Major Flaharty's party on boats passing by to bring them to, but without effect. Damage to the boats or their men unknown. This morning Col. Comfort Tyler was taken from his boats, by an escort of the militia, to appear before the Governor at Washington, the seat of the Territorial Government, about thirty miles from our station. The officer, Capt. Davison, who made the requisition to Col. Tyler, observed to him that he had no warrant. Col. Tyler agreed to the Governor's wishes without that requisite. This day Major Flaharty, who can neither read or write, and is not a magistrate, informed me that he had taken and forwarded to the Governor the affidavit of a man, who deposed before him, that he had seen, fifty miles above our present position in the Petit Gulf, thirteen of Col. Burr's boats containing arms and ammunition, with an unusual number of men. During several days past, some individuals of our party have been obliged, at Washington, to undergo examination, and enter into recognizance to testify, on the part of the United States, against A.B. at the next federal court, to be held on the first Monday in February.

About ten o'clock this morning, Major Floyd communicated to me the following letter, received by Capt. Burney from Major Flaharty:

January 23d, 1807.

SIR:—Not wishing to go to rash measures, I have to inform you that I must comply with the orders of the commander-in-chief, if you keep your present position; and, as I am certain that it can't be injurious to yourself nor any of the people with you, I wish you to move opposite the mouth of Cole's Creek, where the communication is more convenient for you and me. You mentioned in your letter to me, yesterday, that you did not wish to put the militia to any more trouble. Your compliance will save the march of two companies that are ready to join me, if called on.

I am, with much esteem,

Yours, etc.,

JACOB FLAHARTY,

MAJOR FLOYD. *Major, 2d Regiment.*

On perusal of the above letter, which Flaharty could not write, I acquainted Major Floyd that if it was worthy of credit in the intimation it held out of the orders of the commander-in-chief, and the truth of his menaced reinforcements of two companies, it might as well answer our present views and situation to comply as to adhere to the determination expressed yesterday, of maintaining our present position; that, on the other hand, the Governor would be as responsible to us and the law for any impropriety of conduct toward us by the militia, as for any other acts of authority unduly exercised toward us. I therefore suggested to him the substance of the following letter in reply to Flaharty:

PETIT GULF, *January 23d, 1807.*

SIR:—Your communication, by the hands of Capt, Burney, I just now had the honor of receiving. You mention your wish for us to move to the mouth of Cole's Creek; the request I would take a pleasure in complying with, had not Col. Burr directed me to stay where we now are until his further commands. I do expect to have a messenger from Co. Burr to-day, perhaps time enough to move down this evening. At all events, we will determine, to-morrow morning (23d), what step will be proper for us to take. Report says, the officer commanding the district opposite you is determined to prevent the commanding officer of the Mississippi Territory from interfering with the jurisdiction of the Territory of Orleans. This report, if true, may be proper for you to be informed of. At all events, we are awaiting a legal investigation into our conduct; and I contend that, during that investigation, and while we are, properly speaking, in the hands of its authority, the military law has no right to interfere. I am,

Respectfully, etc.,

DAVIS FLOYD.

MAJOR FLAHARTY.

This letter, by means of the unfounded suggestion, submitted to Major Floyd, of the jealousy of the people on the Louisiana side, of any encroachments on their jurisdiction, or by other matter it contained, prevented Flaharty from carrying his declarations into effect, if he really had authority under orders from the Governor so to do; and he was removed from his post opposite to us the following morning (24th), on the arrival of Col. Fitzpatrick, who substituted only a party of ten men, under the command of Capt. Abrams, with orders to board boats civilly, without firing upon them, and seize only such arms and ammunition as they might contain. Col. Burr, this day, returned to the boats from Washington, where he had remained since the 17th under a voluntary submission to the civil authority, which had been exacted of him at Cole's Creek, on his reception there on the 17th by Mead, at the head of five or six hundred of the militia, half armed and generally discontented, in disregard of the connection that had been entered into by Mead and himself. The Acting-Governor, it now appeared, had threatened him with all the armed force of the country unless he submitted. No securities, however, were required for his appearance at the adjourned Federal Court, to be holden on the first Monday in February. His own single recognizance was taken, in the sum of —— dollars. Accordingly, his return to the boats was free. I soon heard from him that Mr. Mead had received dispatches announcing the statements by Flaharty of what had passed between him and Major Floyd, which so exasperated the Governor, that he threatened to have Floyd brought to him in irons, but was induced to retract his menaces on learning Flaharty's character to be fraught with the utmost ignorance and assurance, while Major Floyd's temper was both mild and amiable. Col. Burr also acquainted me with the indignation the Federal Judge, Rodney, had expressed at the exercise of the military law over Col. Burr and his friends, both in the Mississippi and Orleans Territories; the Judge assuring him, in opposition to the U.S. Attorney, Mr. Poindexter, that the civil authority of the Territory was competent to try him; adding, at the same time, that if Wilkinson, or any other military force, should attempt to remove his person out of the Mississippi Territory, prior to his trial, he, the Judge, would again, as he expressed it, put on old " '76," and march out in support of Col. Burr and the Constitution. This day, about three o'clock in the afternoon, my family arrived in the boat of Mr. Thomas Butler, who having, on his way from Pittsburgh, called to take them on board at my house, on the Ohio, there underwent, with eight or ten other gentlemen, a captivity for three days, diversified in its scenes by a mock trial, in my hall, alternate insult and plunder, committed in common on them, my family and property, in a variety of particulars, for which I refer to Mr. Neville's journal.

25th.—Nothing material occurred till eight o'clock at night, when we cast off to drop down about twenty-six miles, to Cole's Creek, opposite which we took another station on the Orleans shore. Here we remained, without any material prospect of a change in our affairs, till the 27th, when we heard that intelligence had reached Mississippi Territory that Col. B.'s drafts on New York had been protested, and the Gov. Williams, who had returned to resume the functions of his office in the Mississippi Territory was reported to be friendly disposed toward us. Col. B. determined to visit the Governor, and set out next morning (28th) for that purpose, and to prepare, probably, for his trial on the following Monday. Reports now reached us of the near approach to Natchez of a division of nine or ten gun-boats, under the command of Commodore Shaw, bearing a special order from the "Secretary of the Navy" to take Col. Burr, or the next in command under him, and to take or destroy all the boats under his command. By this time the effects of general disorder and want of regulation in the use or distribution of liquors and provisions, with a total disregard of all pretense at authority whenever attempted to be assumed by superiors, which had long since manifested themselves throughout all our numbers, now openly broke out among particular leaders, who even threatened to turn out of their boats the provisions, in payment for the demands of some of the men who had become discontented and threatened to leave us

29th.—Nothing occurred till 2d of February, when the Court at Washington had not that day charged the grand jury, who, of course, had not found any bill against Col. Burr, owing to objections, I suppose, made by the Attorney-General, to the jurisdiction of the Court over actions done by Col. Burr, without the limits of their Territory. Next day (Feb. 3d), Mr. N. brought me intelligence of the arrival of Graham at Washington, and of his having had an interview with Col. Burr [in which he said.—]

APPENDIX C

[This brief, which Blennerhassett wrote for his counsel while he was in the Richmond Penitentiary awaiting trial for Treason and Misdemeanor, is alluded to several times in his Journal, beginning with the entry for August 7. This text is reprinted from W. H. Safford's *The Life of Harman Blennerhassett* (1850), pp. 223-239, whose text derives from edition of the Blennerhassett papers by William Wallace. A comparison of this text with the MS in the Library of Congress has been made and substantive changes or omissions have been restored in square brackets. See particularly Articles 14, 15 and 21.]

United States of America *vs.* Harmann Blennerhassett	Brief on behalf of Harman Blennerhassett, confined in the Penitentiary at Richmond, Va., under an indictment for high treason.

CASE

Introduction to Burr. 1. Prisoner first became acquainted with Aaron Burr by a voluntary and unsolicited visit made by A.B. to prisoner at his late residence on the Ohio, in the spring of 1805. Col. Burr arrived about nightfall. He participated during the visit in the general conversation of the company; had no private interview or business with the prisoner, and he took leave about eleven o'clock at night, with his companion, Mrs. Shaw, to pursue his voyage down the river.

2. Some time in the beginning of December following, prisoner, on his return from Baltimore, received a letter from Col.

Burr, couched in polite language, and expressing a regret at not having had an opportunity of improving personal acquaintance with prisoner, owing to the absence of the latter from home[, at the season with Col: Burr was returning by Chilicothe fr. N. Orleans to the Eastward—].

Substance of prisoner's first letter to Burr.

At this time a wish on the part of the prisoner to improve his pecuniary affairs, combining with a natural desire to cultivate an acquaintance by which, he justly thought, he might so much improve his own talents and promote the interest of his children, led him, after some reflection, to write the first letter he ever addressed to the late Vice-President, expressive of a desire [of a complementary nature,] to be honored with a hope of being admitted into participation of any speculation which might, during his tour through the [W.] country, have presented itself to Col. Burr's judgment as worthy to engage his talents. In making this advance, prisoner contemplated not only a commercial enterprise or land purchase [—either of which it was thought the prosperous establishment of the Manhattan Company, might again induce the Col. to engage in] but a military adventure was distinctly mentioned, in which prisoner would engage. A reference, however, to the original letter, or its copy in prisoner's letter-book, will show that prisoner then considered [the] government alive to every sentiment of indignation and resentment that he fancied it cherished against the Spanish Court, for acts of aggression and injustice committed by its troops [on] American citizens and the territories of the United States, and conduct by its minister and immediate representative at the seat of government, little short of direct insult upon our Executive. Under such impressions, prisoner conceived the inevitable necessity of a speedy war with Spain, and observed in his letter to Col. Burr, that in the event of a *Spanish War*, in which case the government and country would call upon the talents, &c., of Col: Burr, the prisoner would engage with him, in any enterprise, to be undertaken for the subjugation of any of the Spanish dominions.

Burr's second visit to the island.

3. This overture, on the part of the prisoner, procured him a visit from Col: Burr at prisoner's late residence, on the Ohio, some time in the month of August, 1806. Col: Burr spent but one night [at the]prisoner's house. Prisoner having next day rode with him to Marietta, within a mile of which place [, the day after] he, the prisoner, took leave of the [Col: then on his way to Chillicothe,] and returned home[, distant fr. Marietta about 15 miles.] Col: Burr arrived on the island about noon, in company with Col. De Pestre and Mr. Dudley Woodbridge, Jun., [who introduced those Gent^{n} to the Prisoner,] with whom Col: Burr had a private interview in the library, which was terminated fully an hour and a half before dinner. Some time after dinner, Col. De Pestre and Mr. Woodbridge having left the table, the subjects of conversation which had been taken up in the library, and there at the utmost dwelt upon for twenty-five minutes, were resumed, and further considered, during not more than half an hour; after which Col: Burr and the prisoner joined the company in the hall, when conversation became and continued general till bed-time.

[In which not more than 3/4 hour was spent in private interview with A.B.]

4. [Prisoner did not arrive at Munsel's Tavern, where Col: Burr put up in Marietta till after a space of time in which the Col: had caused some Coffee to be made to relieve a severe headache, under which the Prisoner that

Went with him to Marietta, where there was no time for organizing treason or military expeditions.

day laboured.] Prisoner remained at Marietta about twenty-four hours, from which, deducting the part of time [allotted] to sleep, to the occupation of Col: Burr in commissioning or contracting with D. Woodbridge, to provide for him those boats and provisions that have been seized, under the orders of the government, receiving the visits of various persons that awaited him at the tavern, &c., an estimate may be easily formed of how short a time the prisoner could have availed himself, to digest the projects or to contrive the means with A. Burr of executing treason against the United States, or of founding empires in other countries.

Nature of such communications as opportunity or inclination did permit A.B. actually to make.

Sentiments of the people in Orleans and Mississippi Territories. Agitated and might produce revolt, which would affect the interests of the Western country, and might induce an examination by the people into the grounds of their connection with the Atlantic States, and probably produce a separation.

5. From such opportunities, however, as the prisoner derived during all the private interviews afforded him, at this time, and the disclosures therein made to him with rapidity, but also with reserve, he was led to conclude, that the sentiments of a respectable majority of the people in the Orleans and Mississippi Territories were disaffected to the present government, to a degree that, in Aaron Burr's opinion, would, at no very distant period, produce a revolt which would probably call in the aid of some foreign succour to support it.

That, in such an event, the States and Territories west of the Mountains would be placed in a dilemma, out of which they [must] withdraw, as they

A.B. had no concern with these things [farther than thinking People sh.[d] be informed before they suffered by the Event.]

might be governed by an Eastern or Western ascendency of interests: that it was the colonel's opinion the discontents, particulary in the Territory of Orleans, would induce the Western country to examine the grounds and interests of its present connection with the Atlantic States, and probably induce a separation; that he, A.B., had no further concern with these things than in a speculative way; but that he thought, as well as the prisoner, that the people should be informed on the subject before they might be drawn unawares to a crisis for which they might not be prepared.

Such an event spoken of, as sooner expected than desired, by some members of the government. People of New Orleans disgusted to a degree that might induce in beginning of revolt, a seizure of bank, &c.

That a separation of the Western from the Eastern States was an event spoken of and apprehended, at the seat of government, by some of the heads of Department, which the maladministration of the country might bring about much sooner than was desired or expected; and finally, the people of New Orleans were so much disgusted with the conduct of government towards themselves, and on Spanish affairs, that he should not be surprised to hear of their beginning a revolt by seizing the Bank and Customhouse there.

Mexican Society wanted to place A.B. at their head; he declined.

He spoke of a society of young men of that city, openly denominated the Mexican Society, seizing and shipping some French cannon lying there, for an expedition against Mexico [, which when] at Orleans they had solicited him to lead, but he had declined to be concerned in.

Burr would not tell Blennerhassett his exact plans at all.

6. In the course of such private conversation as opportunity offered the prisoner to have with Aaron Burr, whilst on the island and at Marietta in the month of August, 1806, prisoner naturally endeavoured to elicit from him a disclosure of some specific project, by referring to the letter of the prisoner whereof the substance is set forth in the second paragraph. But from a reserve and conciseness observable on the part of Col. Burr on such solicitation, and from entire confidence in the honour and judgment of the Ex-Vice-President, the prisoner forbore to urge particular inquiries, that seemed to be displeasing to him, from their tendency to a development of the details of his objects and his means of effecting them.

7. Your client, however, did not take leave of Col: Burr without matter of some satisfaction of his curiosity and interest, sufficient to engage his serious reflections on the expediency of adopting or avoiding that concern, which now seemed to be proffered to the election of the prisoner in his interests. For, after having made the prisoner the general remarks set forth in the fifth article, with the contingency of which Col: Burr declared he had no concern, but which would not be adverse to his own particular views whether they should precede or follow

Expulsion of Spaniards from American territory, or even invasion of Mexican States by A.B. to be probably agreeable to government, if either could be effected without declaring war against Spain, which might offend France.

them, he then signified to your client, "that the expulsion of the Spaniards from the American territory then violated by them, or even an invasion of Mexico, would be very pleasing to the administration, if either or both could be effected without a war being declared against Spain, which would be avoided as long as possible, from parsimonious motives on the one hand, and dread of France on the other; although the then existing circumstances would, to a probable certainty, occasion its commencement before he should engage in any operation."

But such a war must take place before any operations of his plans.

Thus led to believe the government was not adverse to such designs, whilst they were kept secret till their execution should be legalized by a declaration of war, the prisoner tendered his services to Col. Burr generally.

8. At this time, your client neither sought nor received from Col. Burr any information whatever of the use or destination intended for the boats and provisions mentioned to have been contracted for with Dudley Woodbridge, jun., Art. 4, with which the prisoner had no concern, further than as he was a constituted member of the house of Dudley Woodbridge & Co., at Marietta, save that the prisoner informed Mr. Woodbridge, when the latter seemed doubtful of the sufficiency of Col. Burr's credit at New York, that the prisoner would indemnify the

company for all disbursements made on account of the boats and provisions, in the event of the bills drawn for the same on New York being dishonoured.

Design of publishing the Querist.

9. Some time in the month of August or September, 1806, your client, reflecting on the information and views disclosed to him, as aforesaid, by Col. Burr, conceived the design of publishing in the Ohio Gazette, a series of short essays, calling the attention of the people of the Western country to a subject that might engage their interests. Three or four numbers of these papers were published, exhibiting succinctly a general and relative view, in a political aspect, of the Union and the Western country, and setting forth motives of right and expediency which should induce the country west of the mountains to seek a separation from the Atlantic States in a peaceable and constitutional manner; if they should adopt the sentiments of the writer, who took the signature of Querist. The author, in making this essay on the public mind in that quarter, had no view of aggrandizement for himself, or of a political establishment for Col. Burr in the Western country, who (Burr) assured him he neither desired nor would accept any thing within the United States [, they could give him.] Your client was actuated to [attempt] the publication by two motives only, viz., to prepare the country by a proper

To prepare the people for contingencies involving their interests,

direction of its interest and energies for a crisis sooner or later approaching them, not from the views or operations of Col. Burr, but from the state of things on the Mississippi; at which their espousal of an eastern or western ascendency would determine their future prosperity, and to divert public attention from scrutiny into contigent plans or operations against Spain, which, whilst kept secret, government would not disapprove, but when exposed, [they] would be obliged to frustrate, as [they] had done at New York in the case of Ogden and Smith.

and to mask designs against Mexico, which whilst kept secret, would probably not be impeded by government, as was the case of Ogden and Smith.

10. With these views, the prisoner pledged his honour to Fairlamb, the printer of the Gazette, that he should publish nothing that would subject him to legal penalty, and the prisoner would avow himself the author whenever it might become necessary to exonerate the printer from any responsibility. In the same spirit and for the same purposes, prisoner communicated his design, and read the manuscript of one of the first numbers, to John and Alexander Henderson, who solemnly pledged their joint honours to the prisoner, under the sanction of hospitality in the house of said Alexander, never to disclose the name of the author or the communication he then made them, to the purport and [extent] that are set forth in the fifth and ninth articles.

Fairlamb the printer guaranteed safe to publish.

[The general design but no mention of Mexico made known to the Hendersons, who engaged to ask their father's approbation of it and pledged their honours to keep it secret.—]

Visit for further insight into Burr's plans into Kentucky where Burr was acquiring much popularity.

11. Some time in the month of October, 1806, the prisoner made a visit to Lexington, Kentucky, with views of further certifying himself [of] the permissive progress of Aaron Burr's speculations, so far as regarded his own exertions or the observation of government. During prisoner's stay in that country, where he remained a fortnight or three weeks, he observed Burr's popularity daily increasing; heard of no jealousy or suspicions of his views or designs on the part of the government or its agents, nor from any other quarter, till a messenger had been sent to him express from home, stating to him that the people of Wood county had entered into communication with the President or Governor of Virginia, by forwarding to those authorities memorials or addresses expressive of alarm for the safety of the country and their liberties, which they probably represented were likely to be endangered by Col: Burr or the prisoner, of which documents the latter has never seen originals or copies, or of any answers thereto; that [the] inhabitants, at the instance and under the influence of Hugh Phelps, and Alexander and John Henderson, had organized a volunteer battalion of three companies, which they had armed with the arms of the militia, that they had a general muster during the prisoner's absence from home, and were expected, by the report of Peter Taylor and others, on the evening of the day of the muster, to land on the island where the prisoner's family then dwelt, and burn his house; that in all probability the prisoner and [certainly] Col: Burr would be shot, if either returned to the island; and that some kiln-dried corn then preparing at the island, would be seized by the said volunteers as soon as it was put up; Dr. Joseph Spencer, of said county, having in the meantime declared that he and others regretted that they had been obliged, through fear, to sign the resolu-

tion[s] for organizing the said volunteer association, which some others had persisted [in refusing to do, particularly his son Wm and Mr Weld of Bellville—]

12. Agitated by this intelligence, set out for home from Lexington, Kentucky, and reached the island between one and two o'clock on the third of November, 1806. Reflecting on his way that he should be unprovided at home with any adequate means of defence to protect his family and property against the menaced outrages of a lawless multitude with arms in their hands, he was led to call on Dr. Bennet to learn such further particulars as [the Doctor] might have been informed of, since the express left the island for Lexington; and to provide him (the prisoner) with such aid as the Dr. could enable him to procure from his county, against any illegal and unwarrantable attack from the people of Wood county. To effect this latter object, the prisoner freely entered into a statement of the innocence and legality of every step the prisoner should take, in virtue of his concern in the speculations of Aaron Burr, observing that the latter had completed a large land purchase of Col. Lynch; offered to the prisoner such participation in the purchase as he might desire; and expected the prisoner, with such associates as might wish to purchase or procure donations, would leave home for the country where the lands lay, on the Washita or the Red River, in the beginning of the ensuing month; that, in a political sense, Col: Burr, as well as himself, abhorred and abjured all intentions their enemies were imputing to them, of undertaking enterprises illegal or adverse to the United States; and declaring that neither ever had, or would have, any [further] concern with the means of effecting a division of the Union, than a readiness to deliver their opinion in favour of the right of the people to effect such a measure whenever the time might arrive which should render it expedient. The prisoner, then calling the doctor's attention to his alarms for his family and property on the island, from personal enmity borne him by the people of Wood, solicited the doctor to hasten any persons he might know in his neighbourhood, who would wish to emigrate with the prisoner,

to join him as soon as possible on the island, where he did not know how soon he might need their assistance to protect him from such outrages as are stated to have been apprehended in Article 11. To these observations, made chiefly during a ride of five miles, which the doctor was induced to take, for the sake of accompanying the prisoner as far as the ferry, the doctor was pleased to reply, that if he could dispose of his place without too great a sacrifice, he should be willing to emigrate himself; that he had no doubt it would suit many persons in his neighbourhood, to whom he would speak at the muster [to take place] held in a few days; [—and address to pri(soner)] such as he should find disposed, in the manner prisoner had directed him, i.e., provided with rifles and blankets.

13. The prisoner took leave of the doctor at the ferry, about two o'clock, P.M., on Sunday the second of November, and reached the island on the following day. On his arrival, as well as on the road between Dr. Bennet's and his own house, he found the apprehension of an attack on the island from the [P]oint of the Little Kanawha, the head-quarters of the volunteers, had by no means subsided; and was informed an attempt would be made on his person that evening. To meet this contingency, the prisoner prepared some house-arms he had by him during ten years; and with a view to prevent it, he condescended to conciliate Mr. Phelps, the commander of the battalion, by addressing him a letter to thank him for a message he had sent to prisoner's wife some time during her husband's absence from home, [to lull or quiet] her apprehensions from the volunteers [: and solicit an interview with him, for the purpose of removing] whatever misconception of the prisoner's conduct or intentions might have been propagated among his neighbours. But aware of Col. Phelps's predilection for jobbing and speculation, which is notorious to all who know him, and in order to procure an interview with a person who had not been in prisoner's house for nearly seven years, by which the prisoner might induce the influence of said Phelps to moderate the passions and to allay the jealousies of the ignorant and misguided [, which it generally guided in that country—]

the prisoner thought it necessary to hint to him obscurely a desire to promote his interest, by some proposition which might engage his attention. [The letter was couched in the following terms.

Wood C^y^, Nov.3.1806

14. Dear Sir,

Just returned home after a journey of 700 miles, I hasten to express to you, the satisfaction with which I learned, on the road, that you had been invested with the command of three volunteer companies, that had been raised in this county during my absence, as that circumstance afforded me a sure guarantee against the idle reports I had heard, of any misguided violence intended by my neighbours, against my family or property, whilst I was not on the ground to defend them. But the information my wife has given me of the purport of the friendly message you sent her, at a *time* when you thought it would be expedient, has laid me under personal obligations to you, and rendered it a duty with me, to endeavour to revive our former neighborly intercourse; especially, at a time when so much misconception misleads the people, propagated, as I have no doubt I can satisfy you, by yr. enemies and their own; when I shall have the pleasure of an hour's unreserved conversation with you,—in which I expect I can make you some propositions that will engage yr. attention, and be serviceable to yr. interests. I therefore embrace the earliest opport^y^ of soliciting an interview with you: and in consideration of my fatigue, I take the liberty of requesting to see you this evening, and yr. accepting of a bed with us. Or if that should be inconvenient to you,—I shall do myself the pleasure of attending any appoint^t^ you may designate for tomorrow.

H.B.]

[15.] [This] letter might, or might not have had the first effect designed by it, viz., that of putting off the assault apprehended that evening on the island; but it occasioned a visit there, after a lapse of three or four days, from Col. Phelps, with whom the prisoner had a private interview, which was opened by the prisoner with a tender of thanks for the colonel's message to Mrs. Blennerhassett, during her husband's absence. The prisoner then affected to ridicule the reports which he had heard of the meditated injuries [with which his family and property had been threatened] from the Point; suggested to the [C]olonel that he suspected the other party in the [County,] (under the influence of the Hendersons[,] was now becoming so strong that its leaders would probably overturn the [C]olonel's interest, on which alone they had hitherto depended for whatever popularity they had acquired, and cautioned the [C]olonel against any coalition or co-operation they might seek with him, in exciting clamour or suspicion against the views or intentions of Aaron Burr or his friends, which the past conduct of the Hendersons towards him should induce him to avoid. Col. Phelps, in reply, complained much of the ill-treatment he had received from the said Hendersons [, who, he said, had risen in the Co^{y}. on his shoulders, without specifying particulars: observing however, that the Tuckahoes w^{d} soon overrun the County.] Prisoner stated his concern with Aaron Burr in a land purchase; informing the colonel that he, the prisoner, solicited or invited no person to join in the emigration, though many had voluntarily offered to do so, [some of whose names he mentioned;] but added that if the [C]olonel wished a concern for himself or his friends, that he might look to the example of General Jackson, and other characters of distinction, who, the prisoner understood, were going to join in the settlement with many associates; that as to the rumours and suspicions that had been circulated of Col: Burr, or his friends, engaging in any thing against the laws of the United States, such were wholly groundless: but it was not unlikely that the proximity of the purchase to that part of the country where an engagement had already taken [*place,*] or might soon be expected, between General Wilkinson and the Spaniards, would engage Col: Burr and his friends in some of the earliest adventures of the war. General Jackson being already prepared to march with 1000 or 1500 of his Tennessee militia, whenever he should think himself authorized by the orders or *wishes* of the government to put that body in motion. Col. Phelps received this information with declining to embark himself, on account of his family and the unsettled state of his affairs; but said he had no doubt many young men from Wood county would be glad to go with the prisoner, to whom he would recommend the speculation, as he might have opportunities. The prisoner conversed with the [C]olonel on no other topic, except some general propositions for renting the prisoner's place by the [C]olonel's son-in-law, Thomas Creel [, and whatever raillery the Col. underwent at Dinner, on the subject of the volunteer drum and minute-men at the Point, and the chattering of the children about fighting the Spaniards—]

[16.] The prisoner, however, still continuing to receive daily assurances that the people from the Point were [*determined*] to seize and destroy his corn on the island, as well as the boats building on the Muskingum river, which were to convey his family and friends, with their provisions and necessaries to the Mississippi, thought it prudent to write to Dr. Bennet, requesting him to lend him ten or twenty guns for [the] protection [of his friends and himself on the Island and on the River as far as the Falls of Ohio fr. whence they should be carefully returned with pay for any loss or injury they might suffer.] The object of the prisoner being to resist illegal violence offered to him and his friends in their legal pursuits, he conceived he might correctly borrow rifles, the private property of individuals, or even the arms of the militia, whilst they were not wanted between days of muster, to enable him to resist an apprehended [*outrage on the Laws*] of the country, in the persons of the prisoner and his friends. The doctor replied, that the arms of the militia were in the charge and under the control of the colonel, and he could procure no others.

[17.] Prisoner [now] occupied himself with preparations for his removal with his family and friends from the island, which he took every public opportunity to declare would take place from the 8th to the 10th of the next month of December, 1806, generally telling the applicants [for accompanying him], to provide themselves with a rifle and blanket, but accepting the offers of many as associates without either; soliciting no man, nor offering wages or bounties to any; preparing and providing no military stores, or implements of war whatever—unless corn-meal, flour, whisky, and pork be [regarded] as such—until the latter part of November, when he had an interview with Mr. Graham at Marietta.

[18.] Your client, in virtue of a slight acquaintance he had formed in Kentucky, in 1801, with Mr. G., and under an impression that he also was concerned in some of the speculations of Aaron Burr, visited him soon after his arrival, and was received with much ceremony and coldness. Mr. G. described the government as embarrassed by the variety and contradictory matter of statements which had been forwarded from various parts of the western country, of the equipments then providing on the Ohio and Muskingum, some representing them [*more*,] others less [*extensive*,] but all conveying a suspicion that they were destined for an attack on [*New Orleans*,] an invasion of [*Mexico*,] or for transporting emigrants, with their effects, to Col: Burr's Washita purchase; that, however, their real destination was probably New Orleans or Mexico, rather than the Washita. Mr. G. then observed, as he said, in an official character, that he had it in charge to collect such information as might enable the government to stop any military expedition, if such was intended; and in an [un]official character he added, he would advise prisoner, if he was concerned in such designs, to withdraw from them.

[19.] To these observations, Mr. G. was answered by the prisoner, that the latter could not suppose the government disposed to molest individuals not offending against any law, and avowing a lawful object of their pursuits; that the prisoner, although he had no objection to avow and declare to Mr.G., as he had one to every other person, that he was concerned with Col: Burr in a land purchase, whither he should undertake a journey on the 8th or 10th of December, with such friends, from the number of sixty to one hundred, as might be ready to accompany him; would not condescend to answer interrogatories tending to charge him with being concerned in any [*illegal enterprize*]; that the commencement and progress of this journey should be innocent and peaceful, unless it were interrupted by illegal insult or violence, which should be repelled with those rifles with which he had generally directed his friends to provide themselves; and that he hoped the government, or its agents, had no wish or design to commit a wanton trespass upon men peaceably pursuing speculations, which, because, forsooth, their details were not exposed to the world, [the] jealousy and malice of individuals who would not be [*admitted to participate*] in them, had invoked the suspicion of government [to frustrate.]

[20.] Previous to making these observations to Mr. G., your client showed him a letter, of which he offered him a copy, from Col: Burr, dated from Lexington or Frankfort in Kentucky, acquainting the prisoner with the institution of a criminal prosecution against him (Burr) by Mr. [Daveiss], the United States Attorney for the Kentucky District, where Col: Burr observed the detention he should thereby suffer, would retard the establishment of the Washita settlement. Mr. G. dined in company with your client [at the Tavern] the same day. At table he was assured, on inquiry made by him, that your client would take his wife and family with him down the river. After dinner, your client invited Mr. G. to his room, where he observed, he had called him up again to offer him a copy of the aforesaid letter from Col: Burr, and to trouble him to state over again, in order to prevent any misunderstanding of the intentions of government, whatever official warnings he had to give, that prisoner might communicate them to Col:

Burr and his friends, whose duty it would be to regulate their conduct thereby. Mr. G. then replied, that the prisoner might inform Col: Burr "*the constituted authorities* of the country would be expected on the part of the general government, to stop his boats, if they carried an unusual number of men, armed in an unusual manner." Your client then asked him whether more or less single men, or married men, accompanying your client, to the number of from sixty to one hundred, in sixteen or seventeen boats—generally taking their rifles with them, but not their families at such a season of the year, would constitute such a party, and armed in such a manner, as would expose them to the obstruction he threatened? To this he answered, "He supposed not, though it appeared unusual and suspicious for such numbers to go so far to settle a new country without their families."

[21.] The prisoner now thought he had taken leave of this personage, perfectly understanding both himself and the government. On the contrary, your client, on his return in a day or two to Marietta, learned with surprise that this envoy-extraordinary of executive vigilance could not delay a moment to cool the zeal of his mission, by plunging it red-hot into those intrigues which your client's letter to Phelps, &c. had lately somewhat stagnated in Wood county. Laved and refreshed in these pellucid waters, he follows their meanders in quest of that fountain from which they issue, which, like the source of Alcinous, is hid in mystery and darkness. Arrived at the Temple erected to Honour and Hospitality, in Beech Park, on the banks of the Little Kanawha, he is received in the vestibule by John and Alexander Henderson, the consecrated ministers of those divinities. A libation is now ordained to ancient friendship and the household gods. Another is next proposed to the tutelary deities of the place, "Hold!" cries the envoy of suspicion, "the rites of Honour and Hospitality may be administered by their votaries in these sequestered wilds. But I will never participate in such mummery before that altar on which you have sacrificed to treason and to Burr!" His brother priests are now dismayed and almost petrified. "Yes!" continues the [visitor], "the safety of the State demands a greater sacrifice to liberty. Now purge ye of the charge committed to your keeping, of all the crimes intended to be perpetrated against your country." In vain the distracted brothers declare, "No secrets of a dangerous nature were intrusted to their sanctum—they were innocent and submitted also by him who trusted them, to sanction in the breast of an aged parent." "Say you parent, innocent secrets, and submitted for sanction to the breast of a parent? Why not then disclose them to the parent of the State. I am his minister and will take charge of them!"

[22.] Your client hopes that last paragraph may not displease by its length or obscurity. The style he has there fallen into was insensibly suggested and protracted by his reflections on the intelligence he received from Morgan Neville, Esquire, that it cost Mr. Secretary Graham no little labour to work the Hendersons up to break the seal of that Honour and Hospitality which the prisoner imagined would preserve inviolate, [the] confidential communications [he made] to them, and through them to their father, to the effect set forth in the 5th and 9th Articles, [and that the Secretary had described and boasted of the new Ethics (by which) he had succeeded.—]

Margaret Blennerhassett.
Courtesy of Missouri Historical Society.

Aaron Burr, 1802. Portrait by John Vanderlyn.
Courtesy of the New-York Historical Society. New York City.

Blennerhassett Mansion, sketch by Sala Bosworth.
Courtesy of the Blennerhassett Historical Park Commission.

Richmond Penitentiary by Benjamin Latrobe.
Courtesy of Virginia State Library.

Harman Blennerhassett's Notebooks. Photo taken by the editor with permission in the Manuscripts Division, Library of Congress.

Journal of
Harman Blennerhassett Esq
Whilst in the Jail at the
City of Richmond Va.
awaiting his trial for
Treason & Misdemeanor

Saint Louis Dec. 25th
Cr F— d— l— m—
a— l— O.C—

Inscription from Harman Blennerhassett's Journal.
Courtesy of the Library of Congress.

credit in Phila.do by the continuance of Mr. Sanders' attachment— Having no other source of pecuniary supply, to which I can resort for ~~[illegible]~~ sub-sistence of my family, till I can col-lect the wreck of their property, I await the accomodation of such credit or remittances as yr. dispo-sitions may devise for the relief of my exigencies.— yrs &c. H. B. —

What sort of an answer will the pa-tience of a friend or a wretched wife, further travel ~~[illegible]~~ thro' yr. notes, to hear I received? The servant returned with a verbal answer in these 4 words "He will see him". importing, that Alston would see Nicholas, as if seeing N. will in-demnify me for all I have suffered or support my family. Be these things only known to thee my wife, hereafter. But let them, now and ever, be my first of cares, until I set them right, or perish. — Alston, tells me Belknap has confessed, he reco. fr. Smith, $700 for me; which he denied, the night he arrived on the Island fr. Ken-tucky, — the night I left it. midnight

Page from Blennerhassett's Journal.
Part of Entry for August 25, 1807.
Courtesy of the Library of Congress.

Richmd. Penity Virga.
Wedn. Augt. 26. 07.—

The Bird I believe has not flown to day; but may take wing, I know not what moment. I have neither seen nor heard fr. him since his verbal answer to my letter of yesterday. The little animal has clapped its wings in screaming essays towards the Oaks but yet may it remain a little longer on that egg; it has not yet hatched, for the cuckoo that layed it. Duane's cuckoos may lose some eggs.—but they keep up the breed.

Wirt raised his reputation yesterday, as high as Mc Rae sunk his the day before. The former, I hear, paid me some compliments. We have many visitors as usual, of whom I shall only notice Kerr, who sat 1 hour here this evg. Was cautioned by Dudy. Wdge to beware of Bennet. But I have him secured by Tupper, who tells me, he T. will support the declarations made by Bennet to him and me, on B's first visit to me here. Mrs. Smith is suffering something of a seasoning. midnight.—

Page from Blennerhassett's Journal.
Entry for August 26, 1807.
Courtesy of the Library of Congress.

ABOUT THE TEXT

In presenting Blennerhassett's journal, I have been guided by the view that a text which was never intended for publication should not be edited in such a way as to appear as if it had been prepared for publication by its author. This effort to "clean up" the text was the essential misconception of the journal's only other editor, William H. Safford, whose edition, while it has been useful to scholars since its publication in 1864[1], does not accurately convey either the texture or the content of the original. Safford silently modernized and normalized in various ways Blennerhassett's spelling, punctuation, and sentence structure; more seriously, he suppressed passages of the journal which he evidently thought were distastefully personal or irrelevant to the objective progress of "historical" events.[2] The result was an edition of the journal which, while eminently readable, lacks the knotty vitality, even the precision, of its original. "A journal," G. Thomas Tanselle judiciously observes, "as a piece of writing for one's own use, is in its final form whenever one stops adding to it"; in consequence, he continues, "*scholarly editions* of letters or journals should not contain a text which has editorially been corrected, made consistent, or otherwise smoothed out. Errors and inconsistencies are part of the total texture of the document and are part of the evidence which the document preserves relating to the writer's habits, temperament, and mood."[3] These remarks seem all the more applicable when we remember two facts about Blennerhassett's journal. First, it was mostly written under special conditions of duress: imprisonment, facing the possibilities of conviction and execution, with uncertainties about the health and circumstances of his family, and in the constant undertow of financial ruin. Second, despite these anxieties, and partly to relieve them, he kept his journal so decorously and consistently that such flaws as we find are important indications of his moods, of what he cannot commit to writing; therefore I believe I have, in a way, enhanced its readability in transcribing it faithfully from the manuscript, now in the Library of Congress.

Editorial Method

With the aims mentioned above in view, I have attempted to provide a literal, clear-text edition of Blennerhassett's journal that could serve both the casual and scholarly reader. However, typographical considerations as well as this duality of audience have demanded some exceptions to absolutely literal transcription and require the following procedures for recording them:

1. Alterations made by Blennerhassett to his own text have been recorded in the Table of Alterations unless these are obviously "false starts" or spelling corrections.

2. Emendations of the text and most interpolations have been recorded in the Table of Emendations, with these exceptions: (1) Occasional comments on special physical features of the manuscript pages—large blots, tears, some stray marks—have been recorded on the page, in brackets and in italics. (2) The Textual Notes provide a physical description of the manuscript and discussions of several special textual features. (3) All other normalized or silently emended orthographical features are included among the following special procedures:

3. The manuscript has been followed closely in spelling, punctuation, and capitalization; however, the following exceptions will apply: (1) A few emendations in spelling, especially names, have been made for the convenience of the casual reader; these are recorded in the Table of Emendations. (2) Similarly, a mark of punctuation has been introduced or altered to a modern form in order to suggest an unambiguous reading; these may be found in the Table of Emendations. (3) The dashes which Blennerhassett used liberally and in varying lengths have been approximated by the em (—) dash with occasional use of 2-em (——) or 3-em (———) forms.

4. The superior letters in Blennerhassett's frequent abbreviations have been printed in 9 point type, with the period (which may also serve to end a sentence) under the first (w.th) of the raised letters. The line which he also generally used between the period and the superior letters has been omitted.

5. The wavy line or "wiggle" and the straight line, symbols above or below the line that Blennerhassett now and then uses to represent omitted letters, have been emended to the modern spelling of the full word, and the changes have been recorded in the Table of Emendations.

6. A few other conventional handwritten symbols in the manuscript also present problems in typography or readability; these have been silently emended as follows: (1) the symbol (y) for the thorn (þ) has been transcribed as "th"; (2) the longtailed *s* (ſ) is transcribed as *s*; (3) the symbol for the ampersand is always represented by &; and (4) the symbol (A/c) for "Account" appears here as "Acct."

7. *Italics*, except when enclosed in brackets, are only used where the author has underlined.

8. Blennerhassett used his paper fully; his few paragraph designations have been standardized to the two-character indentation, and each new daily entry has been indented in this manner.

9. Where legibility is partial, asterisks have been substituted for missing letters and the words or phrases thus approximated have been enclosed in square brackets.

10. Finally, a word should be said about the format of the journal entries and the way it has been represented here. Blennerhassett generally heads each page, especially during the trial, with the place and date and then a short spacing line (represented here by a hairline rule) underneath. When a dated heading does not represent a new date, it has been enclosed in parentheses here to remind the reader that the page continues an entry. Similarly, to keep continuity Blennerhassett often ends one page with the words that will be repeated in starting the next page; these tags have been silently removed since they are confusing repetitions on the longer printed page.

---

1. *The Blennerhassett Papers*, ed. William H. Safford (Cincinnati: Moore, Wilstach, and Baldwin, 1864; reprint ed., New York: Arno Press/ New York Times, 1971), pp. 303-507.

2. Compare particularly the entries for Aug. 8, 10, 14, 16, 20, 22, 23, 25, 29, 30; Sept. 14, 18, 21, esp. 24, 28 (misheaded "25" in S.); Oct. 2, 7, 18, esp. 27; Nov. 18, 19, and 20.

3. "The Editing of Historical Documents," *Studies in Bibliography*, 31 (1978), pp. 47-8. Emphasis added.

TEXTUAL NOTES

Harman Blennerhassett kept his journal in the three small notebooks shown in illustration number 5; all are in the possession of the Library of Congress. The first two volumes, each approximately 6″ x 3¾″, bound in polished calf, are literally pocketbooks since, in addition to being pocket-sized, each has a slip-pocket on the inner side of the front board, and both books are equipped with closing flaps which once had fasteners. The first volume has 76 leaves, on which the first 144 unnumbered pages carry the journal from July 20 through August 27; the remaining four leaves contain a blank page and then, written inverse to the rest, an otherwise blank page headed "Notes," followed by four pages of writing and a blank leaf. HB evidently did not intend these notes to be part of the journal, and they do not expand upon any detail in it, though he does occasionally allude there to other notes [see 124.23-24] he is taking. The notes in this volume have at least a general relevance to his view of the trial and have therefore been transcribed as the last item in this section. The second volume has 90 leaves, of which all but one, the back of the last (verso) are inscribed, carrying the journal from August 29 through November 4. The third volume is approximately 3¾″ x 6½″, bound in grained calf; it contains 85 leaves, of which 21 are inscribed (parallel to the spine), carrying the journal from November 6 to November 20, where it breaks off in mid page. The remaining leaves are uninscribed except for the last two, which contain (last page, verso; recto pasted to board) the inscription shown in illustration number 6.

The text itself contains a number of anomalies—some of them perhaps no more than stray marks—which have been identified by bracketed superscript numerals in this edition. These should be further described as follows:

1.[41.1] The text reads "was visited in the most friendly manner [/] by too much folly to mean. . . ." This apparent incoherence suggests that HB may have been recopying his notes and missed a line or two. David Wallace is the visitor named two lines farther on; so his name has been supplied.

2.[74.28] Small numerals 2 2 1 1 1 have been interlined at this point, without a caret or any other evident reference to the text.

3.[102.37] Symbols resembling II have been penciled [?] in above the top line and near the top of the page here, without a caret or any other clear reference to the text.

4.[161.4] See Table of Alterations; in the following lines an apparent reference to a parody of Jefferson has been cancelled with a line, possibly by a later hand.

5.[162.20] The numerals 4 2 1 2 have been interlined above these words, without a caret or any other evident reference to the text.

6.[166.25] "Sufferings" was preceded by "seemingly endless," but these words have been cancelled with a line, apparently by a later hand.

7.[168.23] After the words "General Russell of Kentucky" the words "one of the most vulgar blockheads I ever met with," have been cancelled with a line, apparently by a later hand.

8.[168.34] After "Jefferson" the words "and ought to ruin the last remnant of his credit with every decent man in the community," have been cancelled with a line, evidently by a later hand.

Blennerhassett's "Notes" [*62.5*]:
State prosecutions in Republics—
conducted partially, because—

1.st The people considering the sovereign power their individual property,—when led by party or prejudice to think it has been assailed in the hands of their agents, sensibly regard the accused as a personal enemy.—Hence the improbability of his obtaining an impartial Jury.

2.dly The Adm.^{n} feeling itself dependent for its continuance in power on popular favour will encourage the ruling prejudice and directly or indirectly influence returning officials—whilst in other gov.^{ts} the people seldom exercising the power of the state, regard the charge when it occurs, as an affair in the issue of which the Gov.^{t} has more immediate interest than themselves. Hence, acquittals more frequent, in monarchies than in Republics.—In the former the end of the prosecu.^{n} is the future safety and security of the State in all cases, save where the object of the conspiracy has been the usurp.^{n} of the gov.^{t}—in the latter it must generally be the destruct.^{n} of an adverse party, to which the adm.^{n} is personally hostile—

Examples from History.

[*Half-page space*]

In the case of Burr & Associates—the gov.^{t} loads the Federalists w.th the odium of his imputed Treason in exertions for his acquittal—But Gov.^{t} returning officials and large majority of Gr. Jury are of the opposition or Democratic faction, besides the venire is made returnable fr. remote counties a large majority of whose citizens are of the Gov.^{t} party, and cannot fr. their education and habits of life take that enlarged view of the subject they are to judge of, that citizens or Jurors fr. the Body of the State might.—The policy of the Law which requires the Panel to be returned fr. the District or County, in which the crime is charged to have been committed—was devised as well, for the benefit of the accused as of the prosecution.—But here the citizens of Wood C^{ty} and the other counties can be proved *generally* to be prejudiced or personal enemies of H.B.—and where the reason of the law ceases, the law sh^{d} cease with it—A[**th^{s}]

[*Two spaces*]

The accused has some security ag^{t} undue influence over his judges, in such practical participation, as is found, on their part, in the cementing principles of each of the only 3 gov^{ts} that can exist.—Under a monarchy, he looks for it in the Glory and agrandizement of the Crown—under an Aristocracy, in the personal honour of the Rulers of the State; and in a Republic—in the individual virtue and sympathy of all the people.—

In ancient Republics

Where this Virtue had only a real existence it was always dormant during the season of popular prejudice ag^{t} persecuted patriots, as in the case of Aristides at Athens and Coriolanus at Rome.

In modern Republics

It has never appeared save in some of Switzerland, but as a name. For these being all derived fr. a commercial origin, the mercantile principle that engendered them, has ever been commensurate with their duration and every citizen, of a large majority is more a merchant than a patriot by habit—If in quest of popularity—he is a partizan—If under the influence of patronage, a persecutor for the Gov^{t}—

ANNOTATIONS

These have been keyed to the text by page, line, and reference-phrase. Lines counted are all actual lines of print on the page, including dates and hairlines but not the running head. Full annotation of HB's densely allusive diary would require a work at least as long as the copy-text; consequently these annotations have, in general, been limited to HB's references to major participants in the Richmond drama, his loaded comments on acts and testimony involving himself, and those cultural allusions and quotations which suggest the scope of his reading and other interests. References to sources have been given with minimal abbreviation so that these may also serve as a selected bibliography.

4.31-33 *visited by M.r Alston, M.r Mercer, and M.r Randolph, the latter having obligingly tendered me his services as a Lawyer*: HB's mention of these visitors might best be clarified by brief sketches of (1) Alston, (2) Mercer, and (3) Counsel in the trial, among whom Randolph figures significantly.

(1) Joseph Alston (1779-1816) was Burr's son-in-law, having married Theodosia on February 2, 1801. He had attended Princeton for a year in 1795-6 and later studied law with Edward Rutledge. As the eldest son of Col. William Alston, a prominent South Carolina rice-planter, he became one of the richest men in the state and was the heaviest financial contributor to Burr's expedition. He became governor of South Carolina in 1812 and served until 1814. For his early—and in HB's view, disgraceful—attempt to dissociate himself from his father-in-law's projects, see 10.8 and note. HB believed that Alston had guaranteed him against all his losses on Burr's behalf; these losses he eventually estimated at $50,000., including Burr's unpaid drafts of $6,864.96 [see 126.12-17.], losses of $15,000. through forced sale of his household property, and the remainder through the destruction of his mansion. Alston seems to have thought his obligation extended

only to his father-in-law's unpaid drafts, though HB credits him with a payment of $12,500., nearly twice the amount of these.

(2) Charles Fenton Mercer (1778-1858) is a strangely obscure yet significant figure in the journal; HB identifies him by little, apart from remarking the pleasure given him by his friend's frequent visits and other acts of kindness. Mercer was a native of Fredericksburg, Virginia; he was a lawyer, a businessman, and a Congressman for Virginia from 1817-1839; a man of liberal interests and considerable talent, he favored suppression of the slave trade, colonization of Africa by freed Negroes, and a complete system of public education from common primary school to a state university. In 1845 he published *An Exposition of the Weakness and Inefficiency of the Government of the United States*. He never married. What W.H. Safford tells us of HB's first meeting with Mercer in December, 1806 is itself quite interesting. Mercer, who had known Alston while both were at Princeton, was introduced to HB during a western tour. Evidently he had heard that the island estate might be for sale and stopped to inquire about it; however, when he heard that HB wanted $50,000. for the place—a price, the owner declared, that was $10,000. less than it had cost him—Mercer gave up thoughts of purchasing "the most elegant seat in Virginia," yet he warmed to conversation with its owner. The date of this visit was the 6th of December, and HB was full of plans and prospects for the expedition on which he would so soon embark. He related much of this to Mercer, pressed him to join in; praised the moral leadership of Burr, and then listened as Mercer expressed his reservations about Burr's character and his doubts about founding one's future upon such shifty ground. Later that evening, as the two men journeyed to Marietta, Mercer expressed his puzzlement at the contradictoriness of HB's new choice and posed, as Safford relates them, troublesome and impassioned queries to him: " . . . Will a man who, weary of the agitations of the world, of its noise and vanity, has retired to a solitary island in the heart of a desert, and created a terrestrial paradise . . . a man whose soul is accustomed to toil in the depths of literature; whose ear is framed to the harmony of sound . . . ; will such a man start up, in the decline of life, from the pleasing dream of seven years' slumber, to carry fire and sword to the peaceful habitations of men who have never done him wrong?" There were other penetrating rhetorical questions of this kind, and they left HB, Safford relates, in a state "much disheartened as to the enterprise, and nearly resolved to abandon it altogether." From this mood he was only roused by the "persuasive eloquence" and "heroic enthusiasm of his wife," supported by timely

arrival of Comfort Tyler and his people. Thus the Mercer who visits HB in prison is evidently that friend who made the most serious effort to dissuade him from the course of action that brought him to his trouble. [W.H. Safford, *The Blennerhassett Papers*, Cincinnati, 1864, pp. 161-64.]

(3) Edmund Randolph (1753-1813) who had been a delegate to the continental Congress, Governor of Virginia, representative from Virginia at the Constitutional Convention, and the first Attorney General of the U.S., was chief counsel for Burr, the most prestigious if not the most effective member of Burr's "forensic army." See Index, below, for HB's many comments on individuals in the powerful array of counsel for both sides, which Charles Warren has listed as follows: "For Burr there appeared, first and foremost, Edmund Randolph, ex-Attorney-General of the United States, weighty in counsel, deep in knowledge, but ponderous in style; Charles Lee also ex-Attorney-General; John Wickham, the leader of the Virginia Bar, famed for his wit and versatility; Benjamin Botts of Virginia, a lawyer of much tact, local attorney and good fellow; and finally Luther Martin. Burr himself, with his keen and powerful intellect, originated and directed his whole defence. For the Government there appeared Caesar A. Rodney, only recently appointed United State Attorney-General, who took part in the preliminaries of the trial; George Hay, United States District-Attorney, and son-in-law of James Monroe; William Wirt, then thirty-five years old, and practically at the beginning of his brilliant career, and Alexander McRae, Lieutenant-Governor of Virginia, a lawyer of courage and tenacity but lacking in tact." [*A History of the American Bar*, Boston, 1911, p. 268.]

5.3-4 *some good tea and cakes sent me by Mrs Alston*: She was, of course, Burr's daughter Theodosia, who appears indirectly in the journal through the tributes HB pays to her qualities and by way of the gifts she sends him. At one point [143.25-26] he remarks that Luther Martin's "idolatrous admiration of Mrs Alston is almost as excessive as my own. . . ." There was something of a return of hospitality in the "good tea and cakes," since Theodosia, followed later by her husband, had visited the Blennerhassetts at their island home in September, 1806. Milton Lomask has described succinctly the impression she made on her host and hostess: "The Blennerhassetts found her company delightful. Most people did. At twenty-three, Theodosia was precisely the paragon of brains, beauty, and wit that her father had long ago made up his mind she was going to be." [*Aaron Burr: The Conspiracy and Years of Exile, 1805–1836*, New York, 1982, p. 131. For a concise biography see R. Ray Swick, "Theodosia Burr Alston," *The South Atlantic Quarterly*, 74 (Autumn, 1975): 495-506.]

8.20-21 *Quiquid delirant Reges plecuntur Achivi:* "Whatever errors the great commit, the people must atone for." Horace, *Epistulae*, I, 2. 14.

8.23-24 *Write to Emmet to come to the trial*: Thomas Addis Emmet (1764-1827) brother of Robert Emmet, was an Irish barrister who gained a brilliant reputation for his efforts in behalf of the Irish cause; for these activities he was imprisoned in 1798 and later released on condition of his permanent exile. Emigrating to the U.S., he established a successful practice in New York and became one of the most prominent American lawyers of his time. He was an old friend of HB, who had gone east for a reunion with this friend at the time when Burr passed the Island on his return to the east in October 1805.

9.31-32 *saying Mrs Blennerhassett had good reason for her opinion of Col. Morgan*: On his way west in the summer of 1806 Burr accepted an invitation to visit an old friend, Col: George Morgan (1745-1810), at "Morganza," his estate in Washington County, Pa., not far from Pittsburgh. He was escorted there by the Colonel's sons John and Thomas; during their ride and the following visit, Burr—so the Morgans would later testify—made predictions "that the union of the states could not possibly last; . . . that a separation of the states must ensue as a natural consequence in four or five years"; that the western states would secede within that time; more dangerously, he allegedly asserted "the weakness and imbecility of the federal government," and even boasted that "with two hundred men, he could drive the president and congress into the Potomac." Thomas Morgan, in particular, would testify that Burr had taken him aside and had tried to recruit him, saying that "under our government there was no encouragement for talents," and had asked him whether he "would like a military expedition or enterprise." Such testimony, of course, would come later, but it was begun when, soon after Burr left Morganza, Col. Morgan sent an account of these remarks to the President. [M-J. Kline, *et. al.*, eds., *The Political Correspondence and Public Papers of Aaron Burr*, Princeton, 1983, 2:1039, n.2; D. Robertson, *Reports of the Trials of Colonel Aaron Burr*, Philadelphia, 1808, 1:497-506.]

10.8 *that caution Mt A. has exhibited to the world*: HB's allusion is to Alston's letter to Charles Pinckney, governor of South Carolina. The supposedly incriminating "cipher letter" [see 77.26-7], which the President had made public in his message to Congress on January 22, contained a clear reference to Alston, his wife, and his son. On February 6, 1807, Alston wrote an anguished letter to the

Governor in which he vigorously repudiated all knowledge of the schemes which the "cipher letter" appeared to disclose. Some phrases in Alston's letter [Safford, *Blennerhassett Papers*, pp. 227-29] were also directly critical of his father-in-law's presumption, since Alston, unlike many others, appeared to accept the "cipher letter" as Burr's work. Alston later repented this hasty action and, as we see from the journal, stood by his father-in-law during the trial; but HB had his reasons for wishing to remind Alston of this ill-judged and disloyal reaction [see 37.15].

13.17 *in the case of Swartwout and Ogden*: HB meant the case of Bollman and Swartwout. [See 39.21-24 and n.] Wilkinson had seized Burr's agents John Adair and Peter V. Ogden as well as Bollman and Swartwout and had sent them all East for trial; however, in Baltimore Judge J.H. Nicholson discharged Adair and Ogden on the ground that they had not committed a crime in his jurisdiction.

14.22-23 *the Dernean and once redoubted Eaton*: William Eaton (1764-1811) had become known as the "hero of Derne" for the most celebrated of his exploits in the U.S. war against Tripoli. In 1804-5 he mounted a plan to win the Tripolitan war by attacking the city from the rear by land; with the reluctant support of Congress, he raised a mixed force of some 400 men of various nationalities and undertook the long march overland; he subdued the city of Derna and might have taken Tripoli had the war not ended in a truce. At Richmond, as HB makes clear, the "hero of Derne" cut a colorful but absurd figure in his outlandish get-up. This coupled with his heavy drinking, his bluster and braggadocio, made him unpopular with the locals; and the fact that he had so recently been granted a $10,000 indemnification by the government tended to cast some discredit on his testimony. He had been brought to testify to the treasonous character of certain remarks Burr had made to him in their private conversations during the winter of 1806. During the treason trial much of his testimony was forbidden by the Chief Justice because it was not directly relevant to the "overt act" of "levying war" specified in the indictment. [See 38.13 and 39.16-17.] But in the misdemeanor trial he was allowed to present his sensational testimony, but by then its scandal had staled from having been much publicized in the newspapers. Chiefly, as Francis Beirne has summarized, Eaton told the court that "Burr told him that if he could win over the Marine Corps and secure the interest of Truxtun, Preble, and Decatur, he would turn Congress out neck and heels, assassinate the President (or what amounted to that) and declare himself protector of an energetic government. Eaton insisted that Burr had used such expressions as 'hang him,' 'throw him into the Potomac,' and 'send him to Carter's Mountain.' "That is, he would send him back to Monticello. [F.J. Beirne, *Shout Treason: The Trial of Aaron Burr*, New York, 1959, p. 252.]

14.35 *Quis talia fando temperet a lachrymis*?: "Who could talk of such things and refrain from tears?" Virgil, *Aeneid*, ii, 6. [See notes to 18.23, 133.29-31 and compare John Cannon, ed., *The Letters of Junius*. Oxford, 1978, p. 190 n.]

15.1-3 *Gen.l Dayton . . . will offer himself up, tomorrow*: Jonathan Dayton and Burr had been friends since their childhood days in Elizabethtown, N.J.; both had marched to Quebec under Benedict Arnold during the war. For his part in the conspiracy Dayton had been indicted by the Grand Jury on 25 June—along with John Smith, Comfort Tyler, Israel Smith, and Davis Floyd—on charges of treason and misdemeanor; the charges were dropped when Burr was acquitted. Some authorities have lately identified Dayton as the author of the notorious "cipher letter." See notes to 77.27-28 and 83.19.

15.16-17 *D. Woodbridge slept in, whilst I was at breakfast*: Dudley Woodbridge, Jr. had been HB's business partner at Marietta, Ohio. For HB's reaction to his testimony and his character, see 62.27-63.26; 106.28-107.3 and notes.

18.23 *Proh pudor!*: Oh shame! [See note to 133.29-31 and compare John Cannon, ed., *The Letters of Junius*, p. 224.]

19.30-31 *procured . . . copies of the depositions, before the Grand Jury, of Peter Taylor, Jacob Albright and David Wallace*: At the Grand Jury hearing, which lasted from May 22 to June 30, the prosecution, to obtain an indictment for high treason against Burr, HB, and the other associates, had to show that it could prove that an "overt act" of "levying war" against the U.S., an act witnessed by at least two persons, had occurred at the time and place specified, "Blennerhassett's Island . . . the 10th day of December, 1806." As his remarks in this entry and elsewhere indicate, some of the evidence produced at the inquiry troubled HB greatly because he believed it to be perjurious and/or potentially damaging to his case, and because this material was likely to be reintroduced at the trial, which had begun on August 3. Two of the deponents mentioned here, Taylor and Albright, did testify at length in the following days, and in ways that justified HB's anxiety.

Peter Taylor was the Blennerhassett's gardener, whom they had brought from England in 1803; a plain, unlettered man, he proved nonetheless to have a copious memory. He was permitted to testify about his master's activities shortly before and after the President's proclamation against the conspiracy; his testimony was intended, according to Hay, to "directly prove the connection of Burr with Blennerhassett, and with the assemblage on the island." It seemed likely to have a more profound effect. Among other things, he told the court that HB had told him that "Colonel Burr and he and a few of his friends, had bought eight hundred thousand acres of land and they wanted young men to settle it"; however, when he later and from time to time continued to ask what kind of seed he should bring, HB at last "made a sudden pause, and said 'I will tell you what, Peter, we are going to take Mexico; one of the richest places in the whole world.' He said that Colonel Burr would be the king of Mexico and Mrs. Alston, daughter of Colonel Burr, was to be queen of Mexico, whenever Colonel Burr died." Most remarkably, Taylor recounted that when he had asked his master what was to become of the men who might not want to go farther than the lands they had come to settle, HB had said: " 'O by God, I tell you, Peter, every man that will not conform to order and discipline, I will stab; you'll see how I'll fix them.' " Taylor also told how HB had sent him on an errand to a Dr. Bennet of Mason County with an offer to purchase firearms from him; he was, he said, given a letter for the Doctor which he was not to leave with him in any case but "to get it back and burn it, for it contained high treason."

A day later the prosecution expected even greater significance from the testimony of Jacob Albright, a laborer who had been "hired on the island to help build a kiln for drying corn." Hay said the object of his testimony was to prove "the actual assemblage of men on Blennerhassett's island" and "to prove directly the overt act" of levying war. Albright told the court he had been on the island on that cold night of December 9, when with two or three inches of snow on the ground, men were hastily loading Comfort Taylor's four boats for the flight down-river. He recalled that about midnight, as a circle of men were warming themselves around a fire, "a man by the name of [General Edward] Tupper, laid his hands upon Blennerhassett, and said, 'Your body is in my hands, in the name of the commonwealth.' Some *such words* as that he mentioned. When Tupper made that motion, there were seven or eight muskets levelled at him. Tupper looked about him and said, 'Gentlemen, I hope you will not do the like.' One of the gentlemen who was nearest, about two yards off, said, '*I'd as lieve as not.*' Tupper then changed his speech, and said he wished him to escape safe down the river, and wished him luck. Tupper before told Blennerhassett he should stay and stand his trial. But Blennerhassett said no; that the people in the neighborhood were coming down next day to take him, and he would go." [David Robertson, *Reports of the Trials of Colonel Aaron Burr* (1808), 1:

491–97, 506–514; for Tupper's deposition of Sept. 8, 1807, see Lesley Henshaw, ed., "Burr-Blennerhassett Documents," *Quarterly Publication of the Historical and Philosophical Society of Ohio*, 9: 1 & 2 (Jan. and Apr., 1814): 13–27. Henshaw's notes set the time of Tupper's visit to the island as the evening of Dec. 9 and of HB's departure as the early morning of Dec. 10.]

Robertson does not record testimony of David Wallace before the grand jury; however, in his sworn statement, Wallace declared: "Blennerhassett informed me of the intended expedition down the river, wished me to engage said I should be Surgeon Gen! but said he was not at liberty to unfold the object he said he expected 500 men to go from the neighbourhood of Marietta. I told him that 300 men on the Ohio could stop them. Blennerhassett said in that case they would land and fire the houses and towns and draw of the attention of the people. I understood the plan to be to separate the union and to take Mexico. Blennerhassett frequently alluded to his plan [;] in conversation requested me to put up a large quantity of medicines addopted to a Military expedition. . . ." [Henshaw, ed., "Burr-Blennerhassett Documents," p. 58.]

These then, particularly the first two, would be the most damaging testimonies linking HB to Burr and to the "overt act" specified in the indictment; here, on August 12, a week before these testimonies would be heard in the trial, HB is appropriately anxious and indignant as he reads over their earlier depositions before the Grand Jury. " 'Oh God of truth and justice,' avenge such murderous villainies," he may understandably exclaim at this point. But as the trial itself progressed his mind would gradually be put at ease with regard to such evidence as this; it would soon become obvious that, while Burr would get an acquittal out of the court, he must get his money out of Burr. Albright's testimony would be discredited by the fact that, although General Edward Tupper of Marietta had been there in court as Albright testified, the witness appeared not to have known him, and that the prosecution was unwilling to place the General on the stand to corroborate Albright's testimony. Their reason would later appear in a deposition sworn to by Tupper in which he stated that he had no authority to arrest anyone on the night of December 9, that no guns were levelled at him, "nor any incivility offered him." [Milton Lomask, *Aaron Burr: The Conspiracy and Years of Exile*, New York, 1982, p. 267.]

Most important of all, from the defense's point of view, is something HB does not, perhaps could not, observe at this point: none of these witnesses could say they had seen Burr on Blennerhassett Island. Albright would be asked this; Taylor would be recalled specifically to be asked this. By August 20, the defense could express its impatience with a parade of testimony that was becoming increasingly irrelevant; the government must prove that there *was* an "overt act" of "levying war" on the Island, and that Burr was physically or legally present at it, before it could introduce collateral testimony. On that day, after a bit more testimony of the kind had been heard, Burr and his counsel made some observations that forecast the essential course of the trial over the next two months. They "objected strongly to the introduction of collateral evidence, and insisted strenuously that the counsel for the prosecution should adduce, without further delay, all the testimony which they had, relating to any overt acts alleged to have been committed on Blennerhassett's island; and that the relevancy or irrelevancy of the collateral proof offered, depended entirely on the existence of these acts." [Robertson, I, pp. 529–30.] HB, as we see, is too caught up in the immediacies of his life to have an early sense of this strategy; his anxiety prevents him from seeing how readily the defense will dispense with such collateral evidence as the deposition of David Wallace. [Later testimony of the Wallace brothers is described in the note to 30.29–32. For the way in which Dr. Robert Wallace of Marietta and one of his sons, Dr. David Wallace, were "instrumental" in Burr's first visit to Blennerhassett's island, see M. Lomask, *Aaron Burr*, 2:58–9.]

19.34 *that General Tupper arrested me*: See 19.30–31 and notes. Edward White Tupper of Marietta, Ohio, was named Brigadier General of the Ohio militia in 1806. He and Burr had been introduced by Judge Return J. Meigs in 1805, as the former Vice-President was returning from his first western tour. The two exchanged several letters, but no specific mention of an expedition was made until Burr wrote Tupper on November 18, 1806, explaining that "the utmost alarm has been excited in your neighborhood on account of preparations which I am making for about 100 or 150 settlers—The rumors of my building Gun Boats, ships & ca. have been fabricated by a few designing men. . . . " [M-J. Kline, *et. al.*, eds., *The Political Correspondence and Public Papers of Aaron Burr*, Princeton, 1983, 2:1002.] In the deposition he gave at Richmond in September, 1807, Tupper stated that HB, with whom he had had a slight earlier acquaintance, had visited his home and had expressed Burr's wish that Tupper "should join them in the enterprise." Tupper stated that he "would not take his family to settle another new country" but would engage in "an authorized Military expedition." In reply, however, HB had made clear that Burr "only wanted men enough to work the boats," but proved evasive about the military character of the mysterious "enterprise." Tupper stated that HB told him he was disposing of property on his island as a consequence of this "enterprise," but never pressed him further to join it. He deposed that he had met HB for the last time on December 9, the evening of his departure from the island in the early hours of December 10. Contrary to Albright's testimony, he declared that, having heard of the seizure of boats at Marietta and of HB's plans to flee, he merely went to the island to settle some business matters, not to make an arrest. He did recall having attempted to persuade HB to stay and face whatever charges might be brought against him; he did not succeed, however, and HB left with Tyler's boats early the next morning. [L.H. Henshaw, ed., "Burr-Blennerhassett Documents," *Quarterly Publication of the Historical and Philosophical Society of Ohio*, 9: 1 & 2 (January and April, 1914): pp. 13-27.]

20.7 *Nolle prosequi*: "In civil proceedings, an action by the plaintiff not to proceed with his action at all or as to parts of it, or as to certain defendants. . . . The court will not thereafter allow any further proceedings to be taken in the case, nor inquire into the reasons or justifications for the Attorney-General's decision. It is not equivalent to an acquittal and does not bar a fresh indictment for the same offence. . . . In the U.S., the discretion is vested in the prosecutor or such as the district attorney and may be used if the accused agrees to make restitution or to plead guilty to a lesser charge." [David M. Walker, *Oxford Companion to Law.*]

20.13 *read . . . Tully de Officiis: De Officiis* (44 B.C.) [*on Duties*] was the last important philosophical work of Marcus Tullius Cicero (106–43 B.C.). Addressed to his son, it consists of three books, of which the first discusses the morally good, the second the expedient, and the third the apparent conflicts between the two concepts.

20.32-33 *The Hendersons would swear much against me*: See Appendix C, paragraphs 9 and 10, for HB's account of his writing of the "Querist" articles and of the occasion on which he read part of one number to John and Alexander Henderson. [On the hostility of the Hendersons, and HB's sarcastic allegory of their behavior, see Appendix C, paragraphs 11 and 20.] The Henderson brothers were prominent Wood County residents; they were Federalists and neighbors of the Blennerhassetts, with whom, as M. Lomask relates, they "had been at odds for years, immersed in a mutual antipathy, all the stronger because they were Wood County's leading families, its greatest slaveowners. Ethnicity may have been a component of the feud, for the Hendersons were Scots by birth and the Blennerhassetts English, but its sticking point was politics." But, as Lomask further observes, "it is difficult to reconcile Blennerhassett's bizarre remarks to the Hendersons, as reported by them at Richmond, with the long-standing strain between the two families." [For HB's reaction to this testimony, which the Chief Justice permitted in the misdemeanor trial, see 102.4-34 and 104.23-105.3.] Alexander Henderson testified that HB had told them that in Burr's plan Louisiana was to be revolutionized, New Orleans seized, and as many as fifty pieces of artillery belonging to the French were to be taken; that "if Mr. Jefferson was any way impertinent . . . Colonel Burr would tie him neck and heels and throw him into the Potomac;" most astonishingly, he said that HB had told him "that with three pieces of artillery and 300 sharpshooters he could defend any pass in the Allegheny Mountains against any force the Government could send." John Henderson testified to the same effect the following day. There is a similarity here with the Morgans' testimony [see note to 9.31-32], but we note HB's eagerness to cross-examine "Sandy Henderson" as well as the fact that Burr's lawyers prevent him from doing so at any length because of "the apprehended hostility, of the witness." [Milton Lomask, *Aaron Burr: The Conspiracy and Years of Exile*, New York, 1982, pp. 130-31; Francis F. Beirne, *Shout Treason: The Trial of Aaron Burr*, New York, 1959, p. 251; *American State Papers, Miscellaneous*, 1: 525-38].

21.20 *sed ita lex scripta est*: but so the law is written.

21.28-29 *M.r Botts said he saw the Querist at Old Henderson's*: [See Appendix C, paragraphs 9 and 10; also 20.32-33 and note.] Soon after Burr left the Island in late August, 1806, HB began to write a series of four letters to the editor of the *Ohio Gazette* of Marietta. These letters, which began appearing on September 4, were signed "Querist." They maintained that the Federal Government, influenced by the commercial hegemony of the eastern states, was exploiting the agricultural West through its adverse policies with respect to trade, land, and taxation. The Querist proposed to "consider those objections that have occurred to me against the measure of a severance of the Union . . . "; however, his stance, beyond this, was to be disinterested; he had "no intention of recommending either the mode or the time" in which the severance might be effected. "An individual embarked in the vessel of my country, when I alarm my shipmates with my report that the helm is deserted or improperly manned, I do not presume to dictate to them how or whither they should steer till called upon to do so." [W.H. Safford, ed. *The Blennerhassett Papers*, Cincinnati, 1864, pp. 139-40.]

22.1 *my first interview with Graham on Burr's affairs*: In late

October, 1806, the President sent John Graham, Secretary of the Orleans Territory, west through Ohio "with confidential authority to inquire into Burr's movements, put the governors, etc., on their guard, [and] to provide for his arrest if necessary. . . ." Graham reached Marietta by mid-November, where he met HB, who had made his acquaintance in 1801. HB assumed that Graham was one of Burr's people and therefore talked freely with him about what he knew of Burr's plans. See HB's Brief [Appendix C, paragraphs 18-21] for his statement concerning this meeting as well as his humorous, mock-heroic account (so strange in a Brief), of Graham's perfidious visit to the Hendersons soon after. Compare also HB's reference to this at 60.32-33.

25.14-16 *what St. Pierre aptly names the harmony of contrast*: This allusion to the writings of Jacques Henri Bernardin de St. Pierre (1737-1814) is particularly interesting for the light it throws on HB's reading. St. Pierre was an adventurer, naturalist, and visionary social philosopher strongly influenced by Rousseau. His supple style enabled him to produce charming descriptions of natural scenes and to evoke melancholy nature-feeling in a manner anticipating Chateaubriand. Among his most influential works, his *Études de la Nature* (3 vols, 1784) examines nature closely for proofs that "God made nature for man, and man for Himself"; his immensely popular *Paul et Virginie* (1788) is a sentimental and didactic narrative that traces the growth of love between two young people on the island of Mauritius, tutored only by the harmonies of a nature untainted by civilization. His notion of the harmony of "contraries," to which HB refers, is developed in the *Études*; this idea, which St. Pierre regarded as the key to philosophy, is vaguely suggestive of Hegel's "contradictions." Nothing has been made in vain, he argues, everything is compensated by a contrary; therefore "every man who affirms a simple proposition is only half right, because the contrary proposition exists equally in nature." [Arvède Barine, *Bernardine de St. Pierre*, tr. J.E. Gordon, Chicago, 1893, pp. 136-7.]

26.10-11 *interesting french conversation with Col: de Pestre*: When Burr visited Blennerhassett Island on August 27-28, 1806, he was accompanied by Col. Julien De Pestre, a French émigré who had served in the armies of both the French and the English. Burr had made De Pestre his chief-of-staff; so presumably he had met with HB and his business partner, Dudley Woodbridge, Jr., as they arranged for boats to be built and provisions to be supplied for the expedition. The specific *conversation* to which HB refers would have been especially "interesting" to the diarist because De Pestre dropped some hints as to why he was not indicted along with HB and others of Burr's chief associates. Evidently the government had offered to provide "handsomely" for the Col. in the army if he would turn state's evidence; perhaps some pressure was even brought to bear by the action against De Pestre's brother-in-law to which HB alludes. But because the Colonel declined this offer he reappears in these entries as HB's congenial confidant. [For further comment on De Pestre, see 97.37–100.8 and note to 98.23–25.]

28.34–29.8 *Wood, the late Editor of the Atlantic-World*: John Wood, a Scot who had emigrated to the U.S. in 1800, was the author of the libelous *History of the Administration of John Adams, esq. Late President of the United States*, which Burr had worked to suppress in 1802. In 1806, when Wood became an editor of *The Western World*, a Federalist paper which began publication in Frankfort, Ky. that summer, he gladly published Joseph Hamilton Daveiss's articles charging Burr and others with conspiracy. Later, when Daveiss's attacks had proved ineffectual, Wood came over to Burr, moved to Washington, and, having started a paper he called the *Atlantic World*, began vigorously defending in it the man he had so recently inveighed against. For HB's account of Wood's analysis of Daveiss's true motives for his persistent attacks on Burr, see 64.10–65.2 and notes.

30.29–32 *Doctor Wallace is alarmed at my presence here to confront him . . . for he is no Doctor. . . .* : David C. Wallace had sworn that HB had offered him the post of Surgeon General to the expedition; for his affidavit, see 19.30–31 and note. Later, at the misdemeanor trial, he testified to the same and maintained that HB had said that if the flotilla were to be fired on from the bank, " 'in that case, we would land a party, and set fire to every house in town.' " He also narrated the following, which, if true, casts light on HB's disposition to lead: "I rode with Mr. Blennerhassett to see the boats that were building up the Muskingum, where he showed the builder of the boats and myself the articles by which *the people under his command, as he called them*, were to be governed on descending the river." [Emphasis added.] In the cross-examination Wallace reiterated that "this party intended to effect a separation of the Union, and to carry the expedition into Mexico." He supposed that HB had offered the post of Surgeon General "to induce me to join, although I had not practiced physic." He stated, however, that he had studied medicine for seven years at Philadelphia, including one winter's attendance of surgical operations at the hospital there and three years' study with Dr. White.

David Wallace's brother, Robert [see 18.13–14], testified the following day, September 25, that HB had tried to recruit him for the expedition but had not been specific about its nature. "He said he was not then at liberty to reveal the object entirely, but if I would depend on his friendship he would do well for me. He spoke of settlement of the Washita land, but intimated there was something else in view." When he asked whether the Government countenanced this expedition, "Mr. Blennerhassett replied that it was immaterial whether the Government aided it or not; Government was weak; they would have nothing to do with Government, unless it opposed the expedition; in that case they would make resistance." The next day, Robert Wallace continued, he rode back to Marietta with HB, who undertook some recruitment along the way: "he was engaging several young men to go down river with him, offering them lands; among the rest was one Rattburn, a schoolmaster; I told him he was a drunkard, and could do nothing towards the settlement of land. 'No matter,' said Mr. Blennerhassett; 'when he is brought under good discipline, he will make a good soldier; and his allowance will not be large enough to make him drunk.' " Robert also testified that he had been present when HB had offered his brother the post of Surgeon General; he also told the court that his father, Dr. Robert Wallace, who had been present, told HB "he had better give up the enterprise, and stay at home on his island; that it was impossible he could succeed; that his force was too small, and the opposition too great. Mr. Blennerhassett said that General Wilkinson and the army would join them." [*American State Papers, Miscellaneous*, 1:535-36.]

34.10-11 *a pamphlet entitled Agrestis*: Agrestis was the pseudonym of the author of *A Short Review of the Late Proceedings at New Orleans*. See Introduction, above, p. xxvi and n.

34.13-14 *language . . . w.^{d} not be unworthy of a Curran*: John Philpot Curran (1750-1817) was an Irish barrister and member of the Irish House of Commons, where he was notable for his oratorical skills as well as for his strong advocacy of Catholic emancipation and his astringent criticisms of governmental patronage and corruption. Moving to London after his retirement in 1814, Curran frequently socialized with such literary lights as Thomas Moore, Lord Byron, and Richard Brinsley Sheridan.

37.15 *discords fr. the letter to Pinkney*: [See 10.8.] HB evidently hopes to confirm Alston in his duty by reminding him of an earlier failure of it—his letter to Charles Pinckney—which he now repented.

37.18-22 *if it cannot move the Oaks*: "The Oaks" was Alston's plantation in S. Carolina, on the site of what is now Brookgreen Gardens, near Georgetown.

38.30-32 *It will appear . . . how far Hay contends that the doctrine of constructive treason is law*: What HB alludes to here was to be the crucial issue of Burr's treason trial. According to the Constitution, acts of Congress, and terms of the indictment, the prosecution in Burr's case had to prove that an "overt act" of "levying war" against the U.S., an act witnessed by at least two persons, had occurred at Blennerhassett's island on December 13, 1806, as specified in the indictment. Furthermore, the accused had to have been legally present at that time and place. As Ch. J. Marshall was to say in his Opinion, "the whole treason laid in this indictment is the levying of war in Blennerhassett's island; and the whole question to which the inquiry of the court is now directed is whether the prisoner was legally present at the fact." Of course, it had been clear from the start that Aaron Burr had not been physically present at the fact; therefore, even if an "overt act" were to be proved by witnesses, the prosecution, to convict Burr, would have to show that he was present in some other sense. To quote the Chief Justice further, "though the overt act may not itself be the treason, it is the sole act of that treason which can produce conviction. It is the sole point at issue between the parties. And the only division of that point . . . which the court is now examining is the *constructive presence* of the prisoner at the fact charged." [David Robertson, *Reports of the Trials of Colonel Aaron Burr* (1808), 2:428-29. Italics added.]

In the case of Bollman and Swartwout [see 39.21-24] the Ch.J. had argued that the framers of the Constitution had deliberately defined treason in a narrow sense so as to rule out the doctrine of *constructive treason* by which, under English law, the concept of treason could be extended by construction to doubtful cases. Nevertheless, certain phrases in his *obiter dictum*, [especially, "all those who perform any part, however minute, *or however remote from the scene of action*, and who are actually leagued in the general conspiracy are to be considered as traitors."—as cited by Wm. Wirt for the prosecutor and transcribed in Robertson, *Reports*, 2:62] appeared to allow considerable latitude, for proving the constructive presence of the accused, and it was around this point that the prosecution built its case. However, in his Opinion the Ch.J. made it clear that his remarks in the case of Bollman and Swartwout had not been intended to create legal precedent for introducing constructive treason into the U.S. and that, furthermore, the prosecution had not proved either the actual or legal presence of the accused at the scene of action.

Finally, it should be noticed that *constructive treason*, as seen in historical perspective, was not really an issue in Burr's trial, though it appeared at first to be. The English doctrine of constructive treason descends from the statutes of Edward III, gradually coming to mean, as Bradley Chapin states, that "words spoken or written, and conspiracies to levy war could amount to the treason of compassing or imagining the death of the king, and that any attempt to modify public policy by force amounted to treason." In American cases such as those of Fries [see 134.9] and those arising from the "Whiskey Rebellion" the doctrine of constructive treason had been applied in such a way as to elevate riot against the execution of a general law to constructive levying of war, and therefore to treason. But in Burr's trial, as Chapin observes, the Ch. Justice analyzed these American precedents without objection. The outcome of the trial, in Chapin's view, really came down to a defect in the indictment: "Burr stood indicted as having been present at Blennerhassett's island. In fact he had not been. The prosecution had argued that a general change of levying war was adequate and that Burr had been, in effect, constructively present. The defense insisted that the charge needed to be specific and proved as laid." [*The American Law of Treason*, Seattle, 1964, pp. 3, 97, 111.] Perhaps it is only because he is absorbed in his own case that HB does not notice this problem with the indictment when he criticizes the Grand Jury's errors on 13.11-15.

38.35-36 *Bollman's long letter to Duane . . . settles forever, the honour and good faith of Jefferson*: [Compare 46.10-11; see note to 39.21-24.] After his release from custody at Washington by the Supreme Court, Dr. Bollman made a statement to Jefferson, giving his account of the conspiracy. The following day the President asked Bollman to put his disclosures in writing, at the same time giving his word that this material would never be used against him and stating that the document would never leave his hand. Nevertheless, the President did send the paper to District Attorney Hay, but with instructions that it must not be shown to any but his associate counsel. Along with Bollman's statement the President sent a pardon that granted the Doctor immunity for turning state's evidence, though he had as yet done so only in private. Realizing that he had been betrayed, and that the President's position was compromised, Bollman, though he hesitated over a private offer, soon spurned the pardon when Hay offered it to him in open court. This is the background of HB's remark. Bollman went on to write a long letter to William Duane as editor of the *Aurora*; in an effort to set the record straight, he explained that he had not made his statement to the President in the hope of obtaining a pardon and that his only motive for not accepting the pardon offered him in private was his wish to reject it openly. A few days later Duane printed another long letter in which Bollman accused the President of bad faith in letting his, Bollman's, statement out of his hands. This letter was reprinted in the *Virginia Argus* for 25 July; it may be the article to which HB refers. [Dumas Malone, *Jefferson the President: Second Term, 1805–9*, Boston, 1974, pp. 307-8. *Aurora* 8 July and 17 July, 1807; *Virginia Argus*, 25 July, 1807.]

39.7-8 *Eternal justice then support my innocence*: Thomas P. Abernethy observes that "one good reason for accepting the evidence of the journal is that in it Blennerhassett never proclaimed his innocence, but frequently implied guilt. . . ." *The Burr Conspiracy*, New York, 1954, p. 246. But HB does imply his innocence here and also in his "will show what treason" remark on August 27 [61.24-25]; as for his "implied guilt," this generally takes the form of anxiety over the effect of testimony (such as that of Taylor and Albright) he considered false or misleading; finally, we could hardly expect that HB would have felt it necessary to proclaim his innocence (or guilt) to his wife and the few closest friends for whom the journal was written.

39.21-24 *advantage the prosecutors have taken . . . opinion given by Ch. Just. Marshall in the cases of Bollman and Swartwout*: Justus Eric Bollman, Peter Vroom Ogden, and Samuel Swartwout were agents of Burr who had carried ciphered communications, supposedly in Burr's hand, to Gen. James Wilkinson in the summer of 1806. [For an account of these communications see Mary-Jo Kline, *et. al.*, eds. *Political Correspondence and Public Papers of Aaron Burr*, 2:973-90, and note to p. 105.27-8 below.] After his betrayal of Burr, Wilkinson held the three under arrest in New Orleans. Bollman and Swartwout were conveyed to Washington for trial. By the time their case reached the Supreme Court, the charge against them had escalated from that of being accessories in Burr's treason to themselves having levied war against the U.S. Ultimately Justice Marshall dismissed the defendants, ruling that the prosecution had produced insufficient evidence to justify the charge. His Opinion was a landmark treatise on the meaning of treason according to Article 3, Section 3 of the Constitution. He held that for treason to be committed "war must be actually levied against the United States" and that conspiracy to commit treason "is not treason. To conspire to levy war, and actually to levy war are distinct offenses." Furthermore, he argued that the framers of the Constitution, aware of the abuses of the treason laws in England, intended to forbid *constructive treason*, that is, the extension of the crime of treason "by construction to doubtful cases." The portion of this Opinion to which HB alludes above was an *obiter dictum* in which the Ch. J. went on to observe that it was not the court's intention to say that no person could be guilty of treason unless he had actually "appeared in arms against his country. On the contrary, if war be actually levied, that is, if a body of men be actually assembled for the purpose of effecting by force a treasonable purpose, all those who perform any part, however minute, or however remote from the scene of the action, and who are actually leagued in the general conspiracy, are to be considered as traitors, but there must be an actual assembling of men, for the treasonable purpose, to constitute levying war. . . ." [W. Cranch, ed. *Reports of Cases Argued and Adjudicated in the Supreme Court of the United States in the Years 1807 and 1808*. New York, 1812, 4:122.]

39.27-28 *the Little Emperor at Cole's Creek may be forgotten in the Attorney at Richmond*: This sarcastic remark should be correlated with HB's other more detailed references to Burr's behavior when the would-be Emperor's little flotilla reached the lower Mississippi; one notices especially the interest with which HB refers to Cowles Mead's observation that Burr appeared to be "at times deranged" during this period. [See 75.6-8, 98,18-21, and 113.20-114.21.] HB's remarks on these latter pages show that he was primarily critical of his erstwhile leader's preference for deception and flight over honor and fight; hence the irony of his remarks [114.18-19] that Burr "exhibited at that season every derangement but that of avoidable hazard."

HB's attitude is partly explained by Appendix B, above, which includes his own diary of the last fateful days of Burr's flotilla, particularly of the days between the joining of his party with Burr's at the mouth of the Cumberland on December 27—amassing a combined force of not more than twelve boats and one hundred men—and Burr's abandonment of "his people," the faithful of his expedition, at Cole's Creek on February 5. On January 17, at the invitation of Cowles Mead, Acting-Governor, Burr surrendered voluntarily to civil authorities of the Mississippi Territory. An "armistice" was worked out while Burr made ready to appear for trial before the Supreme Court of the Territory. Meanwhile the little flotilla, apparently with HB in command, moved to the Louisiana side of the river, opposite the mouth of Cole's Creek, about halfway between Natchez and Bayou Pierre, there to await, in the cold, dead of winter, the outcome of their leader's trial. About this time also word reached them that Burr's drafts had bounced, and it was rumored that government "gun-boats" were on their way up river to take Burr; furthermore, HB complains, there was a general lack of discipline aboard the expedition's boats; he writes "the effects of general disorder and want of regulation in the use or distribution of liquors and provisions, with a total disregard of all pretense at authority whenever attempted to be assumed by superiors, which had long since manifested themselves throughout all our members, now openly broke out among particular leaders, who even threatened to turn out of their boats the provisions, in payment for the demands of some of the men who had become discontented and threatened to leave us."

The trial of Burr on February 2-4 before U.S. Territorial Judges Peter B. Bruin and Thomas Rodney was marked by procedural and jurisdictional squabbles between U.S. Attorney-General George Poindexter and Burr's counsel, W.B. Shields and Lyman Harding; however, on February 4 the grand jury of the Territory not only quickly returned a verdict of not guilty but also found two grievances against what they considered unwarranted abrogations of the defendant's rights: the "military expedition" against him, and the "military arrests made without warrant." But this discharge from the territorial court only began a new phase of Burr's troubles, and it may be his decision to cut and run on February 5 that HB most deplores. On January 27, Governor Robert Williams had returned to the territory and relieved Cowles Mead. He was considering seizing Burr as soon as he was released by the court on February 4; however, he was only confirmed in this decision a day later after he was visited by Judge Harry Toulmin of the Tombigbee District, who persuaded him to act. But by this time, Burr, who had returned to his boats for one day and had "made a long speech saying he was acquitted, but they were going to take him again and he was going to flee oppression," had slipped away before he could have known of this decision. [Deposition of David Fisk, *American State Papers, Misc.*, 1: 524-5 as quoted in T. P. Abernathy, *The Burr Conspiracy*, 1954, p. 221; see also, M-J. Kline, *et. al.*, eds., *The Political Correspondence and Public Papers of Aaron Burr*, 2:1006-8, 1017-21.]

39.34-35 *another Eugenius; as dear to me as the first was to Yorick*: In Lawrence Sterne's novel *Tristram Shandy* (1760-67), Yorick is "the lively, witty, sensible, and heedless person," of Danish descent—perhaps from Hamlet's Yorick—whose friend and mentor is Eugenius.

40.12-13 *how justly Darwin reckons, the desire of fresh-air amongst our natural appetites*: HB alludes, of course, to Erasmus Darwin (1731-1802), the grandfather of Charles. A physician, poet, and botanist, Erasmus was the author of *The Botanic Garden* (1789-91), a poetical exposition of the system of Linnaeus, and *Zoonomia* (1794-96), which explained the development of organisms according to evolutionary ideas which anticipated later scientific theories. It is the latter work to which HB refers.

41.4-5 *impossible David Wal-*

lace could ever mean *to practice so black a villainy*: [For David C. Wallace's deposition and HB's attitude toward it, see 19.30-31, 30.29-32, and notes.] By "the crime of a 2^{d} perjury to swear away my life" HB presumably refers to Wallace's testifying at the trial as he had sworn earlier in his affidavit, since the two declarations are much the same.

45.11 *I wanted subpoenas, duces tecum*: "The subpoena takes two forms, *subpoena ad testificandum*, when the recipient is called to bring documents or papers relevant to the controversy for examination by the court." [David M. Walker, *Oxford Companion to Law*.]

46.1-2 *Burr can boast, as Chas Fox did*: Charles James Fox (1749-1806) was an English politician and noted orator. In 1783 Fox regained political power by forming an expedient coalition with Lord North, whose coercive policies against the American colonies he had formerly opposed. His task was to explain convincingly his sudden reconciliation with North. In a speech before Parliament on February 17 he said, "I am accused of having formed a junction with a noble person, whose principles I have been in the habit of opposing for the last seven years of my life. . . . it is not in my nature to bear malice, or to live in ill-will. *Amicitiae sempiternae, inimicitiae placabilis.* I disdain to keep alive in my bosom the enmities which I may bear to men, when the cause of those enmities is no more." [Quoted in part from Christopher Hobhouse, *Fox*, London, 1947, pp. 132-33. Italics supplied.] Compare Cicero, *pro Rabirio Postumo*, 12, 32. *Mortalis inimicitas, sempiternas aimicitas.* "Let our enemies be short-lived, our friendships eternal."

46.6-8 *the letter to Pinkney . . . process-verbal of the interview with Jefferson*: Alston's letter to Pinckney [see, 10.8, and note] and Bollman's interview with Jefferson [see 35.35-36 and 46.10-11] were both, in HB's view betrayals of Burr by those close to him, HB contrasted these, by implication, with his own loyalty; though he felt that Burr saw neither the betrayals nor his loyalty in their true light.

46.10-11 *my opinion on Bolman's manoeuvre with Jefferson:* [See 38.35-36 and note.] Evidently HB considers that Bollman's motive in his interview with Jefferson may have been betrayal of Burr (and HB) to obtain a pardon; since the pardon was judged to be irrevocable, the Doctor was able to have the pardon but reject loudly the appearance of having sold out for it.

46.33-34 *Genl Tupper read over a most humorous Lampoon*: Tupper composed a mock-heroic ballad on the seizure, by the Ohio militia under Maj. Gen. Joseph Buell, of the Burr expedition's newly constructed boats on the Muskingum River above Marietta,

December 9, 1806. W.H. Safford printed it as Appendix III, to his *Life of Harman Blennerhassett* (1850). The ballad, entitled "The Battle of the Muskingum, or Defeat of the Burrites," contains such stanzas as these:

When Blanny's fleet, so snug and neat,
Come floating down the tide, sirs,
Ahead was seen, one-eyed Clark Green,
To work them, or to guide, sirs,

Our General brave, the order gave,
"To arms! To arms! in season!
Old Blanny's boats, most careless float,
Brim-full of death and treason!"

A few young boys, their mother's joys,
And five men there were found, sir,
Floating at ease — each little sees
Or dreams of death and wound, sirs.

48.2-21 *settling the Ouashita lands . . . his Eldorado on the Ouashita*: In his special message to Congress on January 22, 1807, Jefferson identified three apparent objectives of Burr's maneuvers; two of these purposes, "the severance of the union" and "an attack on Mexico," he regarded as "distinct." The third objective he regarded as "merely ostensible," a screen or pretext for the other two; it was "the settlement of a pretended purchase of a tract of country on the Washita, claimed by a Baron Bastrop. This was to serve as the pretext for all his preparations, an allurement for such followers as really wished to acquire settlements in that country, and a cover under which to retreat in the event of a final discomfiture of both branches of his real design." [*American State Papers, Misc.*, 1:468.] The "pretended purchase" appears to have been real, but the validity of the title, as HB opines, was doubtful; had the title been good, he supposes, Lynch would not have been "a Bankrupt." Charles Lynch testified at Burr's trial that Burr had purchased his interest in the Bastrop grant during his western trip in the fall of 1806, paying "about four or five thousand dollars" and other considerations for "about three hundred and fifty thousand acres." The other considerations were, first, that Burr would pay Edward Livingston $30,000, which was the sum that Lynch owed Livingston for his claim to the tract; and second, Burr would take up a note that Lynch valued at $30,000 more. [M-J. Kline, *et. al.*, eds., *Political Correspondence and Public Papers of Aaron Burr*, 2: 995 n.] But, as Dumas Malone observes, "the claim acquired by Burr . . . went back to a grant made a decade earlier by the Spanish Governor to the Baron de Bastrop. The conditions of this grant had been met on neither side, and no Spanish patent had been issued. The validity of Burr's title, in the eyes of American authorities, was questionable to say the least." [*Jefferson the President: Second Term, 1805–1809*, p. 256.]

48.7-31 *Tyler and Smith who once had been very intent on settling there. . . . But Major Smith will be here tomorrow and then bursts the bubble*: Comfort Tyler, of Herkimer, N.Y.; Israel Smith, of Cayuga, N.Y., a relative of the Swartwouts; and Davis Floyd, of the Indiana Territory, were secondary leaders of the Burr expedition. They were indicted for treason and misdemeanor by the grand jury at Richmond on June 26, presumably because they had been present on Blennerhassett Island at the time of the "overt act" specified in the indictment. At lines 30-31 HB assumes that Smith, who had been offered land in Burr's Washita purchase, would confirm his own hints about the defectiveness of Lynch's title and/or the unsuitability of the Tuckapaw County lands. [For disclosures that Smith did make to HB, see 53.1-2 and 97.37-98.3.]

50.22-26 *"Colonel Duane, Sir," . . . . this Gabriel of the Govt.*: William Duane (1760-1835) had been editor since 1798 of the Philadelphia *Aurora*, the leading Democratic newspaper. This fiery editor appears to have been the best-informed concerning Burr's activities and most insistent in raising the alarm against them; he had first taken up the subject in the *Aurora* for July 30, 1805, where he answered a series of anonymous "Queries" about Burr's schemes that had been posed in an article in the Philadelphia *Gazette of the U.S.* Soon after Jefferson's proclamation against the conspiracy, on November 27, 1806, Duane announced that Burr's projects had been "penetrated to the bottom" by the vigilant administration, and that Burr's design was clearly "that of raising himself to a powerful station over a separate government and an independent territory — to become himself the lawgiver and the founder of a new power. . . ." [Philadelphia *Aurora*, 1 Dec., 1806.]

54.15-16 *my losses, by Miller's sales of my effects*: Robert Miller of Lexington, Kentucky, was one of HB's major creditors; the diarist tells us later [171.27-28] that Miller held a protested draft of Burr's for $4,000., which HB had endorsed. To recover this he had the contents of HB's home sold at auction; the diarist estimates the replacement value of these effects at $15,000. Miller also obtained the use of HB's island estate itself under a writ of elegit; he planted hemp in the fields there, storing the crop in the empty, damaged mansion. The property continued to disintegrate during Miller's tenure, until, on the night of March 3, 1811, through the carelessness of a Negro maid-servant who dropped her candle as she searched for whiskey in one of the mansion's hemp-filled rooms, the building caught fire and burned to the ground.

59.31-35 *an attempt to take off Mr. Duncan . . . that Wilkinson is not a Spanish Officer or pensioner*: Abner L. Duncan, was a New Orleans attorney who testified that he had advised Wilkinson to alter the "cipher letter." [For his testimony on the General's behalf, see 77.27-28.] Wilkinson had been a Spanish agent since 1787 and had been an American leader of the "Spanish Conspiracy," an early separatist movement in Kentucky and Tennessee which the Spanish colonial officers had encouraged. In their reports he was referred to as Agent 13 and was granted a "pension" of $2,000 a year by the Spanish government. It is estimated that he had received some $26,000 from the Spanish by 1796. The General's Spanish connections were still active while Burr was unwittingly building his own plans around an expected war with Spain. As Dumas Malone observes, "modern scholars with access to Spanish archives now know that Wilkinson was, in fact, receiving money from Spain at the time the conspiracy was brewing, his pension having been recently renewed." [*Jefferson the President: Second Term, 1805–1809*, p. 363 and n.]

60.32-33 *I sh.[d] publicly expose the perfidy and dishonor of Graham and the Hendersons*: For his effort to do so, see his Brief (Appendix C), paragraphs 9, 10 and 18-21; also notes to 20.32-3 and 22.1 above.

62.27-63.26 *Dud.[y] Woodbridge — called me aside this morning, to complain . . . He apologized for his having said, that I had "more other sense than common sense"*: Some have taken this telling remark as the simplest explanation for HB's having come to be where he was when Woodbridge made it [Beirne, *Shout Treason*, 1959, p. 154]; however, it can be read simply as the cautious man's retrospective comment on the adventurous one. The temperate shrewdness — and the fairness —of Woodbridge emerges in his testimony. On August 19 he told the court about his having been in business with HB for "six or eight years" by the time the provisions and fifteen boats for the expedition were ordered in late summer of 1806 through the firm of Dudley Woodbridge and Company. He explained that the boats, only eleven of which were completed, were built by Col. Joseph Barker at his yard on the Muskingum River about seven miles above Marietta and that, on the night in which the boats were to be brought down, the 9th of December, he saw "six or eight armed men of the militia going to take possession of the boats; he therefore took steps to warn HB, Comfort Tyler, Israel Smith and others not to attempt to go for the boats and, "after some consultation," succeeded in preventing them from doing so. In the matter of arranging payment for the boats, Woodbridge also showed his cautiousness; he told the court as follows: "I made the contract for the boats with Colonel Burr and agreed to take a *draft* on New-York. When Mr. Blennerhassett handed me the draft, I expressed my dissatisfaction at the long sight at which it was drawn (being ninety days), observing that it would not become due, until after the time in which the boats and provisions were to be delivered, and that I wished to run no hazard. Mr. Blennerhassett, with some warmth, asked me if I doubted Colonel Burr's honour? When I repeated that I wished to run no risk, he said that *he* would guarantee the draft and be answerable himself; and that in the event of its not being paid, I might charge it to him."

This essential difference between the two partners had made itself felt earlier when, as Dudley testified, HB had tried quite earnestly to recruit him for the expedition in the second conversation they had on that subject; but Woodbridge made it clear that he was a sensible man: "the next week I was on the island, when he went into further particulars. From what he stated, the inference I drew, was, that his object was Mexico. He did not positively say so, but I inferred it from several circumstances, particularly from a map of that country which he showed me. He spoke highly of the country; stated its advantages, wealth, fertility and healthiness. He asked me if I had a disposition to join? I evaded his question, but could not forbear telling him that I preferred my situation to an uncertainty, which was the same as declining it."

Woodbridge's testimony seems to have contributed, indirectly, more to Burr's defense by showing how ludicrously unsuited HB was for any "overt act" of "levying war." "Was it not ridiculous for him to be engaged in a military enterprise?" Burr asked. "How far can he distinguish a man from a horse? Ten steps?" Woodbridge agreed, and added some: "He is very near sighted. He cannot know you from any of us, at the distance we are now from one another. He knows nothing of military affairs. I never understood that he was a military man." He was not only physically but also temperamentally unsuited to military action, Woodbridge thought. Wirt, for the prosecution, asked if HB were thought to be a man of "vigorous talents." It was in the context of his reply to this that Dudley made his cutting assessment of HB's deficiency in common sense: "He is;" was the reply, "and a man of literature. But it was mentioned among the people in the country, that he had every kind of sense but common sense; at least he had the reputation of having more of other than of common sense." His favorite occupations: "Chemistry and music."

It appears, in sum, that though Dudley Woodbridge's testimony may have been damaging to HB's ego, it was not so to his case, or to Burr's. [For HB's view of his testimony, see 106.28–107.3.] This was true even on the subject of money, for we note that when the prosecution sought to make the point that, while HB might not be much use in a military enterprise, his money might be, Woodbridge was at pains to deflate his hearers' notions of the prisoner's financial means. "I believe," he said, "they are not as great as was generally imagined. I gave him six thousand dollars for one half of his profits of our business; he had about three thousand dollars in stock in our company's concern. His fortune is much less than is generally understood. He had not over five or six thousand dollars in the hands of his agent at Philadelphia. His island and improvements cost about forty or fifty thousand dollars. It would not, however, sell for near that sum, except to a person of the same cast with Mr. Blennerhassett. After building his house, his property, exclusive of the island and five negroes, amounted probably to seventeen thousand dollars." Having also heard that HB had secured one of Burr's drafts (that for the boats and provisions) for two thousand dollars, the court were in a position to judge both the extent and the wisdom of his commitment to Burr's scheme. [D. Robertson, *Reports*, 1: 518–24.]

63.32–36 *enquire after an Estate of £6000 a year*: On September 11, HB explained the same expectation to his wife as follows: "I have had two dollars worth of letters forwarded from Philadelphia: first, from Ireland; two from Martin, one telling me to inquire after an estate he thinks has fallen to me of £6000 a year, by the death of Lord Ross, *ci-devant* Oxmantown, and Captain Jones, in the West Indies, next to whom I stand in the entail. I do not wish you to build at all on this intelligence, though it is not at all improbable it may be realized." He mentioned the prospect a bit more enthusiastically on October 7, as if to give hope to his wife: "Perhaps we shall yet enjoy ease and wealth, if Martin's expectations of my succeeding to the estates of the late D. Harman, by the death of Lord Oxmantown and Capt. Jones shall be realized; therefore, I only beseech Heaven to inspire you with the same prospects of contentment with which I can enjoy the remainder of my days in a cottage with you and our boys. . . ." A few days later he drew still more deeply on the imaginary legacy in order to further encourage his wife to put past disillusionments and losses behind her: "Why dwell as you do upon the Island? Have you forgotten Marietta and Wood County, or can you regenerate them? Or, if we should succeed to £6000 or £7000 a year by the decease of Lord Oxmantown, etc., would you bury it with ourselves on the Island? Compose yourself, therefore, till we meet, if it should not be these six months." [To Margaret Blennerhassett, 11 September; 7 and 19 October. W.H. Safford, ed., *The Blennerhassett Papers*, pp. 289, 291–2, 294–5.] The legacy evidently never materialized, for the B's were dogged by poverty throughout the rest of their days; despite their serious efforts to make a profit in cotton from their plantation at La Cache,

La., paradise of equanimity was never regained. [For the rest of their story see Norris F. Schneider, *Blennerhassett Island and the Burr Conspiracy*, Columbus: The Ohio Historical Society, 1966, pp. 30-34.]

64.2-5 *Burr, yesterday informed me, by note, he had an unsettled account with Luckett, who holds 1 of his Drafts for $2500. with my endorsement*: The references to him in the journal reveal that C.F. [?] Luckett was one of HB's more tenacious creditors by way his endorsements for Burr. Safford printed *two* notes of Burr's referring to this matter. The first, dated August 27, is brief and cavalier in its request: "Dear Sir: —Mr. Luckett and I have an unsettled account to a considerable amount. He holds a bill indorsed by you. If you can devise means to procure him any aid at this moment, it would gratify me much." The second contains a hint of apology: "It seems that some misapprehension exists on the subject of the bill held by Mr. Luckett. I could not with delicacy propose to you to take up my bill; but I repeat that it would gratify me that it could be done. My present inability is too manifest." [*The Blennerhassett Papers*, p. 287.]

64.10-65.2 *Wood, this morning gave me some information which if true, proves Burr—as bad a general*: See 141.2-3, and notes, for HB's comments on Joseph Hamilton Daveiss's *A View of the President's Conduct* (1807). There he reprints the sequence of letters in which, beginning in January, 1806, he had consistently warned Jefferson of Burr's activities, in the face of the President's continued near-indifference to his charges. Obviously HB is intrigued by Wood's view that Daveiss's persistent attacks on Burr were not motivated by deep patriotism but by spite against Burr because the great intriguer had not taken Daveiss into his confidence during his western tour of 1805, and also by "enmity of the President," whom Daveiss thought to be "involved with Burr's schemes." This theory, of course, would have been a compliment to Burr, whose cause Wood had lately joined.

72.19-20 *being by summons, or venire facias: Venire facias* names a variety of writs, all involving a summons to appear.

73.20-21 *I passed close by Phelps . . . a picture of the disap.t of his malice*: For HB's account of his previous amicable dealings with Col. Hugh Phelps, see his Brief [Appendix C] paragraphs 11, 13-15, above. However, it was Col. Phelps who had commanded the Wood County militia when, on December 10 it assaulted Blennerhassett's island and sacked his mansion. HB had escaped down river with the flotilla in the early hours of that morning; and his wife, evidently accompanied by their two boys, had taken a skiff to Marietta in hope of persuading authorities there to release the family's large boat so that she might follow her husband. It is said that the mansion might have fared better in the absence of its owners had Col. Phelps remained with his men and prevented their partaking too freely of the alcoholic refreshments they found there; as it was, the Col. immediately took a small detachment and set off down river toward Point Pleasant in hope of apprehending the fugitives. In this, as in his presumed hope of their conviction, he was disappointed.

77.26-27 *It is pretended D. has proved W. guilty of forgery in erasing and altering the cipher letter*: [Compare below 105.24–106.3.] A. L. Duncan, Wilkinson's attorney at New Orleans, testified that he had urged his client to omit those parts of the decoded texts that might implicate him in Burr's proceedings, and that his client had done so only after much soul-searching. Authorities now judge that the notorious *cipher letter*, the most significant document of the Burr conspiracy and probably the most famous writing attributed to Burr, was in all probability not written by Burr but by his friend and associate Jonathan Dayton, who, presumably without Burr's knowledge, found means to substitute other coded versions for two such communications Burr had dispatched to Wilkinson. One, dated July 22 and sent west by way of Pittsburgh with Samuel Swartwout, he removed by sending his nephew, D. F. Ogden, to join Swartwout at Pittsburgh with a sealed letter Swartwout was ordered to substitute for the one he was carrying; for the other, dated July 29, which Dr. Eric Bollman was to carry to New Orleans by sea, it is conjectured that Dayton substituted his own letter in some more direct way.

It has been shown that the two letters that Wilkinson showed Duncan in December 1806, those now preserved in the Newberry Library, are not in the hands of Burr, or Swartwout, or of Charles Willie, then Burr's secretary; in fact, "the hand in the two cipher letters appears to be that of Jonathan Dayton, former Federalist senator from New Jersey, longtime associate of AB and Wilkinson, and enthusiastic partner of their schemes for speculation in the West." [Kline, *et. al*., eds. *The Political Correspondence and Public Papers of Aaron Burr*, 2:985.] Furthermore, as these authorities point out, the inflated style of the letter does not match Burr's spare prose; the personal references in it are inappropriate to its purported author (e.g. that Burr, a doting grandfather, would be starting into the wilderness with his daughter and four-year-old grandson, then seriously ill); finally, some stated details of Burr's plans (e.g. "Naval protection of England is secured. Truxtun is going to Jamaica to arrange with the admiral there and will meet us in Mississippi.") are equally fanciful. Dayton's purpose evidently was to brace Wilkinson's loyalty to the cause by sketching a conspiracy larger than its life; in doing so he played nicely into the hands of its betrayer. Burr must have been astonished at the letter that came before the court; he described it correctly to Alston as "a forgery." It is assumed that his personal code of ethics would have prevented him from betraying his friend's, Dayton's, hand in this "forgery." On page 83 we have HB's impressions of these two friends together.

83.19 *General Dayton was sequestered in another room*: For Dayton's long friendship with Burr, his connection with the conspiracy, and his probable authorship of the "cipher letter," see notes to 15.1-3 and 77.27-28.

85.11-13 *some charming trios of Doctor Calcott . . . for some affecting extracts fr. Ossian*: John Wall Calcott (1766-1821) was an English organist and composer whose many glees and part-songs were extremely popular during his lifetime and won him a profusion of medals and prizes. *Ossian* is an epic in eight books, mostly by James MacPherson (1736-1796), but purporting to be transcriptions from the Gaelic of the legendary warrior-poet Ossian, or *Oisin*.

86.21-22 *—Tutius est igitur, fictis contendere verbis quam puguare manu*: [Ovid, *metamorphosis*, 13.9.] It is safer to contend by means of guileful words than with the hands.

90.1-4 *Hay . . . exhibited a general charge against us . . . of having levied War . . . at Cumberland Island in Kentucky, at Bayou Pierre, on the Mississippi, or at some intermediate place*: In this hearing, which lasted until October 20, the defense was required to show cause why they should not be transmitted to other districts to stand trial for "overt acts" allegedly committed in those districts. At this hearing the Chief Justice admitted, as HB complains, most of the evidence offered. Particularly important at this juncture was the testimony of Sgt. Jacob Dunbaugh who had been given leave by his superior, Capt. Daniel Bissell, to accompany Burr's flotilla after it left Ft. Massac, near the mouth of the Cumberland. Dunbaugh testified that Burr had gathered his people (numbering at most 100), on Cumberland Island but would not divulge his plans to them there because "he said there were too many bystanders present." His testimony was corroborated by that of James McDowell. [40.10-12] Dunbaugh also testified to certain acts which took place later on, at Bayou Pierre, particularly to the sinking of guns in the river near, he said, Petit Gulph, three miles below Bayou Pierre. Concerning this action he testified as follows: "The night we left Petit Gulph, Colonel Burr and Wyllie went into the bow of the boat for an axe, auger, and saw; they went into Colonel Burr's private room and began to chop; he ordered no person to go out, but I did go out; I saw a skiff lying aside of Colonel

Burr's boat. After they had done chopping, Mr. Pryor and a Mr. Tooly got out of the window; I got on the top of the boat, and saw two bundles of arms tied up with cords, and sunk by cords going through holes at the gunwales of Colonel Burr's boat. . . ." [*American State Papers, Misc.*, 1:515; for HB's reference to this incident, see 113.35.]

98.23-25 *the probability of de Pestre's being hanged thro' failure of an enterprise he had sent him on*: As HB explains in the next entry, in October 1806 Burr sent his chief of staff, Col. Julien De Pestre, on an errand to the Marques de Casa Yrujo, the Spanish Minister to the U.S., with letters assuring him that he planned no assault on Spanish territory and that his only purpose was to divide the American Union. De Pestre's mission miscarried and Burr received no help from the Spanish treasury because, as HB notes below, the shrewd minister had long been suspicious of Burr's activities and had been reporting his suspicions to his government.

On the "probability of de Pestre's being hanged," HB's remark was rhetorical because de Pestre had not been indicted along with others of Burr's lieutenants, very likely for the reason that the diarist himself relates on p. 26. [See note to 26.10-21.]

105.23-24 *placed beyond all doubt "his honour as a soldier and his fidelity as a citizen."* HB's ironic allusion is to Jefferson's message to Congress on 22 January, 1807, in which he had paid tribute to the General's exhibition of "the honor of a soldier and fidelity of a good citizen;" after Wilkinson, having disclosed the conspiracy, had shipped Burr's messengers Bollman and Swartwout to Washington for trial and had sent the President the version of the "cipher letter" which Swartwout had delivered. Jefferson did not then know that the General, who had published this letter earlier at New Orleans, had altered it to conceal any reference to his past involvement with Burr's plans; nevertheless, the President may already have had some reasons to doubt the very terms in which he was describing the General to Congress. [See Dumas Malone, *Jefferson The President: Second Term, 1805–9*, pp. 263-4.]

105.27-106.3 *he was confessed, —he altered a duplicate of the original cypher letter*: [For the *cypher letter* see note to 77.27-28.] The General had been badgered into confessing for the first time in open court that he had doctored the letter, supposedly from Burr, which Jefferson had transmitted to Congress as evidence of the conspiracy. But by this time, as HB's tone implies, the letter could no longer be taken seriously as proving anything against Burr, and Wilkinson's credibility had been impugned. When the General appeared in closed session before the Grand Jury on June 15-20 and placed the presumably incriminating letter before them, the members of the panel could see immediately that he had tampered with it in order to conceal his earlier involvement with Burr's schemes. This discovery negated the letter's value as evidence and induced seven of the 16-man panel to vote to indict the General along with Burr. Wilkinson thus narrowly escaped indictment, but faith in his integrity was eroded. After the General's later revelations in open court, those of which HB writes, Hay, the District Attorney, wrote to the President that his confidence in Wilkinson had been "shaken, if not destroyed" [George Hay to Thomas Jefferson, 15, Oct. 1807]; but the President himself never expressed a lack of confidence in Wilkinson after the General had betrayed Burr to him.

106.27-107.3 *thus ended, I wish I could say, my last concern with the Woodbridge family*: HB does not appear to be giving his partner justice here; perhaps he resented the deflating candor of some of Woodbridge's testimony. A review of that testimony [see notes to 62.27-63.26] shows that Dudley did state quite clearly that the expedition's designs were against Mexico, although he does not say that HB said so "unequivocally"; yet his testimony seems to have been what HB says it was reputed to be, "a fair candid and to us, an advantageous testimony." HB's harsh assessment of Dudley, Jr. was too much for Safford, who knew him personally; therefore, he introduces this brief testimonial, one of his few notes to the pages of the journal: "The integrity and respectability of Mr. Woodbridge is undoubted by all who knew him. From a personal acquaintance for some years previous to his death I am enabled to add, that such was the purity of his character, through a long and useful career, as to stamp with untruthfulness any reflection upon his honor as a man or his veracity as a witness." [W.H. Safford, ed. *The Blennerhassett Papers*, p. 424 and n.]

107.11-13 *unless I excepted McClurg, whom I believed to be a man of some genius*: Samuel Mordecai writes of Dr. James McClurg as being "one of the most eminent physicians and talented men of his time. . . . He served in the Medical staff during the Revolutionary war, and was declared to be the most skillful and accomplished medical officer in the division of the army, serving in this part of the Union. He was a member of the Convention that formed the Constitution of the United States, but did not sign it." [*Richmond in By-Gone Days*, 1856, p. 78.]

110.9 *Mr C. kindly pressed me to dine en famille*: John A. Chevallié was, according to Samuel Mordecai, "a gentleman of the most scrupulous politeness, of fine literary attainments, and of extensive and varied information. He was brought up in the ante-revolutionary days of French Society, and his manners conformed to it.

He came to this country as agent for the Count Beaumarchais, who had, either as a secret agent of Louis XVI, or at his own outlay, furnished a large quantity of arms to the United States during the Revolutionary war." [*Richmond in By-Gone Days* p. 101.]

113.25-35 *called the* armistice, *at Natchez. . . .had them all hid and sunk in the river*: [See notes to 39.27-8 and 90.1-4.] On January 17, in order to protect himself from falling into General Walkinson's hands and from the swift military justice that would ensue, Burr agreed to surrender to civil authorities in the Mississippi Territory and to allow his boats to be searched for any military equipment that might be aboard. When the boats were inspected by Col. Fitzpatrick on the 19th, he found no military arms because Burr had arranged for his muskets to be tied into bundles and suspended in the water through holes cut into the side of his boat.

114.31-2 *Then came forward the ingenious Poindexter*: George Poindexter was U.S. Attorney General for the Mississippi Territory at the time Burr was tried there. [See note to 39.27-28.]

117.27-120.10 *Wirt's parallel of Burr's character and my own*: This speech appears in Robertson's notes substantially as HB quotes it except that after the words with which HB's excerpt ends [" . . . froze as they fell." 120.7] Wirt goes on to enforce his point that Burr was the master-mind, HB only an accessory, in heavy discourse that HB may have deliberately omitted: "Yet this unfortunate man, thus deluded from his interest and his happiness, thus seduced from the paths of innocence and peace, thus confounded in the toils that were deliberately spread for him and overwhelmed by the mastering spirit and genius of another—this man, thus ruined and undone and made to play a subordinate part in this grand drama of guilt and treason, this man is to be called the principal offender, while *he*, by whom he was thus plunged in misery, is comparatively innocent, a mere accessory! Is this reason? Is it law? Is it humanity?" [David Robertson, *Reports of the Trials of Colonel Aaron Burr*, 2:97-8.]

121.35 *St* [*****]: Possibly Richard J. Stevens (1757-1837) an English composer known chiefly for his glees, especially his 15 Shakespearian glees, composed between 1782 and 1807.

122.15-21 *Burr and Martin made a considerable blunder today by producing a Major Bruff to the discredit of Wilkinson*: As HB observes, the defense expected the testimony of Major James Bruff to go a long way toward discrediting General Wilkinson. He testified that the General had once tried to interest him in an unnamed expedition—"a grand scheme," certain to make his fortune and "the fortunes of all concerned"—and that he had later gone successively to Secretary of

War Henry Dearborn and Attorney General Caesar Rodney and accused Wilkinson of being a Spanish "pensioner" and a confederate of Burr's. But then the prosecution produced a Commodore Shaw and Lt. E.P. Gaines, whose testimony showed that Bruff, who had recently been court-martialled, had accused the General out of a long-standing hatred. Hence HB's summation that the testimony on both sides tended to make the General and his accuser look like "rivals in their treachery to the state." [*American State Papers, Misc.*, 1:577 and 584.]

122.23–24 *the curtain had risen and Peacham and Locket stood confessed*: In John Gay's *The Beggar's Opera* (1728) Peacham is a receiver of stolen goods who improves his living by informing on certain of his clients through Locket, the Jailer of Newgate, with whom he has an agreement to divide the reward money.

123.30–31 *I had there, the happiness to see Doctor Cummins just arrived*: See 39.21–28 and note. Dr. John Cummins, a physician who had studied medicine with Dr. Benjamin Rush and was the son-in-law of Judge Bruin, lived at Bayou Pierre. He was a heavy financial contributor to the Burr expedition, and the person with whom Burr left the extraordinary maps of the Spanish domains which reveal graphically the full extent of Burr's aspirations. After he abandoned his followers at Cole's Creek on Feb. 5, Burr evidently went into hiding at Cummin's home, since on Feb. 10 one of Cummins's slaves was taken and found to be carrying, concealed in a coat of Burr's that he wore, a note directing Burr's lieutenants Tyler and Floyd to meet him at a place nearby.

123.35-36 *Nothing less than letters of McKee's*: Col. John McKee had been U.S. agent to the Choctaw Indians. In January, 1807, after HB had arrived on the Mississippi with so few recruits, Burr asked McKee to assist him by raising recruits from the tribe; he also obtained some military supplies from the agent. In his testimony at Richmond, however, McKee read letters of his to General Wilkinson showing that he had been corresponding with the General about some employment for himself, since 1805, and that at the time he was assisting Burr, in January and February, 1807, he was writing to Wilkinson in such terms as the following; "I never was a *Burrite*, nor can I ever give myself up to schemes of lawless plunder; it is certain that in my situation I might have engaged in any honorable enterprise, however hazardous, but the late one, such as it has been represented, is such as I hope no friend of mine will ever suspect me of favoring." [McKee to "His Excellency General Wilkinson," 16 Feb., 1807. *American State Papers. Misc.*, 1:595.]

125.27–28 *Yesterday, then I completed my 42^{d} or 43rd year*: Ray Swick, Historian, Blennerhassett Historical Park Commission, states that the Baptismal Records in the archives of County Hampshire, England, show that HB was baptized on October 10, 1764; he could not, therefore, have been born in 1765. [Further information on this and other events of HB's first thirty-two years is to be found in Swick's "Harman Blennerhassett: An Irish Aristocrat on the American Frontier," unpublished doctoral dissertation, Miami Univ. (Ohio), 1979.]

129.15-16 *La guerre des Dieux*: The author was Évariste-Désiré de Parny (1753-1814); the poem is a mock-heroic, erotic work in ten cantos. [Nouvelle éd., complete. Paris: A. G. Debray, 1807.]

133.29-31 *As Junius says of the King*: "Junius" is the pseudonym of the author of a series of political letters, rich in irony and invective, which appeared in the London *Public Advertiser* from 1769 to 1772. In his letter of 6 February, 1771 "Junius" had used the quoted passages in a quite different sense from that in which HB applies it to Wirt here. The King's honor and the people's are one, "Junius" argues, "Private credit is wealth;—public honour is security—The feather that adorns the royal bird, supports his flight. Strip him of his plumage and you fix him to the earth." [John Cannon, ed., *The Letters of Junius*. Oxford 1978, p. 224.] Despite HB's misappropriation of his source here, this allusion and other echoes suggest the influence of "Junius" on "Querist" as well as on the Journal.

134.9 *Dallas and Lewis in the case of Fries*: John Fries was the leader of an armed resistance raised in 1788-9 by certain farmers in Bucks and North-Hamptom counties of Pennsylvania against the federal tax on land and houses. Fries was twice tried for treason and convicted; he was sentenced to be hanged but was pardoned by President John Adams. Alexander J. Dallas, James Ewing, and William Lewis defended Fries in his first trial, before Judge James Iredell; Lewis defended Fries again in his second trial, with Judge Samuel Chase presiding. The case was cited frequently in the Burr Trial because in it, as in the cases arising from the "Whiskey Rebellion," the English legal doctrine of constructive treason, [see 38.30-32], originating in the statutes of Edward III, had been applied so as to enlarge the meaning of "levying war." As Bradley Chapin has observed, the judges in these cases "brought in the doctrine of constructive levying of war, and it remains good law to this day." [*The American Law of Treason*, Seattle, 1964, p. 97.]

139.30-35 *the President's message. . . . the clause relating to the issue of the judicial proceedings against us*: The relevant paragraph from Jefferson's annual message to Congress, Nov. 27, 1809 is as follows: "I informed Congress, at their last session, of the enterprises against the publick peace, which were believed to be in preparation by Aaron Burr and his associates, of the measures taken to defeat them, and to bring the offenders to justice. Their enterprises were happily defeated by the patriotick exertions of the militia, whenever called into action, by the fidelity of the army, and energy of the commander in chief, in promptly arranging the difficulties presenting themselves on the Sabine, repairing to meet those arising on the Mississippi and dissipating before their explosion, plots engendering there: I shall think it my duty to lay before you the proceedings, and the evidence publickly exhibited on the arraignment of the principal offenders before the district court of Virginia. You will be enabled to judge whether the defect was in the testimony, in the law, or in the administration of the law, and wherever it shall be found, the legislature alone can apply or originate the remedy. The framers of our constitution certainly supposed they had guarded, as well their government against destruction by treason, as their citizens against oppression, under pretence of it, and if these ends are not attained, it is of importance to inquire by what means most effectually, they may be secured." [*American State Papers*, 5:484.]

141.2–3 *appearance at this crisis of a pamphlet by J. Daveiss*: [For HB's opinion of this pamphlet after he has read it, see 168.26–169.1 and n.] Joseph Hamilton Daveiss had been, as HB remarks, Federal District Attorney for Kentucky; he was a brother-in-law of Chief Justice Marshall, and, of course, a Federalist. Beginning on January 10, 1806, he wrote the President a series of letters, warning him of suspected traitors, including Burr, who were active in the West. "Spanish intrigues," he declared in his first letter, "have been carried on among our people. —We have traitors among us. A separation of the union in favor of Spain is the object finally. . . . I am convinced Wilkinson has been for years and now is a pensioner of Spain." [Daveiss, *A View of the President's Conduct Concerning the Conspiracy of 1806*, (1807), pp. 68–71.] He was especially suspicious of Wilkinson, more so than of Burr; in a letter of February 10 he sent the President a list of ten prime suspects, with Wilkinson named second, Burr ninth. Other letters, including offers and plans to conduct on-the-spot investigations, followed in March, April, and May. Jefferson was prompt in his answer to Daveiss's first letter and invited the list of suspects contained in his second. However, when he saw this list he was reluctant to believe that all the persons named were conspirators; yet he could plainly see that it was a list of Republicans, compiled by a Federalist who was a brother-in-law of John Marshall; consequently, he tended to disregard his informant thereafter, providing merely a formal acknowledgment of his letters much later, in September, 1806. Undeterred, the indefatigable Daveiss carried his crusade, now directed at Burr, into the columns of *the Western World* and the U.S. District Court of Kentucky, but without success. As HB notes, Jefferson was so annoyed at Daveiss's failure to obtain Burr's conviction, that he had him removed from office. The disgruntled ex-District Attorney responded in the aftermath of Burr's treason trial by publishing, in the pamphlet named above, his eight warning letters to the President, with commentary further embittered by his loss of office. [See T. P. Abernathy, *The Burr Conspiracy*, pp. 89-99; Dumas Malone, *Jefferson the President: Second Term, 1805–9*, pp. 223-25, 237-39, 355-56.] Earlier [64.10–65.2], John Wood, who had published some of Daveiss's material in *The Western World*, related to HB his theory that the District Attorney's attacks on Burr had really been motivated by pique at Burr's failure to include him in his plans.

141.13-15 *explain how readily the Judge must be disposed to favour alike the ruin of Burr, W.ⁿ & Jeff.ⁿ in everything short of murder*: Dumas Malone remarks that this comment of HB's shows he "believed the Chief Justice to be anti-Jefferson rather than pro-Burr." [*Jefferson the President: Second Term, 1805–9*, p. 355.] HB also believed that the Chief Justice compensated for this bias by his liberality toward the government's evidence in the final hearings.

145.23-24 *his back-stairs committees 'till Jack Randolph shall finally sever him from them*: John Randolph of Roanoke had been named foreman of the grand jury at Richmond by Chief Justice Marshall. He was by no means favorable to Burr, but he was a persistent gadfly of the administration and entirely distrustful of General Wilkinson, whom he called "the mammoth of iniquity . . . the only man I ever saw who was from the bark to the very core a villain." [Henry Adams, *John Randolph*, p. 83, as quoted in Milton Lomask, *Aaron Burr: The Conspiracy and Years of Exile*, p. 180.] At the time of HB's remark, Randolph had emerged as leader of the anti-Jefferson faction within his party and constantly sought ways to embarrass the President; his tenacious inquiries into Wilkinson's activities were such a way.

148.24-26 *A desperate democratic printer . . . whose name is Frailey*: Perhaps "Leonard Frailey, Capt. Baltimore Union Volunteers." According to a newspaper account of the incident, "a corps of Patriot Volunteers, commanded by Capt. L. Frailey, whose regular muster happened on the same evening on which this publication [a letter by Luther Martin defending Burr] appeared, presented themselves before L. Martin's house, where Burr, Blennerhassett, and Swartwout, then were at dinner, with charged bayonets playing the rogue's march." [The Baltimore *American*, 19 Nov., 1807.]

150.3-4 *"Blennerhassett the Chemist . . . tune of the public Fiddle"*: The copy of the handbill reprinted in the Baltimore *American* has: "*Blennerhassett the Chemist and Fiddler. . . .*" According to the newspaper account, each of the effigies had a legend or epigram attached to it. Blennerhassett's was: "Alas! are chemistry and bagpipes come to this! — I can't distinguish a *man* from a horse." [Baltimore *American*, 19 Nov., 1807.]

153.4-7 *How far the respectable part of the city will think it worth their while to show they had no participation in this frolic*: On November 5, two days after the "frolic," Judge Walter Dorsey issued warrants for the arrest of several participants, including a George Peterson, perhaps HB's "one Patterson" (152.37). Two weeks later, on the other hand, a committee "appointed at a meeting [Nov. 7] of Democratic Republicans" reported at length on these demonstrations in the *American*; this report described the march as "a peaceful assemblage which met to endanger neither person nor property, but to expose obnoxious characters, and express their abhorrence of treason," and it objected strongly to Judge Dorsey's action. [Baltimore *American*, 19 Nov. 1807.]

168.24 *this American Chesterfield*: Philip Dormer Stanhope, Fourth Earl of Chesterfield (1694-1773) was an English statesman and diplomat, noted for his oratory, his wit, and for his political tracts; but as a writer he is best remembered for the sequences of educational letters he wrote to his natural son and his godson, both named Philip Stanhope. Chesterfield was acknowledged to be the most brilliant aristocrat since the Restoration Wits; no believer in the "natural" behavior later advocated by the Romantics, Chesterfield made his name synonymous with polished manners and self-assured worldliness. For Chesterfield the world's opinion was all-in-all; he counselled self-interest, discreet sexual permissiveness, and the practice of intrigue in preference to the lower vices. Unlike Burr's, his prose style was smooth, succinct, and frequently aphoristic.

168.26-169.1 *I had yesterday put into my hands for the first time Joe Daveiss' pamphlet*: For the authorship and content of this pamphlet, entitled *A View of the President's Conduct Concerning the Conspiracy of 1806*, (1807), see 141. 2-3 and note. Dumas Malone observes that "the President had a copy of the Daveiss pamphlet, whether or not he read it." [*Jefferson the President: Second Term, 1805–9*, p. 355.]

169.4-5 *This performance together with Judge Marshall's last volume of the life of Washington*: Dumas Malone comments on HB's belief that Daveiss' pamphlet and Marshall's volume would "mortify

Jefferson" and inspire him with a more "deadly hatred" of the Marshall clan than ever he had against the Burrites; the biographer concludes that, while Jefferson probably "brushed off" Daveiss' attack, "he undoubtedly resented Marshall's *Life of Washington* until his dying day." [*Jefferson the President: Second Term, 1805–9*, p. 355-56.]

169.18-19 *O caupones maligni!*: O wicked innkeepers. Cf. Horace, *Satirae*, 1, 5.4.

170.4 *so justly condemned by Lavater*: Johann Kaspar Lavater, (1741-1801) the Swiss poet, theologian and mystic, wrote a number of works on metaphysics; however, he is mainly remembered as the founder of physiognomy, the art of judging character and temperament from facial features. In the passage from his *Essay on Physiognomy* (1783) to which HB alludes, Lavater writes: "Fig. 14—We have here what is called the Grecian profile; the famous descent of the forehead to the nose in one continued right line. But can any person, having a sense of truth and nature, suppose this natural and true? I will never more pronounce such words if any such living profile can be found; or, were it possible to find such, if the person who possessed it were not most blockishly stupid. This countenance is, in fact, merely imaginary, and only betokening the vapid and unimpassioned countenance of a maiden." [John Caspar Lavater, *Essays on Physiognomy*, tr. Thomas Holcroft, 19th ed., London, n.d., plate LVIII and p. 432.]

171.30-32 *Now had you seen how "that eye of his"*: See Shakespeare, *Julius Caesar*, 1-2. 122-4: "His coward lips did from their color fly,/ And that same eye whose bend doth awe the world/ Did lose his luster."

171.33 *Vox faucibus haesit*: "My voice stuck in my throat." Cf. Virgil, *Aeneid*, 2. 774: "Obstipui, steteruntque et vox faucibus haesit." ("I stood amazed, and my hair stood, and my voice stuck in my throat.") The ghost of his wife, Creusa, has appeared to Aeneas.

TABLE OF ALTERATIONS

Most of these changes to the MS text where evidently made by HB as he wrote the entries, but some appear to be in his hand at a later date (possibly in 1813, as he revised his notes for the publication he threatened Alston with); and a few alterations appear to be stray marks and penciled cancellings made by W.H. Safford for his edition of 1864. (Would HB have removed the "beloved" that precedes "wife" at page 145, line 34?) Several interesting alterations are discussed in the Textual Notes; all are listed here by page and line. For this count, a line is any actual line of print, including dates and hairlines but not the running head. The revised reading is entered to the left of the bracket.

Page. Line:

2.15 a good house] *interlined with a caret*

3.27 whilst he] *followed by cancelled word, illegible*

4.3 not] *interlined with a caret*

4.15 him] *interlined above cancelled the col.*

4.25 closely] *followed by cancelled* in the order prescribed

7.7 then] *interlined with a caret*

10.25 he] *interlined with a caret*

15.31 fr.] *interlined with a caret*

15.31 of party] *interlined with a caret above cancelled* upon

15.51 wife,] *followed by cancelled* and

15.5 "] *interlined with a caret*

17.32 slept] *interlined with a caret above cancelled* fell asleep

18.4–5 to the house] *interlined with a caret after* So

18.13 Brief] *follows* brief, *partially blotted*

21.24 go] *interlined with a caret*

23.27 day] *interlined with a caret*

24.14 them] *interlined with a caret*

24.19 now] *interlined with a caret*

24.20 one] *written over* the

24.20 ray] *interlined above cancelled* light

24.20 enlighten] *interlined above cancelled words, illegible*

26.11 french] *interlined with a caret*

26.25 an] *possibly, written over* the

27.15 him] *interlined with a caret*

27.35 ch] *evidently fitted in*

33.23 to] *interlined with a caret*

Page. Line:

35.1 repose] —pose *interlined above cancelled letters, illegible*
35.28 wanted] *interlined with a caret*
36.19 channel] *second* n *interlined with a caret*
36.25 you] *interlined above* pleased
36.32 assigned them] *interlined with a caret*
37.3 crammed] *second* m *interlined with a caret*
37.22 assurances] *interlined with a caret*
38.5 comments] *second* m *interlined with a caret*
38.18 against] i *interlined above* n
38.18 He] *written over small h or th*
38.25 I] *interlined with a caret*
39.11 a] *interlined with a caret*
40.3 that] *interlined with a caret*
40.8 not] *interlined with a caret*
40.12 Darwin] *final* g *blotted out*
40.16 of] *interlined with a caret*
41.26 as I felt] as *interlined with a caret*
42.3 addition] *first* d *interlined with a caret*
42.14 partly] l *interlined above* y
43.23 against me] *interlined above cancelled* against me
43.24 because . . . my] *separated by cancelled* I can not do it without showing to their relatives the *(last word interlined above my)*
44.30 I am affected since yesterday] *uncancelled, though* have not been well *is interlined above it*
45.26 and as] *uncancelled, though* that as *is interlined above it*
46.2 say —] *dash interlined with caret*
46.21-22 accommodating] *second* m *interlined with a caret*
46.37 it] *interlined with a caret*
47.9 my] *interlined with a caret*
47.12 and] *interlined with a caret*
47.28 and] *second* and interlined with a caret, cancelled
48.24-25 information] *followed by cancelled, blotted word, illegible*
49.28 more] *interlined with a caret*
50.30 produce or] *interlined with a caret*
52.2 were] *interlined with a caret*
53.15 sit as] as *interlined with a caret*
53.23 him required] *separated by cancelled word, illegible*
54.13 he is] his *altered to* he is *by* e *interlined with a caret*
54.17 sum] *interlined with a caret*
54.34 come] me *interlined with a caret above cancelled letters, illegible*

Page. Line:

55.30 he] *preceded by cancelled* he

56.27 all] *interlined with a caret*

57.6 Prichard] *preceded by cancelled, blotted* Miller

57.24 for] *followed by cancelled word(s), possibly* for pecuniary

57.26 accommodation] *second* m *interlined with a caret*

57.30 travel] *followed by cancelled* travel

61.25 recommended] *second* m *interlined with a caret*

63.29–30 recommendatory] *second* m *interlined with a caret*

64.10 me] *interlined with a caret*

67.8 of] *interlined above* form an

67.31 came] *interlined above cancelled* staggered

68.6 now] *interlined above cancelled word, illegible*

68.29 when] *possibly written over* them

73.1 Judge] *the number* 2 *interlined above*

74.28 Monday] *followed by cancelled word, possibly* last

74.28 express my desire] *numerals* 22 *separated by double spaces interlined above these words*

75.34 Jef. to] *interlined with a caret*

77.23 x-examined] x *interlined with a caret*

78.4 also] *interlined with a caret*

78.27 on] *interlined with a caret*

79.10 little] *interlined above cancelled* small

80.3 day] s *cancelled*

80.31 squall] *interlined above cancelled* by

81.6 an object] *interlined after cancelled word, possibly* the

81.17 1 half] 1 *interlined with a caret*

81.34 on] *interlined with a caret*

82.2 me in] *numeral* 2 *interlined above space between these words*

82.18 Natchez] *followed by cancelled phrase*, of 3.rd ult.o rec.d this day

83.1 Martin] *preceded by cancelled word, possibly from*

84.22 they] *interlined above* knew must

86.22 manu] *followed by an illegible cancelled sentence*

87.28 schemes] c *interlined with a caret*

87.30 clearer] *interlined with a caret above cancelled* better

89.7 He] *preceded by cancelled* O

89.19 that] *written over cancelled word, illegible*

91.13 physiognamy] *followed by 3 cancelled, illegible words*

92.18 and the] *interlined with a caret*

92.20 committed and] *followed by cancelled word, possibly* bound

92.24 Ct.] *interlined with a caret*

97.2 his] *interlined with a caret before cancelled* M.s

Page. Line:

98.13 his] *interlined with a caret*

98.21 had] *followed by cancelled* not

98.21 not to do it] *interlined with a caret*

98.24 hanged] *followed by three cancelled words, partly legible*; at the N_____

98.25 on] *followed by cancelled* thither

102.36–37 For many years] *undeciphered symbols penciled above these words*

104.19 live] *followed by an* x *at edge of page*

105.18 W^{n}] *interlined with a caret*

107.15 him] *interlined with a caret*

108.15 by] b *written over* t

109.34 Moor's] M *written over* n

110.27 took] *interlined with caret before cancelled word, illegible*

117.26 now] ow *interlined above cancelled* ote

126.4 case] e *interlined above blotted* s

127.10 they] *interlined with a caret*

131.20 they] *followed by cancelled* praise

132.34 Martin bears every —] *lightly lined through*

133.30 maintain] *interlined above cancelled* house

136.17 awake] *interlined above cancelled word, illegible*

139.3 3] *illegible characters written above blotted* 3, *possibly* one

139.12 of] *interlined with a caret*

140.11 back] *preceded by cancelled* to support

140.37 when] *preceded by cancelled* rather

141.23 behavior] *interlined above cancelled illegible word*

142.18 B.] *interlined with a caret*

143.5 have been disappointed] *inserted above top line with caret*

143.5 tho'] *inserted above with caret*

143.6 we] *preceded by cancelled* But

143.26 as] *interlined with a caret*

144.1 of these] *preceded by cancelled* these

144.34 wife] *preceded by cancelled* beloved

144.35 trifling] *lightly lined through, possibly cancelled*

145.4 thereby] *followed by cancelled* he w^{d}

146.14 have gone] *interlined above cancelled* move

146.27 arrived here] *entered at top of page above cancelled, illegible words except* hear

148.8 and tho' he] *interlined above cancelled, blotted illegible words*

148.9 boasted] ed *interlined with a caret*

148.25 whose] *interlined above cancelled* his

Page. Line:

148.37 left] *followed by cancelled* Martin's
149.10 there] *interlined with a caret*
149.29 execution] *followed by cancelled* at
150.23 leave] *interlined above cancelled* set out
150.25 would] *preceded by cancelled, illegible word*
151.23 conversing] *preceded by cancelled* smoking and
151.26 I then] *interlined with a caret above cancelled* and
152.32 patroled] *followed by cancelled word, possibly* this
152.34 The mob] *preceded by cancelled* In this instance they
153.2 I have] *preceded by cancelled* for
153.31 by] *followed by cancelled word, possibly* Winshall
154.7 the] *interlined with a caret*
154.21 o'clock] *interlined with a caret*
154.30-31 severe] *interlined with a caret*
154.31 that] *interlined with a caret*
155.25 merchant] 2 *interlined above this word*
155.32 enjoyment] *preceded by cancelled* plentiful
156.1 here.—] *followed by cancelled sentence partly legible*: I write with difficulty . . . read but little by night.—
156.15 &] *interlined with a caret*
156.28 numerous] *interlined above cancelled* genteel

Page. Line:

156.30 whilst] *preceded by cancelled* and
157.11 who] *interlined above cancelled* that
157.24 who] *followed by cancelled* of course
157.27 the] *interlined with a caret*
158.11 he still B.] *he interlined with a caret*; B. *cancelled*
159.34 the] *interlined above*
160.6 bait] a *interlined with a caret*
160.9 be] *followed by cancelled* yet
160.33 Hart] *followed by cancelled* the Schwindler
160.35 set] *interlined with a caret above cancelled* party
161.1 of that name] *interlined above cancelled* for friday
161.4 easily] *followed by cancelled word, possibly* excell
161.4 stage] *followed by two cancelled phrases, partly legible*: His last . . . of Jefferson [*partly blotted*] *followed by* (the order) *bottom left*
162.2 priest of] *followed by cancelled* American
162.20 been further seasoned] *the numbers* 4 2 1 2, *double-spaced, have been interlined above these words*
162.36 town] *preceded by cancelled* this
163.13 Col: D.] *interlined with a caret*
163.31 on which] *interlined with a caret*
163.31 wished] ed *interlined with a caret*

Page. Line:

163.37 which was] *interlined with a caret*

164.5 into] *to interlined with a caret*

164.14 or] *interlined with a caret*

164.17 we] 2 *interlined above this word*

165.7 proposed] *interlined above cancelled* put up

166.10 credit.—] *followed by cancelled* 'tho upon a small scale

166.10 early] *interlined above cancelled* time

166.11 belonging] *interlined above cancelled* upon

166.13 homeward] *followed by cancelled* before night

166.17 care] *inserted at line end to replace cancelled* management

166.25 sufferings] *preceded by cancelled* seemingly endless

166.28 different] *interlined with a caret*

167.1 intention] *interlined above cancelled* design

167.3 Monday] Mon. *written over* Tues.

167.33 with] *followed by cancelled* his worthies—and

168.23 of Kentucky] *followed by cancelled* one of the most vulgar blockheads I ever met with.

168.26 of] *interlined with a caret*

168.32-33 mortify Jefferson] *followed by cancelled*: and ought to ruin the last remnants of his credit with every decent man in the community

168.33 he] *interlined with a caret to replace cancelled* the Chief of Democrats

169.11 young] *preceded by cancelled word, possibly* gentile

172.8 diminution] *interlined over cancelled word, illegible*

TABLE OF EMENDATIONS

This table lists all changes made from the manuscript other than those silently normalized orthographic features listed above in paragraph six of About the Text. Line numbers refer to a count of actual lines print on the page, including dates and hairline rules but excluding the running head. The emended reading is recorded to the left of the bracket.

Page. Line:

3.15 past] pas
3.21 Sattawhite] *possibly*
4.10 Mayo's] Meyo's
4.12 suppose] suppose,
4.14 Mayo] Meyo
4.36-47 Marshall] Marshal
5.17 brought] brõt
5.18-23 ;] : *or unpunctuated in MS*
5.31 talents] ts *blotted*
8.14 accept] t *blotted*
8.28 w.^{d}] .^{d} *blotted*
9.15 When] when
9.28 know] *possibly* knew
10.12 Barton] B *blotted*
10.29 Aug.^{c} 6] 6 *blotted*
11.14 w.th] w.^{h}
12.12 brought] brõt
13.2 and] *blotted*
13.2 country —] *dash supplied*
13.15 Marshall's] Marshal's
13.17 Swartwout] Swarthout
13.22 Robinson] Robison
16.13 Within,] *comma supplied*
16.13 Assembly] *blotted*
16.15 Marshal] Msh.^{l} *possibly*
16.23 Mess.^{s}] Mess:

Page. Line:

16.34-35 acquaintance.] ;
17.17 To which] to
17.27 leaving] *blotted*
17.28-29 Wallace,] *comma supplied*
17.31 fanning,] *possibly*
18.8 sleep,] *comma supplied*
18.13 Brief] brief
19.33 expedition;] *semicolon supplied*
20.2 justice"] *possibly not quotation marks*
20.25 these,] *comma supplied*
25.20 Mississippi] Missisippi
26.9 be] *blotted*
26.26 Negroes,] *comma supplied*
26.27 Scott] *possibly*
27.14-15 Otherwise] Õwise
27.23 Pandora's] *blotted*
27.24 lid] *blotted*
27.35 Treason —] Treason,
27.35 Treason ch.] *comma supplied*
30.12 me,] *comma supplied*
30.13 dust.:] *colon supplied*
33.19 began] begun
33.27 days to] to *supplied*
34.6 McKee,] *comma supplied*

Page. Line:

34.8 prosecut^{n},] *comma supplied*
34.12 Agrestis] agrestis
34.21 produce:] *semicolon supplied*
34.24 proceeded] *blotted*
34.29 first] *followed by period or comma in MS*
34.33 well.] *period supplied*
35.17 do,] *possibly* do —
36.8 the Counsel] the *partly blotted*
36.20 "Admirable,"] *quotation marks supplied*
36.25 "Agrestis] 'Agrestis
37.26 that,] *comma supplied*
38.13 Truxton,] *comma supplied*
38.17 Counsel,] *comma supplied*
38.22 again] again,
38.34 brought] brõt
39.12 that] *partly blotted*
39.13 Meigs] Meiggs
39.19 Who is] is *supplied*
39.24 Marshall] Marshal
39.29 all day,] *possibly* all day
40.4 my walk,] my, walk,
40.23 infest] in fest
40.26 Mississippi] Missisippi
40.37 when,] *comma supplied*
41.2 . . . .] *apparent omission in MS*
41.27 evening.] *period supplied*
42.6 other;] other:
42.18 overt acts] overt — acts *in MS*
42.21 proved, Burr,] proved Burr,
42.25 maintained] d *blotted*
42.36 can't] *comma supplied*
43.5 He] H *blotted*
43.8 otherwise] õwise
43.36 heard of;] heard of:
43.37 $40.;] *semicolon supplied*
44.1 "Falsehood] 'Falshood
44.6 horses] horsed
44.13 Luckett] Lucket
44.26 — Marshals] Marshalls
44.33 asked] asked.
44.33 brought] brõt
45.6 me to] to *supplied*
45.9 committed] com̄itted
46.23 Wood^{ge}, Belknap,] *commas supplied*
46.25 letter,] letter
47.19 Luckett] Lucket
48.6 ever] *partially blotted; possibly* even
48.36 Luckett] Lucket
49.10 Luckett] Lucket
50.3 brought] brõt
50.32 he,] *comma supplied*
51.7 thought] thõt
51.19 otherwise] õwise
51.31 offers to] to *blotted*
51.32 Govt.;] *semicolon supplied*
52.13 in cash] in *blotted*
52.17 Marshal's] Marshall's
53.2 — midnight] — *supplied*
53.11 myself,] *comma supplied*
53.20 ground;] ground,
53.23-24 apartment] apart^{t}
54.18 instruments,] instruments —
54.23 more engaged] more, engaged
54.28 Duane's] Duanes
54.34 Smith,] *comma supplied*
55.31 knew,] knew;
57.33 him,"] *possibly* him."

Page. Line:

58.8 d] *partly blotted*
58.25 walk] *partly blotted*
59.4 I suppose I can] *partly blotted*
59.5 Luckett's] Lucket's, L *blotted*
59.20 recover] *partly blotted*
59.34 brought] *partly blotted*
60.10 the] *blotted*
60.24 recovery,] recovery.
61.10 he has] *partly blotted*
61.11 made] *partly blotted*
61.27 Chief] chief
63.30 McGilli[cuddy] *partly blotted*
64.3 Luckett] Lucket
64.22 Marshall] Marshal
64.31 Marshall-faction] Marshal-faction
65.28 reverse] *blotted*
65.35 after,] *comma supplied*
65.36 fruit,] *comma supplied*
67.6 Bench] B *blotted*
67.16-17 ermine] *blotted*
68.35 pointed;] *semicolon supplied*
69.6 zeal in the] *blotted*
71.22 Luckett] Lucket
71.24 Luckett] Lucket, L *blotted*
72.5 action] *partly blotted*
72.5 summons] sum̄ons
72.19 misdemeanor] misdemesnor
72.23 misdemeanor] misdemesnor
73.7 heard] heard,
73.13 day.] *possibly* day!
73.36 announce] *possibly* announce
74.24 Luckett] Lucket
75.21 misdemeanor] misdemesnor
76.4 misdemeanor] misdemesnor
76.6 midsemeanor] misdemesnor
76.7 appetite] *partly blotted*
76.12 misdemeanor] misdemesnor
76.14 grounds] grounds,
76.25 "What] *quotation marks supplied*
77.6 Marshall] Marshal
77.34 Luckett] Lucket
78.16 Luckett] Lucket
78.33 misdemeanor] misdesmenor
78.34 commence] com̄ence
79.15 recommitment] recom̄itment
79.25 commerce] com̄ence
81.30-31 misdemeanor] misdesmenor
83.6-7 misdemeanor] misdesmenor
84.3 Luckett] Lucket
86.10 common] com̄on
87.23 what] *blotted*
88.12 announced] anounced
88.30 it] *blotted*
89.1 accommodated] accom̄odated
89.27 special verdict] special—verdict
89.30-31 commit] com̄it
90.20 four] four,
90.29 3] *blotted, possibly* 5
90.32 recommitment] recom̄itment
90.33-34 again to] *partly blotted*
90.35 Court,] *comma supplied*
91.4 tongue-tied.] *period supplied*

Page. Line:

91.15 off] of
91.15-16 "This," . . . "reminds] *quotation marks supplied*
91.19 'come] *quotation mark supplied*
91.20 here?'] *quotation mark supplied*
92.20 committed] com̄itted
93.4 Luckett] Lucket
93.6 The Marshal] the Marshall
93.32 committed] com̄itted
94.34 whereof] whof
95.1 *committing*] *com̄iting*
95.25 Dunbaugh] D *blotted*
95.35 intensity] *possibly*
97.20 company,] *comma supplied*
98.1 mentioned] *partly blotted*
98.6 at] *blotted*
98.23 Smith,] *comma supplied*
98.31 Swartwout] Swarthout
99.14 subject can be] subject be
101.1 Robinson] Robison
101.11 firmness,] *comma supplied*
101.32 him,] *comma supplied*
102.10-11 witnesses] witnessis
103.15 command] com̄and
103.18 summons] sum̄ons
103.21 common] com̄on
104.3-4 music,] *comma supplied*
104.19 "How . . . live";] *quotation marks and semicolon supplied*
104.24-25 cross-examination] x examination
104.27 cross-examining] x examining
105.23 cross-examination] x examination

Page. Line:

106.7 cross-examination] xxam.^{n}
106.22 recommitted] recom̄ited
107.17 tone of his bowls] *possibly ; very faint*
108.9 Marshall] Marshal
108.17 flower] *possibly* herb
109.26-27 announce] an̄ounce
110.17 otherwise] õwise
111.9 credit,] credit;
111.25-26 cross-examination] xxamin.^{n}
113.3 examination] xamination
114.22 parallel] paralleled
114.28 cross-examination] xxam.^{n}
115.17-18 cross-examination] xxam.^{n}
115.27 cast, a Mr Trisley,] cast a Mr Trisley.
116.8 cross-examination] xxam.^{n}
116.25 exam.^{n}] xam.^{n}
117.24 cross-examination] xxam.^{n}
118.16 Blen.^{tt}?] Blen.^{tt}
118.25 smiled'] smiled"
119.2 tranquillity,] *comma supplied*
119.14 others;] others.
119.28-30 abandoned; . . . vain;] : *replaced by* ;
120.1 Bonaparte] Buonaparte
120.31 speculations] *partly blotted*
121.17 Robinson] Robison
121.34 Patricolas] *possibly* Paticoles
122.13 8.^{r}] blotted
122.18 General,] *comma supplied*
123.26 Bruff] Brough

Page. Line:

124.4 Col's] Col's.
125.34 day,] *comma supplied*
126.4 case] *blotted*
126.11 seems,] *comma supplied*
126.35 note] not
127.4 &] *possibly* I
128.24 friend] *partly blotted*
129.30 dress] *possibly*
130.8 projects,] *comma supplied*
130.15 these] *possibly* the
130.15 Cummins] Comings
130.21 Cummins] Comings
131.6 Cummins] Comings
131.17 knew] knew
133.6 court,] *comma supplied*
134.8 appropriating] *partly blotted*
134.19 everyone] *partly blotted*
135.3 Moore] Moor
136.14 w^{d}] *blotted*
136.21 cheats] cheat
136.24 Marshall] Marshal
136.26 commit] com̃it
136.28 commit] com̃it
136.31 behind] *partly blotted*
136.32 Duane] *partly blotted*
137.2 Cummins] Comins
137.15 necessary —] necessary. —
137.31 Cummins] Comins
138.5 Burr, Martin,] *commas supplied*
138.6 Cummins] Comins
138.21 commence] com̃ence
139.3 3] *blotted*
139.13 soon] *partly blotted*
139.20 Stell's] *possibly*
139.23 Commins,] Comins
139.30 communicated] com̃unicated
140.22 Marshall] Marshal
140.28 Cerberus] *partly blotted*
141.11 Marshalls] Marshals
141.22 conduct] *partly blotted*
141.24 Cummins] Commins
141.30 Cummins] Commins
142.1 Cummins] Commins
142.8 control] controll
143.22 of] *blotted*
143.36 half-made] *partly blotted*
144.26 Washington?"] *punctuation supplied*
145.6 summoned] sum̃oned
145.23 committees] com̃ittees
146.16 as it was] *partly blotted*
147.4 Blount,] *comma supplied*
147.10 received] *partly blotted*
147.26 Cummins] Commins
147.30 Cummins] Commins
148.6 command] com̃and
148.19 Luckett] Lucket
148.26 Frailey] Freley
148.28 proposed] *partly blotted*
149.28 'choice spirits'] "choice spirits"
150.6–7 'Aaron . . . Union'] "Aaron . . . Union"
150.18 hours before] hours, before
150.27 him] *blotted line under*
150.30 Luckett] Lucket
150.30 Cummins] Com̃ins
150.34 Luckett] Lucket
151.2 Cummins] Com̃ins
151.5 heard,] *comma supplied*
152.23–24 estimate,] estimate.
152.25 heard] *illegible abbrev. in MS*
152.26–27 Ch.Just.,] *comma supplied*
153.5 will] will will

Page. Line:

153.7 Point] point
153.13 by] *partly blotted*
153.26 offering] *partly blotted*
153.30 Point] point
154.5-6 reception,] *comma supplied*
155.11 decided] *partly blotted*
155.17 probably without] probably—without
155.19 N x x x x .] *undeciphered*
156.16 Pollock] Pollok
157.9 recommended] recom̃ended
157.14 Pollock] Pollok
157.14 Joe] Joe.
157.16 Joe] Joe.
157.19 Pollock] Pollok
157.23 Pollock] Pollok
158.25 solicited] sollicited
158.27-28 Lewises?"] *quotation marks supplied*
158.29 sh.[d]] *partly blotted*
159.5 judge of,] *comma supplied*
159.8 Pinkney,] *comma supplied*
159.11 dignity"] *quotation marks supplied*
159.13 print.] print:
161.4 excell] *possibly ; partly legible*
161.9 affairs.] *period supplied*
161.21 (that is] *parenthesis supplied*
162.7 Irishman).] Irishman.)
162.31 answer;] *semicolon supplied*

Page. Line:

164.1 Whilst] whilst
164.9-10 commence] com̃ence
164.18 Marshall] Marshal
164.21 Wilkinson,] *comma supplied*
165.5 Monroe] Monro
165.27 him,] *comma supplied*
165.30 13] *partly blotted*
165.32 Tightman] *possibly* Tilghman
166.2 Joe] Joe.
166.11 belonging to it] belonging it
166.34 Cummins] Commins
167.11 recommends] recom̃ends
167.25 Joe] Joe.
168.5 visits,] *comma supplied*
168.11 Biddle] Biddel
168.12 Cummins] Commins
168.12 Pollock] Pollok
168.16 Pollock] Pollok
168.16-17 Cummins] Commins
168.17 Biddle] Biddel
168.20 Russell] Russel
169.6 Marshall] Marshal
169.6 Washington,] *comma supplied*
169.9 Marshall] Marshal
169.11 Nolte] Nolta
169.34 Bonaparte] Buonaparte
169.36 pleased;] *semicolon supplied*
171.16 Luckett's] Lucket's
171.18 L.] *blotted*
171.24 Luckett's] Lucket's
172.30 selfmanagement.)] *parenthesis supplied*

INDEX OF NAMES

As they appear in the Journal or in Appendix A, B, or C of this book.